WALKING WITH TIGERS

ALSO BY JEFFREY MARX

The Long Snapper

Season of Life

It Gets Dark Sometimes

One More Victory Lap (with Carl Lewis)

Inside Track (with Carl Lewis)

WALKING WITH TIGERS

A Collection of LSU Sports Stories

JEFFREY MARX

JAM PUBLISHING

JAM PUBLISHING

The cover photo of Mike the Tiger, taken by LSU photographer Steve Franz, is used with permission of the LSU Sports Information Office.

"The Best Years of His Life" was first published by *Sports Illustrated* on August 12, 2002. It is included with permission of writer John Ed Bradley.

Other portions of this book previously appeared elsewhere in similar but not exact form. "Bert Jones at Sixty" and "Fifty for Fifty" were posted on LSUsports.net. "Fifty for Fifty" was also published in the *Baton Rouge Advocate*. "Rally Corn" was published in the *Advocate*. "The Long Snapper" and parts of the Gus Kinchen section in "Things People Save" were published in Jeffrey Marx's 2009 book *The Long Snapper*.

Cover and book design by Michelle Neustrom of Baton Rouge, Louisiana.

Author information: **www.jeffreymarx.org**

FIRST EDITION

ISBN 978-0-692-44155-8

For the three people who gave me Louisiana:
Bert Jones, Dale Brown, and Leslie Marx ("Po" to me)

This book is also dedicated to the memory of Wendy Marx,
my only sister and best friend,
and to all who save lives through organ donation and transplantation

CONTENTS

INTRODUCTION

Sports have always played an integral role in my life. As a youngster, I was constantly throwing or hitting or shooting some sort of ball, and I spent summers working as a ballboy for the Baltimore Colts. As an adult, I was drawn to sports stories as a newspaper reporter and then as an author of non-fiction books. And I've always been an avid sports fan.

It was perfectly natural, then, that I gravitated toward LSU sports after moving to Baton Rouge in 2007. The path was neither short nor direct. I grew up in New York, went to college in Chicago, and spent most of my adult life in Washington, D.C. Then I married a beautiful lady from Thibodaux, Louisiana, and migrated south. Thanks to two longtime friendships—see the chapters on Bert Jones and Dale Brown—I already had a strong interest in the LSU Tigers. Living only minutes from campus took that attraction to a whole new level.

I went to football, basketball, and baseball games. I learned what it really means to tailgate. I even added some purple and gold to my wardrobe. It did not take long to realize that all roads in Baton Rouge somehow go—excuse me, *geaux*—through the world of LSU sports. A good number of my new relationships started by sharing a game or even just a sports-related conversation with someone I now consider a friend. That alone—the role of LSU sports in my assimilation into a new community—gave the Tigers a special place in my reconfigured life.

Then I wrote something about Bert Jones. It was a personal story about my friendship with the former All-American quarterback. On September 7, 2011, the story was posted on the official website of the LSU athletics department—LSUsports.net—and the response was remarkable. I'd already known about the passion of the LSU faithful who attended the games. Now I knew how much they enjoyed reading about their athletic heroes as well.

That got me thinking: What if I took a walk through the world of LSU sports—collecting stories along the way—and wrote a book about it?

Twenty-one stories ultimately made the cut. Some are about star athletes, such as Alex Bregman and Leonard Fournette. Others are about lesser known people whose tales are nonetheless fascinating. There are stories about fans and one about a lucky can of corn. I've also included two chapters—in a section called "Back Stories"—that stand apart in the back of this collection. One is part of a story I originally told in another book—*The Long Snapper*—about former LSU football player Brian Kinchen. The other is a first-person story by former LSU football player John Ed Bradley. I wanted it here because it's my favorite piece of writing about any LSU sport.

What a wonderful walk this has been. I hope you enjoy it as much as I have.

Jeffrey Marx
June 2015

WALKING
WITH
TIGERS

Bert Jones at Sixty

September 7, 2011

First I needed reading glasses—that was a few years ago. Then I needed pills for an inflamed hip. The common denominator was clear. Time would not stand still for any of us, and I was marching deeper into my forties. OK, I got it!

But now comes one final blow to let me know that any semblance of youth is officially gone: My favorite childhood sports hero is today celebrating his sixtieth birthday. How can this be possible? Bert Jones is *sixty?*

Bert is not supposed to have lines on his face and grandchildren to visit. He is supposed to be throwing bullets and fighting for first downs—lifting up teammates and even whole communities with weekly proof that just about anything is possible on a field of play.

For LSU football fans, Bert will always be known as the first All-American quarterback for the Tigers. He will forever be the guy who in 1971 led LSU to a milestone win over powerhouse Notre Dame, the guy who in 1972 beat bitter rival Ole Miss on a heart-pounding touchdown pass with no time left on the clock, the guy who in 1973 was selected by the Baltimore Colts with the second overall pick of the NFL draft.

For me, however, Bert became so much more than some big-time football star to be followed from afar. He became a friend. We first met the summer of 1974. I was in Baltimore—down from my childhood home in a suburb of New York City—for a tennis camp that happened to be held at the same school where the Colts conducted their preseason training camp. As a sports-loving eleven-year-old boy, I could not get enough of the Colts.

I watched them practice. I collected autographs. And I actually got to know most of the players. Bert was the first person I had ever met from Louisiana, and he was a relentless ambassador for both the state and his hometown of Ruston. He could not believe I had never been hunting or fishing. He wanted to know what in the world we woefully deprived New Yorkers did for fun.

Some of the players—Bert included—came to treat me like a little brother. They played catch with me. They took me to Baskin-Robbins for ice cream. They talked to me about girls. After a while, the Colts equipment man and trainers were so used to having me around that they let me help with minor tasks such as hanging jerseys in lockers, handing out towels, and pouring Gatorade.

I was even invited to help at Memorial Stadium during a preseason game against the Detroit Lions. This was Friday, August 9, 1974. Anyone into American history would immediately tag it as the day Richard Nixon resigned the presidency. To me, it would always be known as my first day as a ballboy with the Colts.

Once camp was over and I was home for the start of seventh grade, I did the best I could to keep in touch with my new football friends. When the Colts came to play in New York, I helped in the locker room and on the sideline. Each of the next few years I helped at a game or two, and the relationships kept growing.

I had several favorite players, but Bert was the one I admired the most. Starting in 1975, he led the Colts to three straight AFC East titles. In 1976, he was voted the most valuable player in the entire NFL. He was featured on the cover of *Sports Illustrated*, but even that was not enough. He was also on the cover of *People*, one of the magazine's twenty-five most intriguing folks in the world, right along with Robert Redford, Farrah Fawcett, and Jimmy Carter.

It was not fame alone, though, that drew me to Bert. Fame is too vague, and what does it really mean in the solitude that comes with the end of a day? No, the qualities that drew me to Bert were much more tangible than that.

He was the ultimate competitor. As a youngster he had suffered from rickets, which left him pigeon-toed and knock-kneed. But even when he had to wear braces, he never really played games so much as he attacked them. It was the same with professional football. He was always the leader.

Still, the most enchanting thing about Bert was that he always seemed to be having a good time. He always seemed like such a kid, an overgrown country kid with special permission to run and throw and laugh, always laugh, as he claimed victory after victory in an adult world.

Take his way of greeting the hottest, most miserable days of training camp. He would storm onto the practice field with a grin, a hoot, and a holler. "Can't work me hard enough on a beautiful day like tuh-*day*," he would yell over and over. Some of his teammates just rolled their eyes; others actually drew on his enthusiasm.

Take the sworn affidavit he wanted the lovely Danielle Marie Dupuis to sign on the twenty-fourth day of March 1977 as a condition of their impending marriage. "She will never oppose any plans of Bertram Hays Jones to engage in the manly pursuits of hunting and/or fishing," it says. The document was duly signed and notarized. But it was just a joke. Sort of.

Take the way Bert initiated rookies during training camp. He would wrap his body with bed sheets, covering all but his eyes and hands, and would pull a baseball cap low in the front to help conceal his eyes. Then he would surround himself with offensive linemen for protection and break into the rookies' dorm rooms just before curfew—all so he could blast them with baby powder and water.

He got my room, too. I hated cleaning it up. And I loved it. This was the summer of 1979, and I was sixteen. After five years of helping at a game or two each season, I had finally been hired by the Colts. It was my first of four training camps working full time and living with the team, and by trashing my room, Bert was letting me know that I was one of the guys.

Life was good.

Bert always made time for me. He even let me borrow his car once for a date. I got a kiss that night. And I was pretty sure why. The girl knew whose car it was. She was impressed.

Ultimately, Bert finished his football career with the Los Angeles Rams and returned to Ruston in 1982. After graduation from college—Northwestern University just outside of Chicago—I first moved to Kentucky and then to Washington, D.C., as a newspaper reporter.

I never would have guessed that Bert and I would always stay in touch. Most NFL teammates scatter across the country and lose all contact once their playing days are over, so what were the odds of a star quarterback and a mere ballboy maintaining any sort of relationship? Actually, our friendship would only grow as we moved deeper into adulthood.

The summer of 1994, twenty years after initially meeting Bert, I made my first trip to see him and his family in Ruston, and we even went fishing. That, too, was a first for me. Bert took me out on a pond and showed me how to catch a fish, enthusiastically offering a celebratory high-five when I pulled in a largemouth bass. I would make several other trips to Ruston, where Bert was now the owner and operator of a lumber company called Mid-States Wood Preservers.

As Bert's involvement in the lumber industry grew, so too did our chances to see each other, as he traveled at least once a year to meetings in Washington. Bert would always stay in the guest room of my Capitol Hill townhouse, and the Ruston country boy actually came to know my city neighborhood pretty well. One day, he even ran into a neighbor of mine that he happened to know, U.S. Senator John Breaux of Louisiana, and they exchanged greetings in the street right in front of my house.

Bert's youngest of four children, Beaux, also came to know the area because he spent a summer in my house when he interned with a political consultant in Washington. Things had gone full circle: Whereas I had once been the young kid looking to Bert for guidance and approval, I was now the "old guy" dishing out advice and support to his college-age son. I enjoyed Beaux, and it meant a lot to me that my friendship with Bert—always a family man before anything else—now extended to the next generation.

Speaking of family, it was my decision to get married—in 2006—that prompted one of my all-time classic moments with Bert. He had long been encouraging me to marry the incredible woman I had been dating long-distance for more than six years—she lived in Baton Rouge, of all places—and he was thrilled that I had finally pulled the trigger. A few weeks before the wedding, Bert wanted me to know one of his great secrets to a successful marriage. It was the ability to look your wife straight in the eye and say: "Honey, you are absolutely correct. I don't know how I possibly could have been so wrong."

Bert and I were on our way to dinner in D.C. one night when he told me this. We were walking down Pennsylvania Avenue—on a crowded sidewalk—and he wanted me to give it a try. Looking at Bert and attempting to be at least somewhat serious, I said: "Honey, you are absolutely correct. I don't know how I possibly could have been so wrong."

Clearly, I was not good at this. "No, no, no, not nearly sincere enough," Bert said. "You need to say it like you really mean it. Go ahead, try it again."

And so I did. This time we got a few strange glances as I turned to my friend, looked him in the eye, and addressed him with an intentionally elevated and overly dramatic voice: "Honey, you are absolutely correct . . ." I can't say I scored too well on the sincerity meter, but we did have a good laugh. Of course, having heard the story numerous times, my wife, Leslie, now gives me no credibility whatsoever—which is exactly what I deserve—when I halfheartedly employ Bert's well-intentioned line.

I get a much better reaction when I tell her that Bert's peaches are here. Every year, Bert either ships or personally delivers a case of Ruston's famous peaches. He started doing this long ago when I still lived in Washington. Now the deliveries are easier because I live in . . . Louisiana.

Having nothing to do with the first Louisiana native I ever met (Bert) and everything to do with the most important Louisiana native in my life (Leslie), I am now officially a resident of Baton Rouge. Or as one of my New York friends dubbed me: *Yankee on the Bayou*.

I go to a lot of LSU games—football, basketball, and baseball. I love eating gumbo. And I lie all the time—just for fun—by telling people I'm from Thibodaux (not that they ever believe me).

Oh, and one more thing: I get to see much more of Bert than I did when I lived in Washington. We reminisce about memories from the old days in Baltimore, and we create plenty of new memories as well—all of which is perfectly natural and comfortable.

But Bert Jones at sixty? My favorite childhood sports hero embarking upon his *seventh* decade?

Wow.

I knew what to think about the reading glasses and the bad hip.

I'm not at all sure what to think about this.

The Bat Man of Baton Rouge

October 22, 2011

The day has already been good to Jack Marucci. The LSU football team routed reigning national champion Auburn, 45–10, before a raucous afternoon crowd in Tiger Stadium. In addition to remaining undefeated and ranked number-one in the country after eight games of the 2011 season, the Tigers have also made it through another week without any major injuries. This is paramount to Marucci. He is LSU's director of athletic training, making him responsible for the physical well-being of every player in one of the most celebrated of all collegiate football programs.

But Marucci—forty-seven years old, a husband and father of two—is thinking only about baseball on this Saturday night. He is relaxing in the living room of his Baton Rouge home, watching on television as the Texas Rangers host the St. Louis Cardinals in Game 3 of the World Series. Actually, *relaxing* is not quite right. Long before he started making baseball bats as a hobby, even longer before he elevated his hobby into a successful business, Marucci was an excitable fan of the game. Now he is an intensely dedicated observer—one might even say a participant—especially when one of his guys is approaching the plate holding one of his bats.

This time it is Albert Pujols, star first baseman of the Cardinals, one of the most powerful and decorated hitters in baseball—three times the

MVP of the National League—and he is on fire. In the fourth and fifth innings, he hit back-to-back singles. In the sixth and seventh, he crushed consecutive home runs accounting for a total of five runs. It was the first time anyone had hits in four straight innings of a World Series game.

What could Pujols do for an encore? With the Cardinals leading 15–7 in the ninth inning, that is the only question remaining as Pujols approaches the plate wielding his "AP5" model bat handcrafted by the Marucci Bat Company. There are two outs and the bases are empty. The count goes to two balls and two strikes. Pujols fouls off a pitch. Then Darren Oliver of the Rangers offers an 89-mile-per-hour sinker, Pujols unleashes and . . . *bam*. Yet another baseball is headed into the night sky and over the outfield fence.

"Yes!" Marucci lets loose, turning toward his sixteen-year-old son, Gino, who is watching with him. Gino is initially confused, thinking he is seeing a replay of an earlier blast, but then he realizes this is live action—a third straight home run—and he has only one thing to say about Pujols: "That guy is ridiculous."

Babe Ruth and Reggie Jackson are the only other players to hit three home runs in a World Series game. The numbers Pujols has put up tonight are staggering. Five hits in a row. Six runs batted in. Fourteen total bases—a World Series record for a single game. Young Gino had it exactly right: Ridiculous.

The whole unforeseeable journey leading to this shared moment in the Marucci living room is also preposterous. How does someone taking care of the LSU football team become the bat man of Baton Rouge? And how do his baseball bats end up in the hands of so many major league ballplayers? The story begins with the same two Maruccis who are bursting with excitement as Pujols rounds the bases in Texas. It begins with the passion of a father who just wanted to do something special for his son.

The year was 2002. Gino, then seven, already had a favorite sport. He had often heard his dad talk about his hometown Pittsburgh Pirates. Jack could still rattle off all the jersey numbers worn by his favorite players when he was growing up in western Pennsylvania. So it was no surprise that he had handed down to his son the same love of baseball that American dads had for generations been joyously gifting to their boys. There was only one problem as Gino tried to emulate his own big league heroes on the Baton Rouge fields of youth baseball. All the kids were using aluminum bats—metal had long since replaced wood for youngsters—but Gino wanted to be just like the pro ballplayers he saw on television. He wanted to use the same type of bat they used. He wanted wood.

Jack searched the Internet. He called a few bat companies. He talked to several coaches he knew. No matter what he tried, he kept hearing the same thing. Wood bats for kids were a thing of the past. Nobody knew where he could buy one small enough for a seven-year-old.

Jack Marucci was not one to quit. Instead of buying a bat, he found a used lathe and bought it for eighty dollars. He set it up in a tool shed he had in his back yard and went to work. He knew little about making a bat. But he'd always enjoyed working with wood and was sort of a handyman—something he'd picked up from *his* dad—so he was neither intimidated by the unknown nor discouraged by his initial failures. Gino had his bat before long, and it even had his name burned into the barrel. The boy was thrilled.

A few of Gino's teammates then decided they wanted one. So did some friends on other teams. Jack kept returning to his shed. What started as a singular mission on behalf of his son was soon a hobby for the mild-mannered athletic trainer—and a passion.

Marucci enjoyed it so much that he wanted to show an old friend what he was doing. Eduardo Perez, then playing for the St. Louis Cardinals, was in his tenth year of Major League Baseball. Marucci knew him from their time together at Florida State—Marucci as an assistant trainer prior to working at LSU, Perez as a hard-hitting first baseman eventually selected by the California Angels in the first round of the 1991 MLB draft. A dozen years later, on June 25, 2003, Marucci was in St. Louis for the annual meeting of the National Athletic Trainers' Association, and he gave Perez two bats he'd made for him. Marucci was eager to know what the longtime big leaguer would think of his handiwork.

Perez was skeptical about the quality of a bat made by an amateur craftsman. But he felt obligated to try it. "Jack is such a likable guy," Perez says. "I had to at least humor him."

That evening, with the Cardinals preparing for a game against the Cincinnati Reds at the old Busch Stadium, Perez tried one of his Marucci originals during batting practice—and he was stunned. He actually liked it. The wood was really hard and nicely finished—just what Perez always wanted to feel in a bat—and he pounded balls all over the park. He then let one of his young teammates try the second bat—a rising star by the name of Albert Pujols.

The biggest shock of the night, for Marucci anyway, came when Perez approached the plate for his first at-bat of the game, pinch hitting against Reds relief pitcher Felix Heredia to lead off the bottom of the seventh inning. Watching from beneath the overhang on the first-base side of the stands, Marucci saw that Perez was not carrying his regular Louisville Slugger. He was about to use one of Jack Marucci's bats. Marucci panicked. Only kids had used his bats in games! His bats had never felt the impact of a big-league fastball! What if Perez made contact and his bat just shattered all over the place? There was also the matter of using equipment that was not licensed by Major League Baseball. *Contraband* is the word Marucci now uses for that first bat Perez tried.

Fortunately, nobody but Marucci noticed anything unusual about the bat, and it held together just fine when Perez swung on a 2-0 pitch and hit the ball hard to the left side of the infield. He simply grounded out to the shortstop—a routine play—and the game continued. Marucci could return to normal breathing.

Professional baseball players take their bats seriously. When it comes to trying anything new, nothing is more powerful than the word-of-mouth credibility of one player telling another about it. Perez started telling other players about his new bat and the friend who had made it for him. When perennial All-Star Barry Larkin of the Reds later decided to try a Marucci bat—and became the first player to record a hit with one in a Major League game—it was because Perez had encouraged him to do so. Numerous other players learned of Marucci by way of Perez. Marucci would eventually point to his 2003 trip to St. Louis—and the involvement of Perez it initiated—as a major milestone in the transition from just-for-the-heck-of-it hobby to serious bat business.

Even more critical was an ongoing series of conversations the following year in the LSU training room. Former LSU pitching star Kurt Ainsworth—a collegiate All-American in 1999 and Olympic gold medalist in 2000—was then playing for the Baltimore Orioles. The Baton Rouge native had undergone elbow surgery and had chosen to do his recovery work back home at LSU. Lake Charles native Joe Lawrence was a former professional baseball player—he'd made it to the big leagues with the Toronto Blue Jays in 2002—then attending LSU and trying to play for the football Tigers as a twenty-seven-year-old. But he had suffered a knee injury and been forced to spend much of his time in the training room. While helping Ainsworth and Lawrence with their rehabilitation work, Marucci had a captive audience of two baseball experts. They enjoyed hearing his bat stories and happily critiqued his finished products.

This went on for months. Then things took a turn.

With their injuries forcing them to think about futures beyond the playing of games—and with their late twenties looming—Ainsworth and Lawrence came up with an idea one day while playing golf. Bats! What if they joined with Marucci to turn his hobby into a business? They could stay around baseball, leverage their relationships within the game, and probably have a good time while earning a living.

Marucci had two major concerns: How would they keep up with demand? And how would they increase the quantity of bats being made while still maintaining the quality?

"Jack did not want to do it," Ainsworth recalls. "He was not very interested in being in the bat business—not at all. But we finally talked him into it."

The three men would invest in new equipment and build a shop on Ainsworth's property in the Riverbend subdivision near the LSU campus. Marucci would keep cutting bats at night and whenever his LSU obligations would allow him to squeeze in some time on weekends. Ainsworth and Lawrence would sand, paint, and ship the bats—as well as work the phones and visit with old friends to parlay their baseball connections into sales. The training-room trio was not exactly steeped in business experience—cumulative total: zero—but legal papers were signed one day over lunch at The Chimes. They defined the three men as equal partners in the Marucci Bat Company. Beyond that, there was still much to be figured out.

"We had no real business plan," Lawrence says. "We just had a desire to make a good product and felt like something good would eventually happen."

The formation of a partnership was not the only milestone in 2004.

Marucci was thrilled when New York Mets outfielder Mike Cameron became the first Major League player to hit a home run with one of his bats. It happened at Shea Stadium during a June 17 game against the Cleveland Indians.

Marucci was equally excited when Manny Ramirez of the Boston Red Sox—eventual MVP of the 2004 World Series—called on the phone asking for a few bats toward the end of the MLB regular season. Marucci and the LSU football team were at the time preparing for an early-October game against Georgia. With the Red Sox about to enter the playoffs, Marucci worked late nights to make three bats for Ramirez. He even gave them a unique model number: CB24. The 24 was Ramirez's uniform number. The CB was more creative. It stood for Curse Buster—a reference to a longstanding belief that the Red Sox had suffered under a "Curse of the Bambino" since selling Babe Ruth to the New York Yankees in 1919. That, the story goes, was why the Red Sox had not won a championship since the year before unloading the Babe. Marucci enjoyed the naming of those bats. He enjoyed it even more when Ramirez and his teammates finally put the curse to rest by sweeping the St. Louis Cardinals for victory in the World Series.

The following year—2005—Major League Baseball officially licensed Marucci as a bat supplier. With the help of Baton Rouge resident Bart Talbot, who primarily cut and finished plantation shutters for a living, Marucci and his two partners produced about a thousand bats that year. Six years later, still based in Baton Rouge, the Marucci Bat Company now operates with close to forty employees under the name Marucci Sports. Ainsworth says the company is on pace to sell more than fifty thousand wood bats this year. It has also launched a fast-growing line of aluminum bats—working backward from the way the whole thing started, but moving forward in terms of sales and profit.

The entire story might one day be written in a business book, or in a sports book, or perhaps the narrative of Jack Marucci and his bats will be best told without the limits of any specific category. Consider the pieces: The father-son love that started it all. The innocent beginnings in a nondescript tool shed. The allure of our national pastime and the cultural history of Major League Baseball. The unlikely rise of three men who knew little about business but a lot about hard work and the value of relationships. Taking into account both the breadth and depth of those pieces, only one label will be needed: Great American Story.

The story will include the names of famous players who started swinging Marucci bats before most baseball people even knew what they were: Albert Pujols, Barry Larkin, David Wright, Carlos Beltran, Vernon Wells, Raul Ibanez, Chase Utley, Edgar Renteria, Ryan Howard, Mark Teixeira, Sean Casey, Aaron Hill, and others. It will trace the progression of Pujols from early believer to public face of the company and also a minority owner. In fact, Marucci has reversed the usual economics of endorsement. The company has never paid star players to use its equipment as a way to impress consumers. Instead, almost two dozen players have paid the company to buy in as minority owners, thereby ensuring both their immediate support and long-term loyalty.

The story will explore the two main reasons Marucci has been so successful with pro ballplayers—with more than three hundred major leaguers now swinging the bats. Most important is the quality and consistency of the product. Ask any big leaguer who uses Marucci why it's his bat of choice, and the answer is remarkably consistent: Marucci bats are made from great wood and the company delivers only "gamers"—bats that are good enough to use in the heat of competition. When other companies deliver a dozen bats at a time—their standard quantity for a shipment—maybe half of them will be good enough to use in games. The others might be used only in batting practice or even given away as gifts. All-Star Ryan Vogelsong of the San Francisco Giants speaks strongly of the quality issue: "Being a National League pitcher, getting a chance to hit, I won't go to the plate with anything else but

Marucci in my hands." The other reason for success is the personal access and attention Jack Marucci has always offered to big leaguers using his bats. "He always took good care of me," says Sean Casey, a three-time MLB all-star who played twelve years in the big leagues—through 2008—and is now one of the Marucci minority owners. "Jack is just the best. The level of service that he puts into everything, the level of pride—there's a lot of love that goes into those bats."

The story will address the importance of wood supply. Marucci uses mostly maple and some ash. It all comes from an Amish-run mill in Pennsylvania—and the men of Marucci are quick to credit the purity of that wood for the quality of their bats. The wood means so much to Marucci that the company made one of its boldest moves to ensure it would never lose its supply. In 2008, the Marucci Bat Company took on debt to buy the wood mill. "One of the guys there had given us a heads-up that Louisville Slugger wanted to buy it," Ainsworth says. "So we took a gamble . . . best decision we ever made. If we had not done it, we'd be out of business."

The story will discuss how Marucci also started making aluminum bats. Its first metal bat, the CAT5, was launched last year at events tied to the MLB All-Star Game in Anaheim, California. The early buzz—focused on both the ever-growing cachet of the Marucci name and a patented anti-vibration technology built into the bats—is already leading to brisk sales. But bat sales are really only the hook now. Marucci already has plans to move into other equipment and apparel—pretty much anything that has to do with the game of baseball. "We're not just selling you a bat," says Reed Dickens, now the CEO of Marucci. "We're trying to get you to join a cult . . . the cult of Marucci."

The story will portray Dickens as a key figure in the redefinition of the company and the overall vision now driving it. Dickens took over as CEO in August 2009. He is young—thirty-three—but with a wealth of experience. Dickens served as an assistant White House press secretary for George W. Bush and then ran his own public relations firm before joining Marucci. His forte is brand development and growth. When he says the goal is for Marucci to mean to Louisiana what Nike does to Oregon and Under Armour does to Maryland, he is not just talking. He is intentionally setting the bar as high as it can go. His early moves have been impressive. It was Dickens who steered the broadening of Marucci from being a bat business to a sports company. He's also the one who raised several million dollars to "scale up" the company. It was Dickens who emphasized the importance of generating media exposure to help the public connect Marucci's "brand ambassadors"—the baseball stars who were minority owners—to the company and its products. "When I got here, Marucci had already gone from a hobby to a business," Dickens says. "My mission was to take it from a business to a durable brand . . . a megabrand."

Naturally, this great American story will also have to include a few scenes from tonight in Texas: Albert Pujols blasting dingers in the World Series.

Gino Marucci is now gone from the living room. His dad is still sitting there. Jack is processing all that Pujols has just done in one game—one game on the biggest stage of his sport.

Marucci has seen his bats connect on some big swings the last few years. In 2009, All-Star second baseman Chase Utley of the Philadelphia Phillies used Marucci to hit a total of five home runs in six World Series games, tying Reggie Jackson for the most homers in a Series. Last year, shortstop Edgar Renteria of the San Francisco Giants used a Marucci bat to hit his World Series-winning home run in Game 5 against the Texas Rangers. Earlier this year, All-Star Robinson Cano of the New York Yankees won the MLB Home Run Derby with a Marucci.

But this mammoth performance by Pujols?

I don't know if it gets any bigger than this, Marucci tells himself.

"Fun night," he will later say. "Obviously, I'm thrilled for Pujols. He's such a good guy. But I'm also really happy for everybody that's involved with the company. We all take pride in something like this. We certainly don't take it for granted. We never do."

Marucci Sports continues to grow in both sales and stature. In 2013, the company announced that its bats had for the first time surpassed Louisville Slugger in use by major leaguers. Marucci has also made big moves in youth sports. Now led by Kurt Ainsworth in the role of CEO, Marucci has seventy-five employees and will make more than 150,000 wood bats in 2015. Still, with the company rapidly expanding sales of aluminum bats and other baseball products, even that astonishing number of wood bats represents a diminishing share of its overall business. "Marucci has become a full brand for baseball," Ainsworth says, "and now we're launching into softball." Jack Marucci is still the head of athletic training at LSU. Gino Marucci, the seven-year-old boy who just wanted one wood bat, is a sophomore outfielder on the University of Houston baseball team.

Playing Time for the Tuba Dude

November 12, 2011

A blowout of an overmatched opponent seldom yields any highlights worthy of the archives. But here is a moment—late in the 2011 season opener for the LSU men's basketball team—to be savored. With less than two minutes remaining and the Tigers pounding Nicholls State, 96–69, LSU coach Trent Johnson calls to the end of his bench for one of the most unusual athletes in all of college sports. He's calling for a seven-foot-two kid who came to his team from . . . the school band?

Andrew Del Piero jumps into action. Actually he does not jump from his sitting position—arms folded across his knees, size 20 Nikes turned slightly in at the toes—so much as he unfolds himself. As Del Piero pulls off his warm-up top, unveiling his purple number 55 jersey and moving toward his first appearance in an official game, he is accompanied by some intriguing questions: How is it possible that this pale tower of a young man—all arms and legs, punctuated by big, brown eyes and a floppy cut of brown hair—initially landed at LSU as a tuba player? How did he make his way from the LSU Tiger Band to the basketball team? And where will this whole unimaginable journey ultimately take him?

Of course, no one in the Pete Maravich Assembly Center is looking for answers at this moment. All the crowd wants is a basket for the tuba dude!

With 1:42 left to play, Coach Johnson calls a timeout to get Del Piero in the game. Teammates yell and clap for him as he walks onto the floor. The crowd buzzes with anticipation. But nobody makes more noise than the proud members of the Bengal Brass Basketball Band—a scaled-down version of the football band—and especially the four tuba players standing (instruments now resting on the floor) in the last row of section 120. One of them, LSU junior Phil Arceneaux, is jumping up and down as if he's just won the lottery, and he keeps shouting in celebration of his former bandmate, employing his personal shorthand for Del Piero: "DP! DP! DP!"

Del Piero could not be faulted for thinking: *Funny, nobody ever acted up like this when I made all-state band back in high school.* But he is thinking nothing of the sort. In fact, he can hardly think at all. Del Piero has worked long and hard to prepare for this moment, but everything seems to be moving so fast now.

Growing up in Austin, Texas, Del Piero was always "the big kid" in his class. His father, Paul, a software company executive, stood six-foot-eleven and had played varsity basketball at Dartmouth College. So Andrew naturally gravitated toward the game. He joined both school and local Amateur Athletic Union (AAU) basketball teams. But he was not exactly Shaquille O'Neal.

"Nicest kid in the world, and you always wanted to have that size on your team," says Greg Zaney, one of Del Piero's AAU coaches. "But Andrew was not aggressive at all, and he had no coordination. Man, I worked with him so much, and I always tried to be positive with him, but the rest of his body just hadn't caught up with his height yet."

Del Piero was six-foot-four by the time he played on the freshman team at Westlake High School. But he simply was not equipped to excel. As Del Piero now puts it: "I would be the guy running down the floor and tripping over my own feet." His playing time dwindled. The lack of progress cut away at his motivation. And Del Piero felt much more comfortable with another activity that had grabbed his interest. He was becoming a musician.

He had started playing a tuba in sixth grade. Why not? Biggest instrument for the biggest kid, right? *It just seems to fit him*, thought Cheryl Floyd, the longtime band director at Hill Country Middle School. "He was very smart, very dedicated, and very accurate," Floyd says. "Andrew definitely had the desire to be successful. He always wanted to please the teacher, and he always wanted to please his friends."

Del Piero loved learning how to play music. He loved pushing himself. He loved improving. And here was the beauty of it all: As he spent more and more time with his tuba, it was not a teacher or his friends that he pleased the most. It was himself.

With the game clock still frozen at 1:42, a referee hands the ball to LSU forward Eddie Ludwig, who is standing just outside the right sideline on the Tigers' offensive end of the court. Ludwig inbounds the ball to guard Chris Bass and then joins teammates John Isaac and Jalen Courtney on the left side of the floor. The right side now belongs to Del Piero, the main character in the game's only remaining drama: Will the big kid from the band be able to score his first points as a college basketball player?

Clearly, the Tigers are running a play for him.

Del Piero anchors himself in the low post, back to the basket, and he looks out to Bass, who feeds him a shoulder-high pass. Del Piero gathers in the ball and dribbles once with his left hand as he moves into the lane. Six feet from the basket, he pulls up and steps back with his left foot to create space between himself and the player defending him, Nicholls State freshman Lachlan Prest, who is working with a seven-inch height disadvantage. Del Piero jumps, fading slightly away from the goal, ball loaded in his right hand. He starts to fire away, eyes locked on the basket, right elbow perfectly aligned, pointed straight at his target. Everything is happening just the way he has practiced it so many times, and then . . . *whack*. It is Prest hacking Del Piero high on his shooting arm. The ball falls short of the basket. But a whistle blows—foul on the defense—and the crowd roars for Del Piero.

"He'll get a chance to score at the free-throw line!" play-by-play man Jim Hawthorne excitedly tells his audience on the LSU Sports Radio Network.

"And, you know, Jim, he's earned every minute he's going to get on this floor," says former LSU basketball star Ricky Blanton, now a radio analyst. "Coach Johnson mentioned in the pre-game how hard he's worked from the time he left the band to come out here. So this is an awfully enjoyable moment to see this young man out on the floor."

After that one unfulfilling season as a freshman at Westlake, Del Piero would never again play organized basketball in high school. He'd shoot around with friends once in a while, just for fun. But if he was going to be serious about playing anything, it would not be a sport. It would be an instrument.

Del Piero kept getting better with his tuba. And the whole experience of playing it—both the physical and mental aspects—was very gratifying. *Relaxing* is a word he would use, but even that does not fully capture the feeling. "I would almost get like a high," he says. "When you're playing a tuba, you have to move a lot of air, and moving all that air would make me lightheaded and happy. Plus, it was just a fun way to express myself. I'm pretty easygoing, and tuba players are probably some of the most relaxed people you'll ever meet."

Del Piero took private lessons. He attended band camps. He just kept blowing into his oversized horn—kept moving all that air—and eventually something remarkable happened. He went from being known primarily as "the big kid" to being celebrated as the kid who really seemed to be going places with his tuba. Both his junior and senior years Del Piero was named to the Class 5A all-state band in Texas. Attending college on a music scholarship was a realistic goal. And LSU happened to have one of the most accomplished tuba professors in the country, Joseph Skillen, a former Fulbright Scholar who had taught and performed all over the world.

Del Piero packed his tuba—a five-valve Miraphone 186 C model with a lacquered-gold finish—and headed to Baton Rouge for an audition. He still gets a good laugh when he tells of going through airport security on that trip to LSU . . . because he can still picture the poor security guard who did not know how to handle a plane ticket assigned to passenger *Tuba Del Piero*. "True story," Del Piero says. "That tuba cost like six thousand dollars. I was not about to check it with the baggage and get it damaged. So I had two plane tickets. One was in my name. And the other one actually said Tuba Del Piero on it."

The living, breathing Del Piero had no government-issued identification to show for his seatmate. But the security guy ultimately gave in. The audition with Skillen went well. And Del Piero happily accepted a full scholarship to attend the LSU School of Music.

On Saturday, August 30, 2008, the LSU football team opened a new season with a home game against Appalachian State, and Del Piero could not believe how loud the crowd of almost 92,000 was the first time he marched onto the Tiger Stadium field as a freshman member of the band. Del Piero could hardly hear any music beyond the sound of his own tuba, and he immediately knew this was a moment he would never forget. What he did not know was that a middle-aged man named Trent Johnson happened to notice him from the stands—and that Johnson had an acute occupational interest in height. One would be hard pressed to find a basketball coach who did not.

Del Piero is now trying to calm himself at the free-throw line, but it's impossible to pretend away all the eyes that are on him. The eyes of his coaches and teammates. The eyes of everyone watching from the stands—an announced crowd of 7,124. Perhaps he will someday share this moment as a memory and a revisionist account will allow him to say he was thinking only about mechanics: *Do exactly what you've been doing in practice. Just follow through and knock it down.* As nervous as he is, though, what he's really thinking is this: *Just hit the rim! At least hit the rim!*

He bounces the ball once, slightly flexes his knees, stares at the basket, and shoots. The ball grazes the front of the rim, appears to be going in, but then hits the back of the rim and spills out of the basket. "It looked good," Ricky Blanton informs the radio audience. "I tell you, it kind of went in and out."

Teammates Eddie Ludwig and Jalen Courtney offer hand slaps to encourage Del Piero before his second shot. This time he feels more confident. He again bounces the ball once. He takes aim, lets loose of the ball, and it caroms straight off the front of the rim. Another miss. But wait! Nobody from Nicholls State is able to grab the rebound. The ball bounces off the upper body of Ludwig, hits the floor in the middle of the lane, and somehow ends up back in the hands of Del Piero, who is still at the free-throw line. This is not what he was seeking, but he at least has his first positive entry in the LSU record book. A rebound for the tuba dude!

Fans scream with both excitement and instruction as Del Piero holds the ball. They want him to shoot it.

Wow, Trent Johnson thought that first time he saw Del Piero in the football stadium. *Pretty big kid to be playing in the band.* This was five months after Johnson had left Stanford University to become the LSU coach. "I knew we needed some walk-ons," Johnson says now, "and seven-foot-two is seven-foot-two. I mean, you can't coach size, and there he was. I remember telling my assistants we needed to find out who he was." But nothing came of it . . . not until much later.

As a college freshman, the only time Del Piero even thought about basketball was when someone else brought it up. Everywhere Del Piero went around the LSU campus, people had two height-related questions for him. One was simply: How tall are you? And attendant to that: Are you on the basketball team? Clearly, none of those folks had seen video from his one season of high school ball in Texas. But nobody needed background material to appreciate how comfortably the easy-mannered and quick-witted Del Piero generally handled all the talk about his height. Someone would just walk up to him and say: "I can't believe how *tall* you are!" He would playfully respond: "I can't believe how *small* you are!" And the ice was broken.

Of course, it was still within the 325-member band that Del Piero found the most common ground with his peers. He loved the games and the road trips and the camaraderie of it all. For two years he performed at football games, and as a sophomore he joined the basketball band as well. But he also started playing some basketball—casual pickup games in the student recreation center—and that got him thinking: *Maybe I should really give it another try. I can always go back to the tuba when I'm older, but if I don't try basketball now, I'll never know what it might have been like*. When Del Piero contacted the LSU basketball office late in his sophomore year, during the spring of 2010, the coaches remembered him from the band and encouraged him to start preparing for a fall tryout.

With a minute and a half left in the game, Del Piero ignores the fans yelling at him to shoot, and he passes the ball to Jalen Courtney on the left wing. Courtney sends it out to Chris Bass beyond the top of the key—and Bass again directs his teammates to clear the right side for Del Piero. As Del Piero reclaims his position down low, two things are unmistakable: LSU is transforming what is generally considered "garbage time" into The Andrew Del Piero Show. And the crowd is loving it.

Bass feeds a bounce pass to Del Piero, and the big man moves toward the baseline with a single dribble. With 1:19 left, he puts up a hook shot, but it falls short, hitting off the right side of the rim, and Nicholls State pulls in the rebound. "Well, he had some chances," Jim Hawthorne says on the radio broadcast. "It just didn't go down for him."

Del Piero went home to Austin for the summer of 2010, and he trained with a former college basketball coach named Eddie Oran, a longtime assistant at the University of Texas. They worked on basics of offense and defense, and Oran was impressed by the way Del Piero soaked up knowledge by asking questions and taking notes. He put Del Piero through countless drills: shooting, rebounding, passing, developing his footwork. But priority one was to improve his overall fitness. At the end of the summer, Oran saw progress but also knew that more conditioning would be needed before Del Piero could handle the physical demands of big-time college basketball.

When an athlete is dubbed "a project"—at any level of any sport—it does not evoke optimism about short-term success. And Trent Johnson knew he was taking on a project when he invited Del Piero to join the team in the fall of 2010. "He could barely go up and down the court three times without having to stop," Johnson says. "Just because a guy is seven-foot-two, people think he can play basketball. But it's a process . . . especially when you start as late as Andrew did. He had never really been in shape, still had the baby fat. And with a guy that big, you really need to watch out for injuries—stress fractures, knee issues, those types of things. We had to be real cautious."

A plan was agreed upon. Del Piero would be redshirted for the 2010–2011 season, which meant he could practice with the team—but not play in games—without using any of his eligibility as a college athlete. After a year of what would amount to basketball boot camp, Del Piero would then have two years as a full-fledged member of the team. The timing was perfect because LSU had another big man, Justin Hamilton, a seven-foot transfer from Iowa State, whose move from one NCAA school to another required him to sit out a year before he would be eligible to play. When the Tigers were home, Del Piero and Hamilton would practice with everyone else. Whenever the team left town for a road game, they would remain in Baton Rouge and do specialized work with assistant coach Lynn Nance and strength coach Juan Pablo Reggiardo.

Del Piero did a lot of his early workouts in a swimming pool, which allowed him to shed weight and gain endurance without putting too much stress on his joints. His weight started at 290 pounds. The idea was to work off the fat (he would eventually get down to 245) and then replace it with muscle (he would ultimately build himself back up to 265). "Of course, I was always wishing that I could have been on the road trips with everyone else," Del Piero says. "That was definitely motivation for me to keep working, just so I could get to the point where I could really be part of the team."

Nance, who began coaching college basketball in the late 1960s, had never been part of a project like this—or even heard of one. "It was an unbelievable opportunity," he says. "It was almost like taking a kid at the fifth- or sixth-grade level and starting to teach him basketball, except this 'kid' was seven-foot-two!"

The first couple of weeks Del Piero practiced with the team, Nance sometimes noticed other players hiding their faces and giggling. But that did not last long—not once they grew accustomed to how hard Del Piero was working and saw how much progress he was making.

With 1:07 on the game clock and Nicholls State on offense, Chris Bass makes a steal for LSU and pushes the ball up court on a fast break. Nearing the three-point line, he sees Del Piero hustling toward the basket and feeds him a bounce pass on the right side of the lane. Del Piero initially controls the ball, but then he loses it, and it bounces out of bounds. He remains the only LSU player without a point. But Del Piero is nonetheless having a blast. As he jogs back to play defense, a smile spreads across his face.

The more Del Piero practiced with his new band of brothers—his basketball teammates—the more he realized how much his nascent stages of being a college athlete had in common with his earliest days of blowing into a tuba. He loved learning. He loved pushing himself. He loved improving.

Talk to Del Piero about the team's trip to Italy last May for a tour of exhibition games, and one of the first things he'll tell you is how cool it was that he happened to share a last name with one of the most famous athletes in Italy: soccer star Alessandro Del Piero. Based on surname alone, Andrew was a crowd favorite, and fans even rushed him for autographs—the first time that had ever happened to him. But his teammates and coaches are more likely to mention something else that happened. In one of the games, Del Piero threw down an impressive dunk. "It was so great," Justin Hamilton says. "We were all jumping up and down for him."

Equally encouraging to Del Piero is his tale of the triceps. When he first joined the team and began working out with guys who had for years been sculpting their bodies, Del Piero naturally felt a bit inadequate about his physique—and the lack of any visible triceps muscle somehow became symbolic for him. No matter how much iron he pumped, no matter how hard he flexed, he would still see only "flatness"—his word for it—where he yearned to cultivate elevation. But now he's like a child with a new toy when he playfully strikes a triceps pose. "Got to love that little bump," Del Piero proudly announces with a big smile.

Perhaps the most relevant sign of progress came in a recent intrasquad scrimmage, when Del Piero pulled down thirteen rebounds. "The way he's improved, I just love seeing him now," Johnson says. "Andrew is still a work in progress. But his benefit to us has already been immense. He gives us some different looks in practice—you can't simulate that kind of size. And there will be times when he can help us against certain teams. He's going to play in certain situations."

After a three-point basket by Nicholls State, LSU has the ball back, and Jalen Courtney launches a fifteen-foot jumper. The shot is no good, but Del Piero grabs another rebound, his second in only three offensive possessions, and he quickly throws up a short hook shot. Alas, it misses—and that will be the big man's final scoring opportunity of the game. Nicholls State gets a meaningless dunk. LSU dribbles out the clock. And the Tigers own a 96–74 victory.

The box score does not include any points for Del Piero. But it will always show his first playing time—a wonderful milestone for the tuba dude. Walking off the court, he hopes it will also be a steppingstone.

The biggest question remains unchanged: Where will this journey ultimately take Del Piero?

"It's hard to say," Johnson begins. "If he can keep working at it and sustain some confidence, there's no telling where Andrew could end up. He still needs to get stronger. He still needs to learn how to be more physical—how to really knock people around. That's the next phase. And that's what will determine the upside for Andrew."

Johnson pauses. Then he says: "I'm curious to see what happens."

Meanwhile, Tuba Del Piero sits silently in the off-campus apartment of its owner, oblivious to anything happening on a basketball court. Packed in a black canvas bag, the tuba is buried in the bottom of a bedroom closet, wedged between a pile of clothes and an old blanket. There will come a day when Andrew Del Piero again moves air through his favorite instrument in return for bold notes of affirmation. For now, though, he is too busy working on a different kind of playing time.

Andrew Del Piero scored three points while playing a total of only twelve minutes in four games that season. Then—as a senior—he became a starter under new coach Johnny Jones. Del Piero led the 2012–13 team in shooting percentage (55.1) and blocked shots (34) while averaging 4.3 points and 3.1 rebounds per game. The story of his move from the band to the team was prominently featured in The New York Times *and on ESPN's* College GameDay. *Jones called him one of the most improved players he had ever seen. Del Piero now lives in Virginia Beach, Virginia, and works in management with a building contractor. He no longer plays organized basketball. He does play his tuba every now and then.*

Breakfast with Dale

March 30, 2012

Dale Brown won a lot of college basketball games in twenty-five years as head coach of the LSU Tigers. He took two teams to the Final Four and was once named national coach of the year. He prepared Shaquille O'Neal and many others for professional basketball. More than anything else, though, Dale was defined by his devotion to the power of positive thinking and his commitment to enhancing the lives of others. He was Norman Vincent Peale with a whistle and a clipboard—and that is why so many people are now sharing breakfast with him on this pleasant Louisiana morning.

It is the day before tip-off of the 2012 Final Four here in New Orleans—Kentucky against Louisville in one game, Kansas against Ohio State in the other—and the U.S. Basketball Writers Association is honoring Dale with its lifetime achievement award. Three hundred people dining in a hotel ballroom will also see Kentucky star Anthony Davis receive the Oscar Robertson Trophy as national player of the year. But first it is Dale's turn at the podium.

At age seventy-six—fifteen years after retiring from LSU—he pops out of his seat on the dais with the energy of a much younger man. Dale still bears a certain resemblance to comedian Bob Hope. And he still stands perfectly at ease in front of an audience.

"How do I properly say thank you?" Dale asks. "It's almost impossible."

But he came with a plan. With this very moment in mind, Dale recently pulled from his files one of many handwritten letters he had saved from decades of correspondence with longtime UCLA coach John Wooden, his friend and mentor, who died two years ago at age ninety-nine. Dale says that borrowing from Wooden is the only way he can express his gratitude, and so he reads aloud from the letter: "Thanks is a rather simple, one-syllable word that is too often used without feeling, but when used with sincerity, no collection of words can be more meaningful or expressive." Dale looks up and finishes with this: "I say to all of you—thanks."

The response is strong as Dale turns back toward his seat, quickly escalating into a standing ovation, not because of anything Dale just said but because of all he has long represented—everything beyond all the victories and the trophies. Always reaching out to help others. Constantly taking on causes. Never giving up when fighting for what he believes to be right. And doing it all with an overdose of enthusiasm.

I feel fortunate to have seen so much of Dale in action through the years, and I'm glad that he invited me to spend this day with him. I'm standing and clapping right along with everyone else in the ballroom, but my thoughts are also drifting. *How do* I *say thank you?* I have often wondered how I could possibly thank Dale for everything he has done for me—for all he has given me. But this is no longer merely a thought. It now feels like something I must finally turn into action. I pull a notepad from my briefcase, and I start scribbling.

Dear Dale . . .

We first met more than a quarter of a century ago when I was a young newspaper reporter in Lexington, Kentucky. I had recently co-written a series of articles about cheating in college basketball, primarily focused on the University of Kentucky, and Dale had been following the story.

We had spoken several times by telephone, and now I was going to be in New Orleans for a few days, so he invited me to Baton Rouge to be a guest on his weekly television show, *Inside LSU Basketball.* We taped it late the night of Saturday, January 11, 1986. Dale and his Tigers, then ranked eighth in the nation, had already played a road game that evening, losing 88–77 at Tennessee. After flying back to Baton Rouge, Dale had to rush straight to the television studio, but neither the sting of defeat nor the late hour did anything to lessen his energy and kindness. Off camera, Dale playfully emptied his wallet and stuffed my hands with bills, having fun with something we had written about in the newspaper: an old Kentucky basketball tradition of prominent boosters paying players with "hundred-dollar handshakes." We had a good laugh. But Dale was entirely serious once we sat to talk about cheating and the overall state of college sports.

After taping the show, we went to Ruth's Chris Steak House, which was closing by the time we arrived, but not for Dale. One of his best friends, Thomas "T.J." Moran, owned the restaurant and was there to visit with us, so we were free to stay as long as we'd like. It was after two in the morning when we finally said our goodbyes.

"Let's stay in touch," Dale said.

"Definitely," I told him.

But do we ever really know when just meeting someone for the first time?

What a tremendous tribute to you! It sure has me thinking, reflecting. I never would have thought I'd start writing a letter while sitting here at breakfast, but I have long wanted to put into words something I can only hope you already know: the depth and breadth of my gratitude for your kindness and friendship through the years.

We stayed connected by telephone, and every so often I'd find an envelope marked "LSU Basketball" in my mailbox. Dale sent me all sorts of inspirational material, some of it original, but most of it culled from books, magazines, and newspapers. Clearly, Dale loved to read, and he was equally enthusiastic about sharing his findings. (I still keep in my office one of the first pieces he sent me, "The Penalty of Leadership," a wonderful passage from a 1915 magazine ad for the Cadillac Motor Car Company.)

Early 1986 proved to be an interesting time for me to start following LSU basketball from afar. After winning fourteen of their first sixteen games and holding that number-eight ranking when I first met Dale, the Tigers struggled with a string of injuries and illnesses, losing eight of fifteen games the rest of the regular season. They also lost to Kentucky early in the SEC Tournament. But then came magic. With four straight upset victories in the NCAA Tournament, climaxing with a 59–57 come-from-behind thriller against top-seeded Kentucky in the Southeast Regional final, LSU became the first eleventh-seeded team—the lowest seed ever—to reach the Final Four. This group of Tigers did not have the size and star power of Dale's first Final Four team, the 1981 squad led by All-American Rudy Macklin, but that only enhanced the narrative. By staking their claim as a scrappy group of overachievers, John Williams, Don Redden, Ricky Blanton and company were a perfect reflection of their coach. Always eager to share stories of his humble beginnings in Minot, North Dakota, Dale Duward Brown—forever the son of a welfare mother and a father he never knew—had long relished the concept of rising up and thriving as an underdog. The Tigers finally hit the wall, losing to Louisville in the Final Four, but that did nothing to diminish the glow of their season.

I sent Dale a congratulatory note, and we briefly talked about the Final Four the next time we spoke. Mostly, though, our phone conversations went right back to where they had been. We talked more about issues and people and places than we did about games. We talked about politics and philosophy. We talked about life. It was all part of our progression from being acquaintances to being friends.

I think about so many things in my life that never would have happened without you—starting with "Dribblin' for Donors" and all that came with it.

In 1989, my little sister, Wendy—my only sister and best friend—fell ill with Hepatitis B and needed a liver transplant to save her life. She was twenty-two years old, in a deep coma, and I was standing over her bed in a San Francisco hospital when doctors said that she probably had only twenty-four hours to live. That was how I learned about the desperate shortage of organ donors. Almost 19,000 people across the country were waiting for a transplant of some kind, and the medical technology existed to help all of them, but not without a dramatic increase in the number of donors. I knew this was an issue on which I would later want to work, but for now I was singularly focused on Wendy. The severity of her condition catapulted her to the top of the national waiting list, and I trembled with gratitude when a donor was finally found. Surgeons worked straight through the night to give Wendy the liver of a nine-year-old boy who had been killed in an automobile accident. Her comeback—though long and difficult and at times filled with doubts about the outcome—was also the most amazing display of human spirit that I had ever witnessed.

A few months after the transplant, Wendy and I teamed up with Olympic champion Carl Lewis, with whom I was writing a book, to create the Wendy Marx Foundation for Organ Donor Awareness. We worked on projects all over the country, and when Carl and I later formed another group called the U.S. Sports Council on Organ Donation, Dale immediately joined us as a charter member. I did not really expect Dale to do much beyond lending his name to our efforts, but that was only because I did not yet know him as well as I would.

Dale certainly surprised me when he just called out of the blue one day to offer an idea: "Let's do a big basketball game for organ donation. I've got the perfect game." CBS already had it scheduled for national broadcast the afternoon of Saturday, January 22, 1994: LSU against North Carolina, the reigning national champion, live from the Louisiana Superdome. What an opportunity to get out our message! And so we immediately went to work on a new program—we named it "Dribblin' for Donors"—to use the platform of college basketball to promote organ donation.

I was then living in Washington, D.C., but Dale invited me to Baton Rouge, and off I went. He gave me a desk across the hall from his office in the Pete Maravich Assembly Center, and we spent two months on marketing and logistics. We worked with business leaders and media organizations. We reached out to schools and hospitals. Collaborating with the Louisiana Organ Procurement Agency (LOPA), we mobilized hundreds of transplant recipients and donor family members to help us parlay all the exposure into a successful launch of Louisiana's first statewide computer registry for donors.

After years of hearing about Dale doing so much for others, I was now seeing for myself how much he cared about the world around him. The time he devoted to people involved with organ transplantation was impressive enough. But I also saw Dale help so many others who needed a lift, including kids with cancer, homeless families, and prisoners in the Louisiana State Penitentiary at Angola. One of his favorite people in the LSU basketball program was a mentally challenged young man he had brought on board as an equipment manager. Dale was equal parts go-getter and go-*giver*, and the regularity with which he served others was beyond anything I had ever seen.

Wendy and Carl joined us for the big game in the Superdome, and what a day it was. Every fan entering the stadium was offered a "Dribblin' for Donors" brochure. Before the start of the game, Wendy and Carl walked together to center court, where Carl introduced Wendy to the crowd of about 30,000, spoke briefly about organ donation, and then sang the national anthem. "Dribblin' for Donors" messages ran on the huge stadium scoreboards during the game. And CBS announcers Jim Nantz and Billy Packer did a live interview with Carl so he could reach their audience about organ donation.

There was also some impressive basketball action, though not much of it went in favor of LSU. The final score was North Carolina 88, LSU 65, but the lopsided nature of the game took nothing away from all that was accomplished. As Dale, Wendy, Carl, and I walked toward the postgame news conference, Dale stopped and said: "You know, it really does humble you, something like this. You look at all the bright lights and the television cameras, all these thousands of people who come to see us, all the hype we put into a damn basketball game. A *game*. But then you stop for a minute and think about something that really matters. You think about all the people waiting for transplants, the people who have had them, the donor families—all these people we have met and everything they've had to endure. Man, I'm glad we did this. Win, lose, or draw, I'm just *so* glad we did this."

I will never forget what the people from LOPA told us—that Louisiana had never experienced a bigger boost for organ donation. Wow! And it all happened because of you. What more could you have done? Well, you did sort of give me my wife!

When I first met Leslie Herpin—dark eyes and hair, bright smile and personality, a native of Thibodaux—it was nothing more than a passing introduction made by mutual friends. We all happened to be together for dinner one night while I was working with Dale, and that was that. Or so I thought. Five years later, Leslie and I again crossed paths, and this time we looked at each other quite differently. We began a long-distance relationship—Leslie living in Baton Rouge while I was still in D.C.—that went more than six years before we finally decided to get married. On June 24, 2006, at beautiful Oak Alley Plantation in Vacherie, we stood on the front balcony of the big house and took turns saying "I do." We built a home in Baton Rouge, and I began my new existence as a resident of the state to which Dale had so warmly introduced me. After spending my childhood in New York, my college years in Chicago, and most of my adult life on Capitol Hill, I was now eating piles of crawfish, chasing armadillos out of the yard, and shopping for hurricane supplies. I had to make a few adjustments, but life was good.

Thank you for Leslie!

Thank you for Louisiana!

Thank you for the whole chain of events—all our many links of friendship—that started with a few seemingly insignificant phone calls all the way back in 1985. It is a long chain of good fortune and fellowship. And the best thing is that we keep getting to add more links.

We're neighbors now. Dale and his wife, Vonnie, live less than a mile away. So Dale and I get together quite often. We also talk on the phone all the time. But our best talks occur when we are walking. Dale walks a few miles almost every day. He has several favorite routes through the streets of our neighborhood, and he usually covers them alone, hands locked behind his back, head down, music flowing through his earplugs. Whenever we walk together, though, Dale leaves the music at home and our conversations jump all over the place: personal and family updates; people, events, or issues in the news; books we're reading (we often borrow from each other); sports; philosophy; whatever. We once walked for two and a half hours without realizing how long we'd been gone, and by the time I got home, Leslie was worried that something had happened to us. Something had, too. Friendship had happened.

Another time, Dale and I were exchanging childhood stories, and we somehow got to talking about lessons learned from our parents. Knowing that Dale had always revered his mother (who raised him alone) and had always been disgusted by the mere thought of his father (who abandoned the family before Dale was born), I was initially confused when he declared that the most important things he learned from his parents were love and loyalty. But then he explained: "The love my mother showed to me and my sisters was the most consistent, selfless love I've ever seen. She didn't have much in the way of material things, but what a perfect example of love she was able to give us. And then my father was the one who taught me about the importance of loyalty. He had none. Zero loyalty to his wife and children. Sometimes we can learn just as much from the absence of something as we can from the presence of it."

Long before this walk, I had concluded that love and loyalty were motivational North Stars for Dale. By staying locked in on them, he never had to worry about losing his way. Now I also understood why they held such critical roles in his view of the universe.

It's not as if you're about to slow down! I remember something you said when you were leaving LSU—you said that retirement would either be a rocking chair or a launching pad. Trust me, nobody expected you to opt for a chair. Fifteen years later, I know you're still not ready to choose comfort over action. You're way too busy with your charitable foundation focused on education . . . too busy with your work on behalf of Native Americans . . . too busy helping flood victims in North Dakota . . . too busy giving speeches all over the world . . . too busy with the recent releases of your new motivational book and a years-in-the-making documentary on your life. You are too busy being you!

An award for lifetime achievement in basketball is one thing, but you should really be getting one for overall achievement in life. Of course, I'm well aware that you would immediately reject such an idea. I can already hear you pushing back with one of your favorite old lines: "Flattery is like perfume. Taking a sniff is okay, but you better not swallow." Well, as you finish reading this, I hope you will make an exception. Just this one time, accept the flattery! Allow yourself the luxury of truly absorbing why you deserve to be showered with honors and thanks. It is because you have done so much . . . for so many . . . for so long.

I thank you for allowing me to be one of the many. With respect and appreciation and love, I thank you, my friend.

When the breakfast program ends, people rush the dais for autographs and pictures. Oscar Robertson and Anthony Davis oblige a good number of admirers with signatures and smiles, and then they are gone. Dale is the last man standing, still signing and smiling, greeting old friends and making new acquaintances. "You have a business card?" Dale asks a young man who has questions about coaching. "I have some material I want to send you." The man might have his doubts—just as I once wondered if Dale and I would actually stay in touch—but Dale will indeed put together a package for him. They might even end up being friends.

For now, though, Dale has places to go. This afternoon he'll coach the West team in the Reese's College All-Star Game at the Superdome—the first game of any type he has coached in many years—and he has invited me to sit on the bench with the team. After the game, Dale will be the guest of honor at a hotel reception to benefit the American Cancer Society—yet another good cause to support—and I'm looking forward to sharing that with him as well.

We are still adding links to our chain.

On our way out of breakfast, Dale has no idea what I'm folding up and tucking into my briefcase. I will wait for one of our neighborhood walks to give him my letter.

The Hit Man of LSU

June 5, 2012

Tyler Hanover has been around baseball long enough to know good hitting mechanics from bad, and the LSU third baseman has an idea for a new instructional video: "How *Not* to Hit" . . . featuring his teammate and buddy Raph Rhymes. Hanover thought of this months ago, and he's dogged Rhymes about it ever since. "Guaranteed to be a big seller," he's saying now. "With everything Raph does wrong, what a great video for every coach and Little League kid!"

This time the teasing comes after practice on a sunny Tuesday afternoon in Baton Rouge. It is a big week for the Tigers, as they will play Stony Brook starting Friday in a super regional of the NCAA tournament. The winning team advances to the College World Series in Omaha, Nebraska. The loser is done for the year. For now, though, the mood is light in the LSU players' lounge at Alex Box Stadium.

Standing on carpet but pretending to be Rhymes in the dirt of a batter's box, Hanover grips a bat and mimics one unorthodox hitting element after another. He starts with what baseball people call an "arm bar"—meaning the front arm is locked straighter than it ought to be. Once settled in his stance, bat held high while waiting for an imaginary pitch, Hanover wiggles the bat when it should be still. Then—with the "pitch" coming—he makes a big kick with his front leg. Swinging now, Hanover opens his front hip more than any hitting coach would recommend. And he practically throws his body into the ball—"lunging" at it (baseball parlance)—right along with the bat.

"Completely the opposite of everything we have ever been taught to do," senior Grant Dozar declares.

Rhymes offers no retort.

Leaning back in a chair and laughing, he simply watches as Hanover transitions into the role of announcer and playfully introduces his make-believe video: "Ladies and gentlemen, boys and girls of all ages, here it is—Raph Rhymes hitting the way every instructor tells you how *not* to hit. The arm bar! The bat wiggle! The leg kick! Excessive leg movement! Head movement! Front hip flying open! Lunging! We'll cover it all!"

Rhymes laughs again.

And why not?

It is easy to laugh when you were initially cut from the team and now you are the leading hitter—with an eye-popping .452 batting average—in all of Division I college baseball. It is easy to laugh when you are doing things never before done in the 120-year history of LSU baseball. It is easy to laugh when you are living out your childhood dream in a glorious reality bordering on the absurd.

The dream was three generations in the making.

In the mid-1950s, LSU had a third baseman named Ray Rhymes. He later had a son—another Ray but known as "Bubba"—who fell in love with baseball. And then came Raphael Rhymes, who would go by Raph (pronounced "Rafe," as in safe).

One day in 1991, Bubba pulled up to the family home in Monroe—back from his management job with a health-care agency—and took in a sight he would forever carry with him: his only son, two years old, standing in the front yard and taking his first swings with a plastic bat.

Raph's mother, Carol, had gotten him started by gently tossing a plastic ball underhand to him, and the boy kept hacking away. He was having a blast.

Raph would learn to enjoy hunting and fishing. As he got older, he would play golf and other sports. But baseball would always come first. Bubba coached. Raph played. And he never had more fun than when he was running around a ball field with friends.

Raph heard lots of stories about LSU baseball and one day his dad finally took him to Baton Rouge to see a game. The boy was hooked. Raph's childhood heroes played for the Tigers.

One of the most exciting things that ever happened to him was meeting LSU star Ryan Patterson. Raph and his friend Hudson Biedenharn—both thirteen at the time—were in Baton Rouge with Hudson's parents to see LSU play in a regional of the 2003 NCAA tournament. During one of the games in which the Tigers were not playing, some of the LSU players sat in the stands of the original Alex Box Stadium to watch. An usher let the boys from Monroe move down to be near them. Raph could hardly believe it when he realized who was sitting right next to him: Ryan Patterson! One of the best hitters in the Southeastern Conference! Raph was amazed by how nice Patterson was to him—and that alone made Patterson his all-time favorite player.

LSU advanced to the College World Series that year, and after seeing the boys have so much fun at the regional games, Murray and Kathy Biedenharn took them to Omaha for the big event. By losing their first two games, the Tigers were eliminated before the Biedenharns and Raph even arrived, but the trip was still a wonderful adventure for the boys. Improvising, they adopted the Rice Owls as their stand-in team and did not miss a beat. Just watching the games was great. But they also enjoyed the ballpark food, the souvenir stands, and the whole scene at historic Rosenblatt Stadium. They collected autographs from players and staked out the press-box entrance so they could get ESPN analyst

Harold Reynolds to sign baseballs. Kathy Biedenharn wanted photos of the boys in the stadium, and as they posed in the box seats behind home plate, Raph—wearing a blue Rice Owls T-shirt—made an unusually bold statement for a boy who was generally quite reserved: "I'm going to come back here. Y'all are going to see me play here one day for the LSU Tigers."

The dream had always been to play for LSU. Now—for the first time—there was a final destination attached to it.

Rhymes became a hard-hitting second baseman at Neville High School in Monroe—three times an all-state selection—but did not get any scholarship offers from major colleges. So he made what felt like an obvious decision. Rather than going to a small school where he knew he could play, he would chase his dream by enrolling at LSU and attempting to join the team as a walk-on.

Tryouts went well in the fall of 2008—Coach Paul Mainieri was impressed enough to keep Rhymes with the squad for about a month of practices—but the timing for any walk-on to make the final roster was problematic. The Tigers were loaded with talent. Coming off a season in which they made it to the College World Series, they were returning a group with a strong chance of contending for a national championship. Then there was the matter of a new NCAA rule. For the first time in college baseball, the size of a team would be restricted. Without adding a single walk-on, the new limit of thirty-five players meant that Mainieri would have to release five guys from the previous year's team. As much as he liked Rhymes and wanted to give him a chance, he couldn't bring himself to tear out the heart of another young man who had already given so much of himself to the team.

The next to last week of fall practice, Mainieri pulled Rhymes aside on the field and told him he was being released. Mainieri voiced his genuine hope that Rhymes would try again the following year, but for now there was simply no room on the squad. As much as it hurt to be cut, that was not the hardest part for Rhymes. The hardest part was calling his parents to share the news.

"Once I had lasted that long, I knew they had gotten some hope that I might actually make the team," Rhymes recalls. "I talked to my mom first, and I was crying. It was tough. And then having to tell my dad was definitely the toughest. He had been my coach forever. He had been to every game I'd ever played since . . . forever. I mean, how do I tell him I'm not going to be playing baseball? And I wasn't sure if I was ever going to play again."

It was not the last of his challenges as a freshman. Things were not going well with his longtime girlfriend, Garnett Robinson, who had made the move with him from Neville High to LSU. By his second semester on campus, Rhymes was not only without baseball. He was also without the girl he'd thought he would someday marry.

College was not off to a great start.

For the rest of the school year, the only baseball Rhymes played was on PlayStation. Instead of suiting up for the Tigers, he returned to being a fan, usually attending at least one game a weekend when LSU played at home. There were times it was hard to watch—moments when Rhymes would sit in the stands and ponder how cool it would be to be playing second base . . . playing the outfield . . . whatever . . . *just to be out there.* But his intermittent longings never eclipsed his devotion as a fan.

The highlight of the 2009 season came after school let out and Rhymes was back in Monroe for the start of summer: LSU beat Rice in a super regional. The Tigers—led by pitchers Louis Coleman and Anthony Ranaudo along with slugger Blake Dean—were going to Omaha for the College World Series!

Rhymes had a routine for enjoying the World Series games. Whenever LSU played, he went to the home of his best friend from high school, Will Hardy, and they watched with a group of buddies on a big flat-screen TV in the den. That room was jubilant the night of Wednesday, June 24, 2009, as the Tigers routed the Texas Longhorns, 11–4, to win the World Series and claim their sixth national championship in two decades. Watching the LSU players dive into a celebratory dog pile on the field of Rosenblatt Stadium, Hardy and the other guys could not help but mess with Rhymes: *Could have been you, man. Think they're going to make a ring for you?*

"As humble as he is, Raph just wanted to tip his hat to all the guys on the team and be happy for them," Hardy says. "Deep down, I'm sure he felt some regret about not being part of the team and part of that championship. But he would never say it."

Rhymes soon heard from Jeff Willis, coach of LSU-Eunice, a junior college with a strong baseball program. Willis had tried to get Rhymes to join his team straight out of high school, and now that Rhymes was out of the game, the coach wanted to make another recruiting pitch.

"We'd love to have you," Willis told Rhymes.

"Let's do it," Rhymes said.

The sequence of events still leaves him shaking his head.

"If my girlfriend and I had still been together, I would have stayed at LSU to be with her," Rhymes says. "I know I wouldn't have gone to Eunice. And then I don't know if I ever would have played baseball again. I probably would have gone back to the walk-on tryouts to give it another shot at LSU, but who knows what would have happened from there?"

Even Willis was taking a chance.

"We always knew that Raph could hit," he says. "But we didn't know what to expect of him coming off a whole year without playing."

What Willis got was the 2010 Division II National Junior College Player of the Year. Playing second base, Rhymes led LSU-Eunice to a junior college national championship, batting .483 with twelve home runs and a whopping ninety-eight runs batted in. "Nintendo numbers," Willis calls them.

Paul Mainieri was now in the awkward position of wanting to recruit a player he had earlier sent away. Rhymes was in Orange Beach, Alabama, enjoying an early-July vacation, when he saw the 225 area code pop up on his phone. Mainieri was hoping that Rhymes would meet with him to discuss the possibility of returning to LSU and playing for the Tigers.

As much as Rhymes loved the beach, he did not take long to start packing. He was in the LSU baseball office the next day. Mainieri told Rhymes how much he would enjoy coaching him—and he offered a scholarship.

"Do you want to go home and think about it?" Mainieri said.

"I don't have anything to think about," Rhymes replied. "I'm ready to be here."

The evening of Friday, February 18, 2011, LSU hosted Wake Forest in a season opener that drew a school-record crowd of 10,055 to Alex Box Stadium. Bubba and Carol Rhymes were there to cheer right along with everyone else as their son finally made his dream come true. Just wearing that gold number 4 jersey and walking up to the plate for the first time—batting second in the lineup as the designated hitter—was enough to make him tingle. He was officially an LSU Tiger!

The excitement only built from there. Rhymes got the team's first hit of the season—smacking a single into center field—and the crowd went wild. Standing on first base, a six-foot-tall, 180-pound package of joy, Rhymes looked into the stands and let the emotion wash over him. *This is why I came here*, he told himself. *Man, this is going to be fun.*

LSU won in a 15–4 blowout. But that was not the end of the first-night initiation for Rhymes. Half an hour after the game ended, Rhymes walked out of the LSU locker room to meet up with family and friends, and he was greeted by a throng of fans—young and old—waiting outside the stadium for autographs and pictures. It was a standard rite of LSU baseball, but Rhymes was amazed by the number of people. He signed baseballs and T-shirts and ticket stubs. He signed hats and bats and game programs. Rhymes did more than scribble his name and mug for photos. He engaged everyone he met with eye contact and a sincere greeting, he shook hands or knocked knuckles with every kid who wanted in on the action, and he offered a welcoming icebreaker to make each youngster feel comfortable.

"Hey, dude, how's it going?"

"What's up? You play baseball, too?"

Whenever an admiring boy or girl thanked Rhymes for his autograph, his response was: "Thank *you*."

All of this was just as important as that season-opening hit in the first inning. Because when Rhymes looked at those youngsters, he did not see a bunch of unknown faces. He saw himself. He saw a wide-eyed boy on a day when LSU star Ryan Patterson took the time to make him feel like a friend.

Mainieri studied the "unique qualities" Rhymes displayed as a hitter—that was how the coach defined the arm bar, the bat wiggle, and the leg kick; not as weaknesses but as unique qualities—and he decided to leave them alone.

"If you watch the greatest hitters in the history of baseball, they all have some unique quality," Mainieri says. "So you can't cookie-cutter your hitters. You can't make them all into the same guy.

"The basic premise of hitting is to get the bat from your stance to the hitting spot as quickly as possible—with good timing and good hand-eye coordination. And that's what Raph does the best.

"My feeling is that a player has to show failure before I'm going to change anything he does. If it ain't broke, why fix it, right?"

Mainieri identified one element of the Rhymes swing that trumped any other: the ability to keep his bat remarkably flat as he ripped it through the hitting zone. That allowed the bat to stay in the zone fractions of a second longer than most hitters got, and that alone could make the difference between getting a hit and swatting only air.

Rhymes still had adjustments to make in his first year as a Tiger. SEC pitching was the best he had ever faced. After playing second base his whole life, he was uncomfortable appearing only as a designated hitter—feeling that he was not contributing enough by playing only on offense. And then there was the elbow that did not cooperate. Soon after Rhymes finally got a chance to play defensively—Mainieri making him an outfielder because freshman JaCoby Jones was a more athletic second baseman—something happened to his right elbow while he was warming up for a mid-April game against Auburn. After only seven games as an outfielder, Rhymes could no longer throw, so he returned to being the designated hitter.

Rhymes at least felt more at ease in the role than he had earlier, and he ended the season as the second-best hitter on the team. All-American Mikie Mahtook led the Tigers with a .383 batting average (which also led the SEC) and Rhymes hit .360 (sixth-best in the conference). The Tigers failed to make either the SEC or NCAA tournament. But the individual numbers posted by Rhymes—first in junior college and then at LSU—were enough to get the attention of professional scouts.

With the Major League Baseball draft approaching, more than a dozen scouts arranged one-on-one meetings with Rhymes the last week of the LSU season, and he told them all the same thing: "It means a lot to me that you're interested. But don't waste a pick. I'm coming back to LSU." Still, once the draft began, Rhymes heard from several teams starting in the fourteenth round: "If we pick you right now, will you sign?" Rhymes was flattered but no more ready to leave college than he had been. On Wednesday, June 8, 2011, the Pittsburgh Pirates selected him—just in case Rhymes changed his mind—in the fortieth round. Rhymes was alone in his apartment when the Pirates called to share the news, and a flood of congratulatory calls and texts soon followed.

One of the texts was from Mainieri, with whom Rhymes already had an end-of-season exit meeting scheduled for later in the day. Rhymes called the baseball office to make sure the meeting was still on.

"Yeah, sure, I'll see you over here at two o'clock," Mainieri told him.

Then the coach panicked. Why did Rhymes feel the need to check about the meeting? Mainieri was already losing Mahtook and several other key players to pro ball. Was Rhymes also planning to sign a contract and leave?

Once settled on a couch in Mainieri's office that afternoon, Rhymes clearly stated that he was staying at LSU. Then he offered one of the most unexpected collections of syllables his fifty-three-year-old coach had ever heard: "Would it be OK . . . would I be allowed to give up my scholarship so you can use it for someone else?"

"What?" Mainieri said. "Are you serious?"

"Well, yeah," Rhymes said. "If you could use the money to go out and get another player to make us a better team, and I'm allowed to do that, I would like to do it. My family is fine. My parents can handle it, and maybe it'll make the difference between someone else being able to come here or not."

Down the hallway from Mainieri's office, an old Vince Lombardi quote hangs on a wall in the team meeting room: "The quality of a man's life is in direct proportion to the intensity of his commitment." Moments after being consumed by the thought of losing Rhymes, Mainieri was now overwhelmed by the intensity of his selfless commitment.

Rhymes would never want to know who ended up with his scholarship money. All he asked of Mainieri was that he'd keep this conversation between the two of them.

Mainieri gave his word, and his eyes started leaking. He stood to thank Rhymes. He hugged him. Then Mainieri wiped away his tears of pride and hope. He was proud of the man Rhymes had become—clearly a leader for the year ahead—and he swelled with great hope that special things would happen with his 2012 Tigers.

Rhymes had off-season surgery—ulnar collateral ligament reconstruction (commonly known as Tommy John surgery)—to fix his bad elbow. Rehabilitation was grueling. But he was determined to stay on schedule and to battle through it.

He had two personal goals for his junior season. One was to earn a starting spot in the outfield. The other was to be a leader whose hard work and consistency could serve as a model for his teammates. "That was it," Rhymes says. "I didn't set any personal, like, statistical goals or anything like that."

Rhymes quickly earned the job of left fielder and settled into the critical role of cleanup hitter (batting fourth in the LSU lineup). It was not a standard spot in a batting order for someone who was more of a singles hitter than a power slugger. But Rhymes was not a typical singles hitter. He was not a typical hitter, period.

In the first seven games of the season, Rhymes had seven hits in twenty-three at-bats, which gave him an early batting average of .304. Then he went on one of the most remarkable hitting sprees ever seen at such a high level of collegiate baseball. In twenty-one games from February 28 through April 1, Rhymes went 46-for-85, which translates to a staggering .541 average. Midway through the regular season, Rhymes was batting .491—and with a team-leading thirty-four runs batted in through the first twenty-eight games.

"I've spent my entire life in baseball—started at age three, standing in a dugout next to my dad, who was a coach—and I've never seen anything like it," Mainieri says. "I mean, hitting a baseball, especially with the type of pitchers our kids are going against, is probably the hardest thing to do in all of sports. You're taking a round bat to hit a round ball. And you have to hit it squarely. It seems like an oxymoron, doesn't it?"

Not to Rhymes. As the man who regularly throws batting practice to him, nobody knows that better than Mainieri, who constantly marvels at the consistency of his star hitter.

"Raph never tries to do too much," Mainieri says. "If I pitch him inside, he's going to pull it down the left-field line. If I pitch him away, he'll hit it to right field. And if I throw him one down the middle, I better make sure I get behind that screen we use, because otherwise I'm going to catch a baseball in the nose. Raph uses the whole field as well as anyone I've ever seen. And he never gets bored hitting singles."

In addition to his penchant for spraying lined shots all over the field, Rhymes also had an uncanny knack for finding open spaces with balls he was not able to hit as solidly. Teammates would sometimes tease him about that: *Are you surveying the field before you hit? Taking pictures before the pitch and then aiming at whatever holes you see?* They figured Rhymes must possess his own radar system: *Raph*dar. They even had a name for a favorite section of outfield grass—a patch just beyond the reach of the second baseman and equally difficult for the right fielder or center fielder to defend—into which Rhymes would mysteriously drop bloop singles as if on command: the *Raph*muda Triangle. Whereas the long-ball hitting of the great Babe Ruth had long before been responsible for the term *Ruthian* meaning any superb or oversized performance, the term *Raphian* now had a chance of entering the local lexicon as a word that means collecting small chunks of something good. Rhymes did mix in a double or a home run every now and then. For the most part, though, he just hit single after single after single.

Teammate and close friend Mason Katz matter-of-factly referred to Rhymes as a machine. Admiring fans offered other labels. On social media, Rhymes was called a monster, a beast, an animal, a straight stud—all intended as terms of endearment. One excited tweeter shared this over-the-top conclusion: "Raph Rhymes is the Greek God of hitting."

He hardly had the build for such lofty status. But at least he now had the right coif to play the role. Prior to this season, Rhymes had always kept his light-brown hair pretty short. He decided to let it go a bit, just to try something new, and now he was sporting some serious locks—the flow spilling out from under his baseball cap and far beyond anything he had ever intended. With his bat so hot, however, Rhymes didn't want to test the baseball gods by doing something as monumental as getting a haircut.

It would be silly to call a string of six hitless at-bats a slump. For Rhymes, though, it was at least an aberration. It happened in back-to-back games—early in April—at Florida. Rhymes even struck out once—only the seventh time he'd done so all season. Then something scary happened. He was hit in the head by a pitch and knocked woozy. Rhymes had suffered a concussion. Fortunately, it did not turn out to be severe. A few days later, with LSU fans still in the dark about his condition, Rhymes tweeted three words—"Life is good"—to assure his followers that all was OK.

Rhymes missed three games before happily returning to the lineup. The Tigers then played seven games in ten days—and Rhymes was right back to his old ways. In fact, he actually raised his average, hitting a preposterous .654 (17-for-26) during that stretch. Teammates joked that maybe they needed to get hit in the head, too. Rhymes was consistent in his response: "Uh, no, I definitely don't advise anybody to go up there and take a fastball to the head."

That post-concussion flurry of hits set off a sixteen-game hitting streak for Rhymes. It also led to a rush of media attention, as the final few weeks of the regular season were coming and Rhymes still led the nation with a batting average that hovered around .500—give or take a few points depending on his daily output. The *Baton Rouge Advocate* started running a regular graphic in its sports pages—"RAPH RHYMES WATCH"—to help chronicle his journey. Out-of-town writers and radio stations called for phone interviews. Television cameras and microphones became a routine part of his days.

There was good reason for all the commotion. Twenty-one years had passed since the last time anyone in college baseball had hit .500 or better for a full season. In 1991, someone named Ron Dziezgowski went 44-for-88 while playing for Duquesne, and even that was not as impressive as what Rhymes was doing. Rhymes had already been to the plate more than twice as many times as Dziezgowski had batted—meaning he had defied the laws of baseball averages for far longer—and Rhymes was competing in the toughest conference in college baseball.

Media folks and fans alike were understandably charmed by the story of a former walk-on who had once been cut by the team and was now the nation's leading man. They also happily embraced Rhymes because of his low-key approach to all that swirled around him. No matter how much the spotlight shined on him, he was never anyone but the same modest, unassuming person he had always been—"a good old country boy from Monroe," as Coach Mainieri fondly calls him.

Rhymes routinely talked about something he had learned long before arriving at LSU: "I know that if I ever go around thinking that I have baseball figured out, that's when it's going to come back and get me. That's when the game is really going to humble me. So I just want to go about things as, *Well, I've done whatever I've done, but how can I get better? What should I be doing to get better?*"

His out-of-control hair notwithstanding, Rhymes insisted that he was not much into the superstitious nature often associated with baseball people. Still, he definitely had his ways of doing things.

If it was a Friday and the Tigers were playing at home that evening, he would pick up his lunch—always a grilled-chicken sandwich—at Zoës Kitchen in Perkins Rowe. He would take his sandwich to Alex Box Stadium and eat it in the locker room. Then he would head to the indoor batting cages, always alone. This was still about five and a half hours before game time. Rhymes would put on some music—didn't matter what it was; whatever happened to be playing on the iPod kept by the back door—and he'd hit baseballs off a tee for a while. He might take fifty swings. He might take closer to a hundred. Part of it was physical: to start getting loose and to make sure he was hitting the ball solidly. Part of it was just to clear his mind. He'd keep swinging, smacking baseballs into the heavy netting, until he felt comfortable. Then he'd return to the locker room. Most of his teammates would by then be arriving, and he enjoyed hanging out with them before taking the field for their standard pregame work.

If his parents were in town for the game—and they usually were—he had one other pregame routine. He'd look for his mom in the stands. Carol Rhymes would always be somewhere on the first-base side of Alex Box. She would hold up a hand with four fingers stretching skyward, four digits to represent Raph's uniform number and wish him good luck, and Raph would instantly transition from being everyone's All-American to his mother's only son. He would blow her a kiss.

Once the game started, when it was his turn to bat, Rhymes always had the same walk-up song, Cali Swag District's "Teach Me How to Dougie"—a seemingly incongruent blast of big-attitude hip hop to announce the country boy from Monroe. Rhymes loved the energy of that song. It was now that his updated batting average, whatever the bloated figure of the moment, would glow in big numbers on the giant stadium scoreboard. Rhymes would never look up at it. He did not want to think about his average when there was work to be done. In fact, he never really wanted to think about it—didn't even want to know what it was.

"Statistics are something that's happened in the past," Rhymes says. "I'm sure the time will come—probably when I'm older and have a family—when I'll want to look back on everything that's happened this year. I mean, no question, it's been an amazing experience. But I don't want to think about any of that when I'm trying to hit. Plus, it's just bad karma to be looking at stuff like that."

The best hitters in LSU baseball history had never come close to hitting .500 for an entire season. Only three had managed to breathe the rare air of the .400 level: Russ Johnson (.410) in 1994, Eddy Furniss (.403) in 1998, and Todd Walker (.400) in 1992. So it was understandable that anyone with an interest in LSU sports was talking about Rhymes. Everyone knew that he would soon own the best single-season batting average in school history. But could he stay above .500 for an entire season? What would it take for him to do that?

Mainieri answered those questions with one of his own: "How in the world would I know? I've never seen anyone do it!"

In the second inning of a May 11 game against Vanderbilt, under the lights at Alex Box Stadium, Rhymes hit a chopper down the third-base line and legged out an infield single. It was not a thing of beauty. But people tracking his average and pulling for him no longer cared about aesthetics. A hit was a hit. Playing in his forty-sixth game of the season—the fiftieth for the team (with only eleven losses)—Rhymes was now 86-for-171 at the plate. With the rest of that game plus six more remaining in the regular season, he stood on first base with a batting average of .503.

Rhymes had two more at-bats that night: He fouled out to the first baseman and flied out to left field. No big deal. Even the hit man of LSU sometimes made back-to-back outs. But things got worse the next night. That was when his sixteen-game hitting streak ended—and with an ugly assortment of futility. Again playing Vanderbilt, Rhymes twice hit into double plays, once grounded out to the shortstop, and then struck out with two men on base and no outs in the eighth inning. It was the first time in thirty-one games that he had not somehow reached base. Six fruitless at-bats after his average had temporarily settled at .503 the night before, Rhymes was now hitting .486—not that he knew what the numbers were. More than anything, Rhymes was consumed by the painful thought that he had let down his team, then ranked third in the nation, in what ended as a 6–3 loss to unranked Vanderbilt.

Before he even walked off the field, Rhymes knew what he wanted to do. His long hair had been getting on his nerves for a while now. Away from the ballpark, without the aid of a hat, he never knew what to do with it anymore. It was that wild. His mom had been wearing him out with her warnings about getting a haircut—about changing *anything* while he was hitting so well. Now, though, after such a dreadful night at the plate, he could finally have someone cut away without any fear of upsetting anything. Once in the locker room, Rhymes enlisted the help of an equipment manager, fellow student K.J. Fort, who used both scissors and clippers to liberate Rhymes from the burden of his messy mane. The cutting took on something of a ceremonial tone. Teammates Kevin Gausman and Kurt McCune each participated by taking a snip or two. McCune then tweeted a photo of Rhymes getting his cut—along with a brief explanation: *Baseball is a very superstitious sport #raphrhymes #hair #seeya.*

His average has not touched .500 again.

With ninety-nine hits in 219 at-bats, Rhymes would need an unthinkable streak of twenty-one straight hits to revisit that lofty plateau. But it hardly matters that .500 has turned out to be unsustainable. This season will always be remembered for Rhymes giving it a chase—the most serious chase in the history of LSU baseball. Plus, it would be terribly incomplete to define what Rhymes has done solely by the rise and fall of cold numbers. His story will always be warmed by the bigger picture of where he came from and where he's already landed: recently named both SEC Player of the Year and a first-team All-American. It is a story of perseverance and a second chance made good—a story of uncommon excellence paired with remarkable humility.

As teammates Tyler Hanover and Grant Dozar continue to give Rhymes a hard time in the LSU players' lounge—still teasing him about the way he hits—three handwritten letters Rhymes has had for weeks sit on a shelf in his locker down the hall. He gets some sort of fan mail almost daily. But these are the only letters he has stored away. He likes to read them as reminders of what it means to be an LSU baseball player and of what it means to be the type of person he has always wanted to be.

One of the letters is from a boy named Greg in Belle Chasse, Louisiana, on the West Bank of the Mississippi River in Plaquemines Parish. "I'm a huge fan of yours," it says. "You are my favorite because of your will to never give up. I love your story of how you finally made the team."

Another letter, this one from a high school baseball player in Sheboygan, Wisconsin, is remarkable not for its content but for the way Rhymes responded to it. The writer, seventeen-year-old Tanner Reklaitis, asked Rhymes to sign two photos, one for him and one for a friend. He also asked Rhymes to sign a baseball. The letter says it was the first ball he'd ever sent out for an autograph—but there was no baseball to be found in the large envelope waiting for Rhymes. A note at the bottom of the letter says, "No ball, would not fit," with the scribbled eyes and mouth of a sad face inked next to the words. Rhymes felt bad about that. What to do? He eventually walked from the locker room to the front desk of the LSU baseball office and asked longtime secretary Virginia Robertson if he could please have a ball to send to the boy. Handing Rhymes a ball, Robertson had one of the same thoughts she always did about him: *Such a nice young man*. She also had another thought: *Who does that? Who goes and finds a ball for some random kid in Wisconsin?*

The final letter came from someone Rhymes knew while growing up in Monroe. Roy Heatherly had for seventeen years lived there and been one of his dad's good friends. Now a newspaper publisher in Jackson, Tennessee, Heatherly recently drove to Ole Miss for a weekend of baseball because LSU was playing there and he wanted to see Raph in action. Heatherly and Raph spent a good bit of time together between games—and Heatherly could not have been more impressed. Soon after returning home, he wrote a letter to Rhymes telling him how great it was to see him and celebrating the way he had become "such a great role model" for young people. "You have grown up into a man of character," it says. "No matter where God takes you next, you will bring honor and dignity to it."

With words such as those sitting in his locker—words such as those filling his heart—it hardly even matters how many more hits Rhymes has left in his bat. He is playing the one game he has always loved most—playing it right where he's always wanted to be. He is already a champion. He will always be one.

LSU lost to Stony Brook in the super regional. Raph Rhymes ended the 2012 season with a .431 batting average—best in the nation and still the LSU record for a single season. As a senior in 2013, Rhymes made good on his childhood statement that he would someday return to Omaha and play in the College World Series. The Tigers were eliminated in two games. Rhymes is now playing professional ball as a minor leaguer in the Detroit Tigers organization.

Mack is Back

July 6, 2012

She had been gone only a month, but Brittany Mack was already missing Tiger Park—home to so many memories as an LSU softball star. It was also the longest she had been away from her boyfriend, Josh Oakes, from whom she'd been pretty much inseparable since they first shared a couple of Mountain Dews early in her freshman year.

Now she was coming back as a local hero: the first player selected in the 2012 draft of the National Pro Fastpitch League. As a rookie pitcher for the USSSA Florida Pride, Brittany was returning to Tiger Park for a four-game weekend series against the Carolina Diamonds. The series was scheduled for Baton Rouge because LSU coach Beth Torina also coaches the Pride during the summer, and she wanted to give Louisiana softball fans a chance to see some of the nation's best players. The Pride alone features nine Olympians. But the weekend would be all about the former LSU All-American now wearing jersey number 44 in the red, white, and blue of the Pride.

"MACK is BACK!" screamed the promotional material. Print ads even used Cajun spelling in support of her new team: "Geaux Pride!"

As the weekend approached, friends and fans called, texted, and tweeted Brittany to tell her how awesome it was going to be to have her back in Tiger Park.

"You must be so excited," they told her.

"You don't even know," she responded.

Actually, the people closest to her thought as they chuckled to themselves, *you are the one without a clue*.

Her four years of college had passed so quickly. One moment Brittany was arriving on campus as a highly recruited flame-thrower out of Round Rock, Texas. Next thing she knew, she was closing out her LSU career as a fan favorite and 2012 Southeastern Conference co-scholar athlete of the year. She now bounced from memory to memory in a personal feast of reminiscence.

She had so many highlights.

As a freshman: pitching a no-hitter against Texas State.

As a sophomore: winning eight of her last nine decisions.

As a junior: recording career highs in wins (20) and strikeouts (209) . . . being named first-team All-SEC and third-team All-American.

As a senior: getting her first career hit (Brittany rarely batted in college) and knocking in the only run of the game to defeat twelfth-ranked Georgia on LSU's Senior Day . . . collecting a career-high 17 strikeouts against Missouri in a super regional game of the NCAA tournament . . . advancing to the 2012 Women's College World Series and throwing a two-hit shutout against South Florida for LSU's lone victory in the series.

Above all else, though, Brittany had come to cherish her position as a role model for young girls who admired both her talents and her spunk. Early in her collegiate career, she sometimes lost her cool on the field or in the dugout, throwing her glove or otherwise letting loose with an outburst. But when she came to understand that young eyes were always upon her, she committed to a self-imposed rule: Whenever fans saw her express emotion, it was going to be the positive kind that any parent would want a child to emulate. Brittany became a high-energy leader known for her celebratory fist-pumping on the field and her fun-filled interaction with fans after games. She also created a program called "Geaux Play" to support children with special needs participating in the Miracle League Association at Cypress Mounds. As a result of her efforts, LSU fans donated more than four hundred gloves, bats, and balls, as well as other athletic equipment.

Then there was her boyfriend and all that came with a relationship now in its fourth year. The first time Brittany and Josh went anywhere together—to join a group of friends playing pool at a Tigerland bar—Josh stopped at a gas station for a soft drink while Brittany waited in his Jeep. She could hardly believe it when he returned with two Mountain Dews: one original flavor and the other Code Red. "You want one?" Josh asked, not knowing that Brittany was practically addicted to Mountain Dew. She happily opted for the Code Red. It was not exactly love at first sip, but Josh was off to a great start. Soon thereafter, he and a few buddies joined Brittany and some of her LSU teammates for a night in New Orleans, and Brittany and Josh had their first kiss. After going their own ways for the holidays—she with her family in Texas, he in his hometown of Shreveport—Brittany and Josh got together back in Baton Rouge the evening of January 1, 2009, and officially declared themselves a couple.

When Josh looked at Brittany—five-foot-ten; sturdy, athletic build; long, dark hair; rosy cheeks and soft, hazel eyes punctuating her big smile and welcoming countenance—he saw only beauty. It made no difference when she was not wearing makeup, her hair was pulled back in a ponytail, and she was still wrapped in soiled athletic gear after practice or a game. Josh would always tell Brittany the same thing: "You're beautiful!"

Away from the softball field, Brittany had never been the most confident person in the world, so she loved hearing that from Josh. She also loved just looking into his eyes without hearing a word. Josh was six-feet tall, his height a nice bonus for a young lady who stretched almost as high. She liked his straight, black hair. But those eyes—deep brown and accentuated by thick, dark eyelashes, as if he were wearing what Brittany called "guy liner" (the male version of eye liner)—it was those eyes that always pulled her in and allowed her a direct path to his core.

Josh became a softball fan.

Brittany learned how to hunt and fish. She started riding four-wheelers and dirt bikes. His things.

They went to church together—Josh introducing Brittany to Healing Place Church in Baton Rouge and Brittany regularly attending services for the first time since her childhood. Josh had two tattoos: the face of Jesus on his right biceps and a cross (along with the word "Forgiveness") on his back. Brittany thought it was great that Josh could always be so committed to his spirituality and also be so playful when it came to just about anything else. He was the first guy she'd dated who would walk down the aisle of a grocery store gobbling like a turkey—just to see how people reacted. So what if he sometimes embarrassed her? He also made her laugh. Brittany laughed a lot when she and Josh were together.

It did not take long for the arguing to start.

"I love you," Brittany would tell Josh.

"I love you more," Josh would reply.

"No, I love you more!"

They sometimes went back and forth this way to the point that friends would just want to gag.

"The big thing for us," Josh says now, "is that we really got to be best friends. We always wanted to be able to tell each other everything. And we've always done that."

Well . . . almost always.

He did not tell her about his plan to get the pet she so desperately wanted. There was a period of weeks once they had moved in together when Brittany was lobbying for a kitten and Josh kept repeating his "no cat" rule: "Not going to happen, Brittany." Then he surprised her with a furry little feline. She cried tears of joy and appreciation.

There was also the fib he told prior to Brittany leaving in late May for the College World Series in Oklahoma City. Josh insisted that there was no way his work schedule would allow him to make it—he has his own business distributing food to retail stores—and he really laid it on thick. He was so upset that he would not be able to share such a special experience with her. Brittany was warming up for her June 2 start against South Florida when Josh surprised her by sticking his head into the bullpen. Again, tears flowed.

Josh always enjoyed a good surprise.

Brittany always enjoyed a good cry.

She knew she would not play tonight in the opening game of the series. Brittany is scheduled to pitch tomorrow. But this still had all the makings of a huge night. Brittany was thrilled about sharing the beauty of her college ballpark with her new friends in the professional league. There was also going to be some sort of post-game ceremony. Brittany knew little about it but did not need a lofty GPA—hers was 3.6 as a kinesiology major—to conclude that LSU was going to do something nice for her.

The Pride helped by winning the game. Two-time Olympic medalist Cat Osterman gave up only five hits and rookie Kristyn Sandberg, Brittany's closest friend on the team, drove in the only run of the night with a pinch-hit double in the sixth inning. The mood was perfect for Brittany and the "home" crowd of 1,037 to enjoy whatever was coming next.

Brittany was told that she would participate in a ceremony to unveil a large banner in celebration of her time at LSU—and that the banner would later be installed on a wall in Tiger Park. Brittany's parents, Scott and Jan, joined her on the infield dirt between home plate and the pitcher's circle, as did her sister, Courtney; Coach Torina; Pride general manager Don DeDonatis; and league commissioner Cheri Kempf. With her Pride teammates kneeling in the grass outside the first-base line and a good number of former LSU teammates also watching from field level, Brittany pulled away a white blanket to reveal the banner, and everyone loved it. Cameras flashed. Fans and players clapped.

But there was more.

Torina took Brittany by the shoulders and turned her around to reveal an additional surprise.

It was Josh—wearing both a red "Mack" jersey and a big smile.

As soon as Brittany saw him, he dropped to his right knee and spoke as best he could: "Brittany, you know that I love you more than anything else in the world. You know I want to spend the rest of my life providing for you and being the man that you deserve to have."

Of course, her tears started flowing immediately. Her body shook. As silent as the ballpark now seemed, it crossed her mind that everyone in the stands might actually hear her crying. So what? All she wanted to do was stare at Josh and take in every ounce of the moment. Looking into his eyes—her all-time favorite eyes—she could see how thoroughly happy he was.

"Will you spend the rest of your life with me? Will you marry me?"

"Yes!" she said. "Yes!"

Actually, she had started saying it before he was even done.

Josh reached into the right pocket of his khaki shorts and pulled out the ring he'd kept hidden since April: three round diamonds set atop a perfect circle of 14-karat gold. He had initially thought about doing this on April 29, Senior Day at the ballpark, but then thought better of it because he did not want to steal any attention from the other seniors being honored. Josh now put the ring on Brittany's finger, and everyone cheered.

Andrea Duran of the Pride turned to teammate Kristyn Sandberg and asked if they should dogpile Brittany.

"Let's go!" Sandberg said.

Everyone else followed. But the players did not dogpile. They just hugged a lot. They smiled and laughed a lot.

Brittany recently wrote in a blog for the team website that "the basics" for her were: "me + family + softball = a fantastic life!" Her equation was now on full display for all to see. Only one small piece was missing. And that would be easily addressed.

Once all the celebrating was done, Brittany left Tiger Park with Josh and Sandberg. It was almost eleven o'clock when they pulled into the IHOP on College Drive. Still wearing their game uniforms, the young women drew curious looks as they were seated. But the uniforms were not the most unusual sight of their meal. That distinction would go to the item that Brittany had somehow forgotten when writing about the basics of her life. The waitress did not bring her only a glass of Mountain Dew. She brought her both a glass and a big carafe of it. How many people had ever seen that?

Sandberg wanted a picture of Brittany in all her glory.

With "Pride" plastered across the front of her jersey, a stack of pancakes on her plate, a shiny, new ring on her finger, the glass of Mountain Dew in her right hand and the carafe in her left . . . Brittany offered a smile for the ages.

And she even suggested a caption for the picture: "The greatest night of my life!"

Brittany Mack and Josh Oakes got married March 30, 2014. They live in Shreveport. Brittany no longer plays professional softball. She coaches youth teams and is in graduate school to become a physical therapist.

Bennie Gets a New Number

August 2, 2012

Bennie Logan is laboring through the opening session of preseason football practice. Time after time, he explodes out of a three-point stance and charges toward an imaginary quarterback. Then he joins his fellow defensive linemen for a series of drills that violate the serenity of morning: lots of slamming into sleds and working on techniques to blow up an offense. "Violence!" demands LSU defensive line coach Brick Haley. "It all starts right now!"

None of this is new to Logan. The six-foot-two, 295-pound defensive tackle is entering his fourth year with the Tigers—his junior season due to a redshirt year—and he already looks like an NFL player. His massive upper body challenges the confines of his purple jersey. His powerful motor never stops.

Only one thing appears wrong on this steamy Thursday morning. Instead of wearing his usual number 93—a fittingly large jersey number for a defensive lineman—Logan is sporting number 18. The teens are generally for smaller players at the "skill" positions, so why would any self-respecting lineman allow himself to be wrapped in such puny digits?

LSU offensive lineman Josh Dworaczyk offers a first-look fashion critique of Logan's new number: *goofy*. "But we'll get used to it," Dworaczyk says. "And it's such a great honor for Bennie. That number 18 has really become a big deal around here."

The number has been worn by many players throughout the 120-year history of LSU football. But its lofty status is relatively new. It started with a playful conversation in early 2004. LSU had recently defeated Oklahoma in the BCS national championship game, and quarterback Matt Mauck, soon to be leaving Baton Rouge for the NFL, was visiting with athletic trainer Jack Marucci. "Hey, who's going to get my number 18?" Mauck wanted to know. "We can't have just anyone wearing it."

Marucci laughed. But he knew that athletes can become quite attached to their jersey numbers—and he could tell that Mauck was not entirely joking. Marucci had come to know him as one of the most dedicated and genuine leaders he'd ever seen on a football team. The longtime trainer was especially impressed by the way Mauck had diligently worked his way back from a severe foot injury to lead LSU to its first national championship since 1958. So out of respect for all that Mauck had contributed, both on and off the field, Marucci talked to LSU equipment manager Greg Stringfellow about picking a player worthy of filling Mauck's jersey—worthy in terms of character and the potential to be a strong leader. Their choice was freshman Jacob Hester, an all-state fullback out of Evangel High School in Shreveport.

Hester had planned on sticking with the number 13 he had worn since his Pop Warner football days. But when he learned that Mauck wanted to bequeath the number 18 to him—and why the former Tiger wanted to do so—Hester was deeply moved. "That meant the world to me, especially as a freshman," Hester says now. "I didn't even hesitate. I just said, 'Of course, I want to wear it.' And I knew I would always think of that number as something very special."

Hester even put it on a personalized license plate for all to see—"LSU 18"—but that was nothing compared to the way he displayed it on game days. Although he was never the most physically gifted member of the team—generously listed at six-foot, 225 pounds—Hester was a hard-working, hard-nosed bruiser who parlayed endless energy and drive into remarkable results. In 2007, his senior season, Hester led LSU in rushing yards (1,103) and touchdowns scored (thirteen) as the Tigers again won the national championship. When the team went to the White House to celebrate, Hester was chosen for the honor of presenting President George W. Bush with a bronze football to commemorate the occasion.

With Hester departing campus—the San Diego Chargers selected him in the third round of the 2008 NFL draft—another deserving successor needed to be chosen for LSU jersey number 18. But who would it be? What had started as an attention-free handoff from Mauck to Hester was by now a matter of considerable interest. After four years of Hester adding to the stature of number 18, players and fans alike wanted to know who would be next to wear it.

The honor went to tight end Richard Dickson, but the process was not as simple as it had been when Hester got the number. After watching Dickson catch two touchdown passes to help LSU defeat Ohio State, 38–24, in the national championship game on January 7, 2008, head coach Les Miles did not initially embrace the idea of Dickson—then a sophomore—giving up the number 82 he'd been wearing. "Richard had made a name for himself, and everyone was used to seeing him in that number 82, so we had to be pretty persuasive with Coach Miles," Hester says. Dickson did not know Miles had finally given the go-ahead until arriving for the start of spring practice and finding a number 18 jersey in his locker. He was thrilled to see it. "For me," Dickson says, "it was just amazing to be considered on the same level with the guys who had already worn it."

Nobody issued a formal announcement that a "tradition" was now in place. No rules were written. The process just evolved. LSU football insiders often use three words—character, perseverance, and leadership—in explaining what it takes to wear number 18. They also stress the importance of being successful both on and off the field. Each number 18 is now chosen with input from team trainers, equipment managers, the sports information staff, and all former number 18s going back to Matt Mauck—with Les Miles still having the final say.

After Dickson left LSU and signed with the Detroit Lions, number 18 went to running back Richard Murphy in 2010 and to safety Brandon Taylor in 2011. Both often spoke in general terms about the honor of wearing the "legacy" jersey, but when Taylor was preparing for the NFL draft, he learned that it also came with tangible benefits. "Every team that I met with, every scout asked about the number 18 and what it meant to me," Taylor says. "They all want good leaders on their teams. So I have to believe that wearing number 18 actually helped me in the draft." The San Diego Chargers—who still had Jacob Hester on their roster—selected Taylor in the third round of last spring's draft.

Soon thereafter, Taylor and Bennie Logan were together one day in the LSU training room. This was after Logan had been offered number 18 for the 2012 season but before any public announcement of it. In a behind-the-scenes passing of the torch, Taylor told Logan: "Just continue doing all the right things. It's not about being an All-American or any of that stuff. It's about your loyalty to LSU."

"Loyalty is all I know," Logan recently tweeted.

And his tweets tell us a lot about him.

"Respect all but fear none!!"

"They gonna love me for my ambition . . ."

"Hungry, humble, and focused #God1st"

"I wanna be great not average that's why I stay on the grind!"

"A grind ain't nothing to a guy who came from nothing!"

"Small city big dreams, I been waiting on these days since I was 16!"

Growing up in the tiny town of Coushatta—the parish seat of rural Red River Parish in northwest Louisiana—Bennie Cordell Logan was the son of a carpenter and a nurse. But his father was never around as much as Bennie would have liked him to be, and his mother was gone way too soon. Bennie was only in fifth grade when Sandra Logan died after suffering a stroke. As the fourth of eight siblings, Bennie learned at a tender age what it meant to sacrifice for others and to cherish with all his heart the people closest to him.

He also learned to dream. His biggest dreams were about football—not only playing it, but also using it as a vehicle to better days for both himself and a future family of his own. He understood that blocking and tackling at Red River High School was a long way from his ultimate dream of playing for his favorite professional team, the New York Giants, but Logan had a plan.

First stop: LSU.

Logan was thrilled to join a program with a growing reputation for putting defensive linemen into the NFL (including first-round picks Glenn Dorsey and Tyson Jackson in the two drafts preceding his arrival). After redshirting as a freshman and playing in only three games in 2010, Logan became a major force last season, leading the defensive line with fifty-seven tackles, including six in the national championship game loss to Alabama. He was somewhat overshadowed by fellow defensive tackle Michael Brockers, who was later selected by the St. Louis Rams in the first round of the 2012 NFL draft. But Logan would not be in the shadows for long.

With the 2012 college football season soon to begin, ESPN.com has shined a spotlight on Logan by naming him the best defensive tackle in the Southeastern Conference. He's also on the preseason watch list for the Outland Trophy, which goes to the best interior lineman in college football, and countless NFL scouts have identified Logan as someone they'll definitely want to study in the coming months. None of that will change his approach to football—or to life.

"He's just an old construction worker," says Haley, the defensive line coach. "He packs a lunch. He puts on his boots and his hard hat. And his whole attitude is: *Let's go have us a good day of work.*"

"Hard work. Dedication. A team guy. He's always helping us teach the younger guys. Those are the first things that come to mind. He's just that guy who other people look to as the standard . . . always leading by example."

Someone who regularly faces Logan from across the line of scrimmage—even if only in practice—offers a glimpse of what LSU's opponents will see when they line up against the newest number 18.

"Mad Dog, that's what I call him," senior Josh Dworaczyk says. "Off the field, Bennie is the nicest guy you'll ever meet. But he puts the pads on, and he's got a mean streak about him. He's like a junkyard dog. You know, 'Don't mess with me, because it's going to get ugly.' That's Bennie. As a teammate, you just love the guy, and you're definitely glad you don't have to play against him in the games."

It is evening now. With the first day of practice behind him, Logan relaxes in the campus dormitory serving as temporary home during football camp. He taps on his cell phone and pulls up a photo texted to him by a buddy. Richard Cannon, a hometown friend still living in Coushatta, had come across it on a website devoted to LSU sports: the first available shot of Logan in his new jersey. Logan peers into the phone, studies the frozen image of himself standing on the practice field between drills, sweaty and drained, and he could not feel better about the man he is becoming. He could not feel better about having been chosen to wear that number 18.

It was never part of his plan. The plan was only about hard work—

only about working his way right into the NFL. But that new jersey of his—the honor it signifies—is something he can carry with him for a lifetime: a wonderful symbol of both the plan and the process.

Employing the magic of technology and the tips of his thumbs, Logan opens his Twitter account so he can share the photo with his 2,300-plus followers.

"My new number," he tweets. "#honor #history #tradition"

Never before has a behemoth lineman been so moved by the thought of carrying such a small number into battle.

Bennie Logan is now in his third year with the Philadelphia Eagles. Two more LSU football players have worn number 18 since Logan left for the NFL: linebacker Lamin Barrow in 2013 and running back Terrence Magee in 2014.

Fifty for Fifty

September 6, 2012

As a Northerner by both nature and nurture—born and raised in New York, schooled in Chicago, happily settled on Capitol Hill in D.C. for most of my adult years—I never could have guessed that I would celebrate my fiftieth birthday as a resident of Louisiana. Yet here I am. I moved to Baton Rouge because my wife is from Thibodaux and already lived here when we married in 2006. And I'm enjoying it.

This is not to say that the transition to "Yankee on the Bayou" has been entirely seamless. But I love being married. People here have been quite welcoming. And I've been able to lean on an old friend—the world of sports—for the comfort of familiarity.

Of course, in Baton Rouge, the world of sports means LSU sports. My first writing project here was a book, *The Long Snapper,* about former LSU football player Brian Kinchen. But I'm not referring only to my work. I'm talking about life as a whole. The entire culture of LSU sports—my enjoyment of both the games and the people around them—has played an integral role in making me feel at home here.

With that in mind, I do not want any gifts on this day I turn fifty. I instead want to *give* something. It is a list of fifty things I love about LSU sports. They are not ranked . . . just listed in no particular order.

I'm calling it my fifty for fifty. And I'm sharing it as a "thank you" for all that the games and people of this town have already gifted to me. I hope you enjoy it.

1. Football tailgating. RVs and grills galore. Jambalaya and so much more. Did I mention adult beverages? These are the best ballgame bashes in America.

2. All things Shaquille O'Neal. I love the ESPN commercial in which he rescues Mike the Tiger from a tree. I love that even though Shaq left school early to enter the 1992 NBA draft, he now has three degrees including a doctorate in education. I love that he has an annual golf tournament to support a Life Skills Program for LSU athletes. I love the Shaq statue outside the basketball practice facility. LSU has never known a more entertaining and far-reaching ambassador for the purple and gold.

3. Marucci baseball bats. All Jack Marucci initially wanted to do was make a wooden bat for his son to swing in Little League games. Ten years later, Marucci bats are used by hundreds of Major Leaguers including Albert Pujols and Bryce Harper. Not bad for a guy whose day job is head athletic trainer for LSU.

4. The book *It Never Rains in Tiger Stadium.* Author John Ed Bradley first made a name for himself as an offensive lineman for LSU. He was a captain of the 1979 Tigers. But John Ed writes football way better than he ever played it.

5. Bert Jones. When I first met the former LSU All-American—in 1974—he was a quarterback for the Baltimore Colts and I was an eleven-year-old ballboy for the team. We "worked together" for years with the Colts and ended up friends for life. Bert and his family are very special to me.

6. The whole "Geaux" thing. "Geaux Tigers!" is a battle cry for all. Geaux Givers is a program for LSU athletes to do community service. And so on. Anyone unwilling to embrace local spelling rules should probably geaux elsewhere.

7. The tuba dude. How many basketball teams have a seven-foot-two center who began college in the marching band and then put away his tuba so he could try dribbling to a different beat? Walk-on Andrew Del Piero hardly got any playing time last season, but one would be hard pressed to find a more enchanting story.

8. The Intimidator at Alex Box. A giant tiger roars on one side of the billboard overlooking the right-field bleachers. But the most intimidating feature on the board is the list of years LSU has won national championships: six times from 1991 through 2009.

9. Dale Brown. Without the former LSU basketball coach—a close friend for many years—I never would have met my wife. In 1993, Dale invited me to Baton Rouge to work with him on a big game to promote organ donation (a cause to which I was deeply committed because my sister had undergone a lifesaving liver transplant). The game was a great success, but meeting Leslie while here would end up being far more important to the rest of my life. Years later, we again crossed paths and began a long-distance relationship that eventually led to marriage. Thank you, Dale!

10. Purple and gold. In addition to all that they represent, they just look good together.

11. Mo Isom. The former LSU soccer goalie became widely known when she tried out for the football team as a kicker. But that storyline is *nothing* compared to her life journey: battling bulimia as a teen, later losing her dad to suicide, surviving a horrific car crash that only strengthened her faith. She is one of the most inspirational public speakers I've ever heard. LSU is lucky to have Mo. The world is lucky to have Mo!

12. Michael Bonnette on Twitter. As sports information director, Bonnette (@LSUBonnette) shares plenty of good Tiger nuggets. Most entertaining, though, is a regular sampling of gems related to his son Max, who recently started first grade. Example: *Max is convinced that I have Santa Claus' phone number. He said, "Dad, just give me his cell b/c I need to talk with him."*

13. Ricky Blanton doing radio for LSU basketball. His knowledge and love of the game are boundless. His experience as a player and his passion for LSU elevate his commentary. Plus, he's a longtime friend.

14. Jacques Doucet's charity softball game. The WAFB-TV sportscaster's annual "Celebrity/Sorta Celebrity" game is not exclusive to LSU athletes and coaches, but it is highly dependent on them. Among those who have played are Ben McDonald, Warren Morris, Glenn Dorsey, Joseph Addai, Devery Henderson, Kevin Faulk, Josh Reed, Rudy Macklin, Brandon Bass, and Marcus Thornton. It's a good time for a good cause: supporting military families.

15. The Golden Band from Tigerland. Number of members: 325. Number of notes to let us know who they are: four. *Daaa Daa Daaa Da!*

16. Visiting with Paul Dietzel. At eighty-eight, the head coach of the 1958 national champion Tigers remains one of the best storytellers in town. We first met five years ago over beignets at Coffee Call, and I've enjoyed staying in touch with him.

17. Walk-On's Bistreaux & Bar. Although not officially part of LSU, it is a popular piece of the LSU sports landscape, and its founders are former Tigers. Jack Warner and Brandon Landry were basketball walk-ons who shared a vision and turned it into a landmark on Burbank Drive.

18. Raph Rhymes. After failing to make the baseball team as a freshman walk-on, he went to junior college and hit so well that Paul Mainieri recruited him back to play for LSU. Last season he led all of college baseball with a .431 batting average. He also might have led the nation in visiting with fans and signing autographs. Raph is one of the most humble, likable athletes I've ever been around.

19. The Jeff Boss Locker Room. With all the legendary players and coaches who have passed through Tiger Stadium, the LSU locker room is named for a longtime equipment manager who died in 2003. As a former equipment guy—all those childhood years with the Baltimore Colts—I love that Jeff Boss will always be remembered for the time and care he put into his job.

20. Ben McDonald broadcasting baseball games. The most decorated player in LSU baseball history combines country comfort with interesting insights. Ben is also one of the nicest guys you'll ever meet at a ballpark.

21. The speed factory known as women's track and field. Going back to 1987, the Lady Tigers have claimed exactly half of all national championships available to them: twenty-six of fifty-two when counting both indoor and outdoor NCAA titles. It is one of the greatest runs—pun intended—in the history of any college sport.

22. The grounds crew at Alex Box. Show me another grounds crew that performs choreographed dance routines between innings of a baseball game. Show me another that cares enough about its work to post a sign saying "Rake like a champion today" on the side of the dugout where it runs onto the field.

23. The Etta James Memorial Meet. When NFL linebacker Bradie James was a sophomore at LSU—in 2001—he lost his mother to breast cancer. Now the annual gymnastics meet carrying her name raises both attendance figures for the LSU program and money to fight cancer.

24. Barkevious Mingo. The All-Southeastern Conference defensive lineman will be huge for the Tigers this season. Freakishly athletic for a big man, he is one of the most enjoyable players to watch. He also has the best name in college sports—even getting bonus points for his nickname, KeKe, pronounced "Key-Key."

25. The photo mural of 2009 baseball dogpile. It fills an entire wall in the LSU players' lounge at Alex Box. Outfielder Leon Landry is forever frozen in air while flying into a celebratory heap of Tigers after winning the College World Series. This wall of joy should always inspire LSU ballplayers toward greatness.

26. *Ole War Skule: The Story of Saturday Night.* Narrated by John Goodman and released last year, this feature-length documentary on LSU football is packed with wonderful interviews and footage.

27. Coach Stud. The nickname alone might have landed him on my list. But I've known LSU offensive coordinator Greg Studrawa since his days at Bowling Green in Ohio, and he's one of my favorite people in college football. As passionate as Coach Stud is about the X's and O's of a playbook, he also knows his greatest contribution is molding his "boys" into men of impact and integrity away from the fields of play.

28. Baseball players with kids after games. They're certainly not the only LSU athletes who pose for pictures and sign autographs for kids. But they do it more consistently than anyone else—graciously working their way down the equivalent of a receiving line always waiting for them outside of Alex Box. It's part of the Mainieri Way.

29. The 1958 plaque. Attached to an exterior wall of Tiger Stadium, the bronze plaque honoring the 1958 national football champions is tired and worn. But the story it tells never gets old. The famous Chinese Bandits are listed along with the White Team and the Go Team. For the season, LSU allowed fewer than five points per game, outscoring its opponents by a stunning margin of 282 to 53.

30. Glen "Big Baby" Davis reading to children. The former LSU basketball star—now in the NBA with the Orlando Magic—is doing important work with his literacy program. Plus, there's just a certain charm to such a large man (six-foot-nine, 290 pounds) sharing a story with a group of tiny tots—especially when he's as playful and engaging as Big Baby.

31. The memorabilia at TJ Ribs. The only Heisman Trophy in LSU history. A rim Shaq tore down while dunking in the Pete Maravich Assembly Center. A collection of vintage Pete Maravich photos. Way more signed and framed items than anyone should try to count.

32. The return of Johnny Jones. How many people ever experience the joy of landing their dream job—no matter what their occupation? Johnny has an ideal combination of personality and background to rebuild both the men's basketball roster and the overall stature of the program. I'm pulling for him.

33. The Jack and Priscilla Andonie Museum. Most people don't even know about this small but splendid sports museum next to the Lod Cook Alumni Center. It is one of the most impressive on-campus sports shrines in the nation.

34. Video of the Warren Morris home run. With two outs in the bottom of the ninth inning and LSU trailing Miami 8–7 in the final game of the 1996 College World Series, Morris unloaded the most dramatic hit in school history: a two-run, walk-off homer to win the national championship. No matter how old the video gets—no matter how many times it is shown—the excitement never fades.

35. Mike the Tiger. He is the most majestic of mascots. Mike VI is a very cool cat with some serious quarters: 15,000 square feet of habitat in which to relax while waiting for his next trip across the street to Death Valley.

36. The "WIN!" bar in Tiger Stadium. A piece of old crossbar—from a goalpost first used in 1955—is mounted above the double doors through which the LSU players enter the field. Tradition dictates that they reach up and touch the bar as a sign of commitment to victory.

37. Three generations of Mainieri men. Paul is the only one with a job on campus. But generation up (his dad Demie) and generation down (sons Nick and Tommy) also spend a lot of time around the baseball program. As kind and enjoyable as they all are, they make it easy to understand my law of Mainieris: The more of them I see, the better my day.

38. Charles Alexander and his C'Mon Man Cajun Seasoning. One of the best running backs in LSU history—a 2012 inductee into the College Football Hall of Fame—is still adding spice to life in Louisiana.

39. Annie Alleva. The wife of athletic director Joe Alleva is a tireless supporter of local charities. She has the heart of a champion.

40. Eating grass at Tiger Stadium. I've never sampled the turf myself, but anyone who follows LSU football knows what I mean. A few blades of grass sure have gotten a lot of attention.

41. Skip Bertman as a public speaker. He's long retired from coaching baseball and serving as athletic director. But the stories—filled with both inspiration and humor—just keep on coming.

42. LSUsports.net. The official website of the athletics department is always one of my first early morning clicks.

43. LSU vs. Alabama football. The history is long and rich. And the rivalry only grows with time.

44. The Football Operations Center. Athletes win championships. But it sure helps to have a spectacular $15 million facility—built in 2006—as your home base.

45. Crowds at Alex Box Stadium. For seventeen straight years LSU has led the nation in total attendance for home baseball games. Last season's figure of 472,391 (in forty-four games) is the highest in the history of college baseball.

46. The giant Eye of the Tiger. Staring from midfield throughout football season, it is the handiwork of LSU sports turf manager Eric Fasbender. He uses strings and a tape measure for the general outline but then goes freehand with his paint sprayers, creating a dramatic display of purple, gold, and white.

47. The Bengal Belles. Established in 1996, this high-energy, fun-loving group of female fans is best known for its festive luncheons during football season. Think of them as giant pep rallies with lots of lipstick. But leader Aimee Simon and a dedicated membership of close to a thousand also have a serious mission: They have raised almost a million dollars for LSU's Cox Communications Academic Center for Student-Athletes.

48. Football jersey number 18. It goes to the player who best represents what it means to be a Tiger in terms of leadership and character. The tradition began with Matt Mauck, quarterback of the 2003 national championship team, who bequeathed his number 18 to fullback Jacob Hester. Now it is worn by defensive tackle Bennie Logan.

49. James Carville cheerleading for the Tigers. Whenever the football team is hot, national media folks know exactly where to turn for some good local color. The political consultant—a loud and proud LSU alum—never disappoints.

50. The ever-growing legend of Billy Cannon's Halloween run. If you're still reading, I can't imagine you need any explanation on this one.

The Graduate

December 14, 2012

It is a huge day for the big man. He has just finished a telephone interview with a Baton Rouge radio station. A lady friend is checking one last time to make sure his oversized gown is free of wrinkles. Now—at 8:05 on a chilly but otherwise delightful Friday morning—he must go. Stanley Roberts, all seven feet and 369 pounds of him, starts moving toward the door of the LSU campus apartment he's called home for the last few years.

At age forty-two, Stanley never moves with anything near the fluidity he used to exhibit on a basketball court. He is also temporarily hampered by an aching right ankle. But so what? Such a minor inconvenience is nothing set against all that has led to this joyous day.

The great expectations and the rise to stardom.

The ugly downfall and the years of disarray.

The renewal of hope.

"Time to do this," Stanley says, a purple cap protected in a plastic bag and held in his left hand, his purple gown draped over the same arm. As he reaches for the doorknob, his eyes pause at the same place they usually do when he's leaving the ground-floor apartment just across Nicholson Drive from Bernie Moore Stadium and the Pete Maravich Assembly Center. That was the whole point of long ago posting one of his favorite passages—from the book *A Return to Love* by Marianne

Williamson—on the inside of the door. It would always be the last thing he'd see on his way out into the world.

Our deepest fear is not that we are inadequate.
Our deepest fear is that we are powerful beyond measure.
It is our light, not our darkness, that most frightens us.
We ask ourselves, who am I to be brilliant, gorgeous, talented, fabulous?
Actually, who are you not *to be?*

Morning sunshine greets Stanley as he puts black dress shoes to concrete on the sidewalk outside his apartment. Moving both gingerly and excitedly, Stanley says, "Let me get my slow limp going." He's referencing only that sore ankle. But he could just as easily be talking about the entirety of his meandrous and almost unthinkable journey: nearly a quarter-century of hard-to-fathom twists and turns leading to the finish line he's about to cross. This has not been a sprint.

The first steps came in the late 1980s, when the calendar defined Stanley as a teen but his size and athletic ability already made him something of a legend in the small community of Hopkins, South Carolina. Stanley lived with his parents and two siblings in a cramped trailer on rural Congaree Road, his mom working nights as a custodian at the University of South Carolina, his dad often gone for months while logging long-distance miles as a truck driver. But the game of basketball was opening paths to all kinds of possibilities. That's what happens when you stand seven feet toward the sky and pack 270 pounds of potential . . . when you can bang with behemoths yet also have the skilled hands of an artisan and nimble feet of a dancer.

"Stanley could take the ball off a rebound and—as big as he was—he could just push it up the court himself," says his high school coach, Jim

Childers. "Stanley could pretty much do it all. Once he was set up in the low post, there was really nobody who could handle him. He had great hands, great feet, great moves to the basket. He even had a nice little hook shot. And then he could also step out and shoot a jumper—had a real soft jumper. He was basically unstoppable."

Nobody much cared that Stanley had been academically ineligible to play as a ninth grader and therefore did not get started with high school ball until he was a sophomore. During the next two years, 1987 and 1988, he carried Lower Richland High to consecutive state championships. As a senior, Stanley averaged almost 25 points, 10 rebounds, and 6 blocked shots per game. He was a consensus All-American—so named by McDonald's, *Parade*, and *USA Today*. The Associated Press said he "may be the most highly recruited player ever" from South Carolina.

College coaches came from near and far to pitch their schools. Stanley never paid much attention to the non-stop recruiting mail—he just kept packing it away in boxes—but sometimes all the talk and all the adults leaning on him became a bit much. And that was before things turned ugly.

None of it would have happened if Stanley's brother, Wayne, two years his elder, had not shot a bullet into the chest of another young man. But he did. Wayne never challenged the fact he had killed eighteen-year-old Gerald Rowe, also of Hopkins, during a brief but intense encounter on an otherwise quiet street the evening of Tuesday, April 21, 1987. Only the circumstances were contested. One version of events centered on an argument over a girl. Another focused on the involvement of a gang—the "B-Loves"—in what might have been a turf battle. Whatever the reality, Wayne insisted he was simply defending himself. Without provocation, he said, three men surrounded and threatened him with what appeared to be an iron bar and an ax handle, a friend slipped him a gun in the heat of the moment, and he fired it in panic. This much was certain: Wayne was charged with murder. And the ominous weight of his criminal case—a possible life sentence hanging in the balance—was later injected into Stanley's college recruitment.

First, Isabella Davis, Wayne and Stanley's mom, reported that the local magistrate who conducted Wayne's preliminary hearing had called to push Stanley to sign with the University of South Carolina. Then there were other callers who threatened that Wayne would be treated more harshly if Stanley signed with anyone but the home-state Gamecocks. Conversely, if Stanley were to sign with South Carolina, it might very well help either with Wayne's case or with the way he'd be treated if he ended up in prison. Twenty-five years later, Stanley still measures his words when discussing how stressful the situation became for him. His voice weakening, he says, "I couldn't live my life as a normal kid."

Isabella wanted Stanley to wait until after the trial to pick a school. But the legal system was not concerned about any such thing, and the trial kept getting pushed back. Wayne told Stanley to go ahead and make a decision—and to make it without worrying about him. For one thing, Wayne knew exactly what had prompted him to fire that gun, and he wanted to believe that everything would eventually work out for him. Plus, he truly wanted what was best for his brother.

Ultimately, the decision belonged to Stanley alone.

It came down to this:

Would he yield to pressure and appease the locals by signing with South Carolina?

Or would he pack up and seek a new beginning far from all the madness? Would he head to Louisiana, following Jim Childers, who had already announced he'd be leaving Lower Richland to join the LSU coaching staff?

A single soundtrack kept replaying itself in Stanley's mind. It belonged to the only college coach who once sat in that trailer on Congaree Road and told him: "There is something very important you need to understand. I'm here to recruit you as a human being first and a basketball player second. No question, we can win a lot of basketball games together, but I want to help you become the best person you can be. If I'm not doing that, then I might as well just choose another line of work."

That coach was Dale Brown of LSU—and Stanley would never forget the power of those words. They were the words that made him an LSU Tiger.

After four days of hearing legal arguments and sworn testimony, a jury deliberated for only two hours before accepting the self-defense explanation of Wayne Roberts and declaring him not guilty. Stanley was sitting in the courtroom when the verdict was announced on Thursday, February 25, 1988, and he could not have been more relieved as he stood to hug his brother. *The whole mess is finally behind us*, he told himself. But he was not entirely right.

A few months later, with his senior year of high school winding down, word circulated that Stanley had been targeted with death threats. People close to the young man Wayne Roberts had killed were supposedly interested in retaliation. FBI agents shadowed Stanley for a while—sticking with him right through graduation. And Stanley was encouraged to get out of town as soon as he could. A few hours after collecting his diploma, he was on a plane headed for Baton Rouge and LSU. There was no celebrating with friends. There would be no summer of hometown freedom and fun before the start of college. But at least he could stop looking back over his shoulder to see who might be coming.

Childers still prefers not to think too much about the way Stanley's high school days ended. It was such a painful time for the young man he'd come to think of almost as a son. Childers would much rather reflect on the earlier, carefree days when Stanley would stop by his house for a meal or just to spend time with his family. Now an assistant principal of a high school in nearby Columbia, South Carolina, Childers still chuckles at the way Stanley would melt into a couch and watch cartoons for hours. "Nothing but a big, old kid," the coach would whisper to his wife. And then there was the way Stanley so comfortably interacted with young Amy Childers. The coach's only daughter—eight years old when Stanley started playing at Lower Richland—had a severe case of cerebral palsy. "A lot of people are kind of standoffish around someone like Amy," Childers says. "They're really not sure how to react with a handicapped child. But Stanley? No hesitation whatsoever. He would just pick Amy up from her wheelchair and carry her around. He'd hold her up over his head, and she would just laugh the whole time. She was always smiling and laughing whenever Stanley was around."

Stanley was always smiling and laughing, too.

Dale Brown was in his seventeenth year as LSU coach when Stanley arrived on campus in 1988. Brown had twice taken teams to the Final Four in the 1980s. He knew what talent looked like—and he had already concluded that Stanley was one of the most promising prospects he'd ever seen. "Tremendous size, obviously, and with great hands, great footwork, great shooting touch—just an unbelievable talent," Brown says. "It didn't take a genius to see the kind of player he could be."

There was one temporary roadblock to success. After failing to make the minimum required score of 700 on the Scholastic Aptitude Test, then mandated by an NCAA rule known as Proposition 48, Stanley was academically ineligible to play as a freshman. He was still expected to meet the demands of a rigorous conditioning program on his own—"Lucky me!" Stanley now says with a laugh—but he could not participate in team practices or play in games. The idea was to keep time free for an incoming student presumed to need help adjusting to the challenges of collegiate studies. With Stanley, however, only limited pieces of that extra time were dedicated to academics. He did just enough work to survive his initial onslaught of classes. Larger chunks of his time were devoted to less strenuous pursuits—endeavors such as general goofing around and concentrated partying.

"Socializing," Stanley says. "I always enjoyed my socializing."

Stanley was not happy about missing his freshman season. Watching games from the stands was tough. But it allowed him a vision of things to come. He watched with delight as classmate and friend Chris Jackson (now Mahmoud Abdul-Rauf) unveiled a dazzling array of offensive skills that landed him on the cover of *Sports Illustrated*. The smooth-shooting, six-foot-one guard set a NCAA scoring record for a freshman—averaging 30.2 points per game—and was named both Southeastern Conference player of the year and a first-team All-American. Stanley looked forward to seeing what he and Jackson would be able to accomplish together as sophomores.

Oh, and there was one other player—a year behind them—who triggered additional excitement by signing a national letter-of-intent to join them at LSU. He was another big kid: a seven-foot center finishing high school in San Antonio, Texas. His name was Shaquille O'Neal.

In the fall of 1989, expectations for the LSU basketball team were higher than they'd ever been leading up to the start of a season. Jackson, already a bona fide star, would now play with two of the most talked-about young giants in the nation—twin towers destined to be the envy of every college basketball program. When The Associated Press released its preseason poll, LSU was ranked second in the nation behind only Nevada-Las Vegas—a remarkable place for the Tigers to be after finishing the previous year with a 20–12 record and no ranking at all.

"We don't want to be just great," Dale Brown told a writer for the *Baton Rouge Advocate*. "We want to be the best." The coach also offered a well-traveled line as a warning label for anyone thinking that LSU could just coast to victory after victory: "The only place success comes before work is in the dictionary."

The Tigers had two exhibition games before the start of the regular season. Brown held Stanley out of the first for failing to keep up with his academics. Then the Soviet Union National Team visited Baton Rouge for a highly publicized contest that sold out the PMAC. Finally playing in an LSU uniform for the first time, Stanley introduced himself by pouring in 25 points against one of the most experienced national teams in the world. The Tigers defeated the Soviets 114–109.

LSU then won seven of eight non-conference games—losing only to Kansas—before the start of SEC play. Stanley was averaging 17.6 points and 12.5 rebounds per game. O'Neal was just behind him with averages of 15.9 points and 11.1 rebounds. Watching his young big-men compete against each other in practice and together in games, Brown sometimes allowed his thoughts to wander into the future. He could already see long and prosperous NBA careers ahead for both Stanley and O'Neal. He also saw one of them ending up as a better professional player. It was Stanley.

Unfortunately, as the season progressed, Stanley never really embraced the notion that going to class was an essential component of the college experience. He was not a late sleeper. Stanley was always up and about. It was just a matter of choices. He valued time with his girlfriend—and with other friends on campus—way more than he enjoyed the constraints of a classroom. "I was horrible about going to class—hated going," Stanley says. "That was my biggest problem."

It was also how he became the most frequent visitor to what LSU players called The Breakfast Club. This was not a prestigious venue. It was a place of punishment. When a player was caught missing a class, a tutoring appointment, or a mandatory study hall, he had to attend the "club" for an early-morning running session—usually at 5:00 or 5:30—under the supervision of assistant coach Johnny Jones. The workout typically included multiple rounds of running up and down steps in Tiger Stadium—from the bottom of the end zone all the way to the top row.

"That generally got their attention," Jones says.

The Breakfast Club was not only about physical exertion, though. It also provided an opportunity for Jones to visit with individual players about anything that might be happening in their lives. After several heart-to-heart talks with Stanley, Jones realized that the regimen of school just wasn't his thing.

"He knew his talent level," Jones says. "He knew that one day he would be playing professionally. And it was almost like he didn't want to wait anymore for that. That wait—especially after having to sit out his first year—was just frustrating to him. He enjoyed basketball practice and the games. But he didn't enjoy the school part of being at LSU, the going-to-class part."

None of that context did anything to lessen Brown's anger one day when he heard that Stanley had missed yet another class. This time the head coach decided to personally conduct a one-on-one session of The Breakfast Club.

"Coach Brown worked the heck out of me that morning . . . ran me to death . . . had me lifting weights," Stanley says. "He was hoping he could change some of my thoughts—maybe even get me going to classes."

After the workout, Brown waited for Stanley while he showered and dressed. The two of them had breakfast together at Broussard Hall—Brown not only eating with Stanley in the athletic dormitory but also sharing a full menu of motivational talk and fatherly encouragement. Then they walked together to Stanley's first class of the day. Before entering the classroom, Stanley gave Brown a big hug and thanked him: "Love you, Coach. I really appreciate everything you're doing for me."

Brown turned and left for his office with a warm feeling of accomplishment. *He finally gets it*, Brown thought. *This is what coaching is all about*.

A few minutes later—once certain that Brown was out of sight—Stanley was gone, too. Forget class. He was too tired for that.

Later that morning, Brown could hardly believe it when someone called to report that Stanley had failed to attend two more classes. *What? I took him to the first one myself!* Brown stormed out of his office and eventually found Stanley on a couch in the student union—sleeping. Brown woke him up.

"What happened?" Brown demanded. "How in the world did you miss class?"

"Coach, all that running this morning, it just about killed me," Stanley said. "I didn't want to fall asleep in class. So I left. I figured I'd just get in a nap before my next class."

The whole season brought a dizzying mixture of hope and frustration. On the basketball court, Stanley displayed only the promise of great things to come. Off the court, his lack of discipline became both an irritant for his coaches and a threat to his future.

On the court: He was LSU's second-leading scorer (14.1 points per game) behind the otherworldly Chris Jackson (27.8) and its second-leading rebounder (9.8 per game) behind the soon-to-be-legendary O'Neal (12.0). In one game, a dramatic, overtime victory against a run-and-gun Loyola Marymount team ranked twentieth in the nation, Stanley matched a shooting-percentage record that could only be tied but never broken: He was a perfect ten-for-ten from the floor.

How tough was it to play against Stanley? After countless hours going against him both in team practices and in unofficial workouts—long hours spent banging bodies in the seclusion of the PMAC basement gym known as The Dungeon—O'Neal knew as well as anyone. Years later, in a *Sports Illustrated* story written once O'Neal was one of the biggest stars in NBA history, the man known as Shaq would say of his former LSU teammate: "I can truly say Stan made me. If it wasn't for him, I'd probably be like everybody else: seven-foot, can't play. But I had to get mean. I had to learn how to dunk on somebody that size. Once you know how to dunk on somebody that size, you know what to do against all guys."

Off the court: What Stanley lacked in commitment to his classes he made up for in devotion to two other areas of his life—eating and having a good time. No matter how much Brown talked to him about the weight he was gaining, Stanley was never really interested in cutting back on his relationships with knife, fork, and spoon. When he consistently weighed in at more than 300 pounds—and not by just a biscuit or two—Brown finally demanded that he take action. He stripped Stanley of his starting job and told him he would remain a substitute player until he lost 25 pounds. The punishment lasted a dozen games—more than a third of the season—but Stanley took it with his usual laid-back acceptance of whatever came his way. He conjured up a rationalization that was almost unthinkable for a young athlete already accustomed to the shine of stardom: "I think I play better coming off the bench than starting."

One night, Brown stopped by Stanley's dorm room—unannounced—just to check on him. Stanley was feeling pretty good. He'd been drinking beer and still had a cold one in his hand. Brown was livid—alcoholic beverages not being part of the diet he had in mind for any of his players, let alone for one supposedly trying to drop weight. Brown took the beer from Stanley's hand and sat him down for another talk: all the usual stuff about wanting to see him do the right things, wanting to see him succeed, wanting to make sure Stanley knew how much he cared about him. Once the talking was done, Brown was almost out the door when Stanley stopped him: "Coach, if you're taking my beer, you should probably take this, too." He was pulling a duffel bag—the rest of his beer stashed in it—from under his bed. Brown would carry this story with him for the rest of his career. He would carry it not as an indictment of youthful transgression, but as a celebration of one of the core qualities that always made Stanley Roberts so likable: his absolute transparency.

That initial poll ranking the Tigers second in the nation turned out to be overly generous. After thirty games, including a one-and-done loss to Auburn in the SEC Tournament, LSU entered the NCAA Tournament ranked nineteenth with a 22–8 record. The Tigers lost to Georgia Tech in the second round. Then came another major blow. After two straight seasons as consensus SEC player of the year, sophomore Chris Jackson announced that he was leaving school early for the NBA.

There were rumors that Stanley would do the same. He had averaged a double-double—17 points and 10.2 rebounds per game—after returning to his starting role for the last four games of the season. Professional scouts had been dropping hints about his value. He was never going to make academics a priority. So why not move on and collect hefty paychecks while still playing basketball? Stanley surprised a lot of people when the deadline for entering the June 1990 NBA draft passed without him putting in his name. Stanley would be LSU's highest-scoring player returning for the next season. And—with a year of shared experience—he and O'Neal could very well be the best pair of big men in college basketball.

That all changed when Stanley got his year-end grades and learned that he would again be academically ineligible to play basketball during the fall semester. All the skipped classes and missed assignments had caught up with him. He could still try to study his way back to eligibility in time to rejoin the team for the SEC portion of the schedule. But Stanley knew himself better than that. Rather than staying in Baton Rouge and hitting the books, he chose to play a year of professional ball in Europe as a steppingstone to the 1991 NBA draft.

Stanley signed with a Spanish team called Real Madrid—and off he went with passport in hand. The capital city of Madrid was a long way from his childhood trailer on Congaree Road in South Carolina. But basketball was basketball. Stanley figured he could dribble, shoot, and bang the boards in any language.

Spain did not go well.

Stanley partied too much.

He went clubbing and stayed out all night. He drank booze and got into cocaine.

"Just had a great time . . . *thought* I was having a great time," Stanley says. "Now I look back and see how stupid I was."

He missed practices. He was never in the best of shape. His team kept fining him—Stanley estimates he lost $150,000 that way—but he just kept going through the motions until he could get back home.

His NBA draft stock dropped because of his less-than-stellar performance overseas. With his size and talent, though, Stanley was still impossible to ignore. On June 26, 1991, the Orlando Magic selected him with the twenty-third pick in the first round of the draft.

Stanley put up decent numbers as a rookie—averaging 10.4 points and 6.1 rebounds in about twenty minutes per game. But he missed a bunch of games with injuries. Orlando general manager Pat Williams would have preferred that he had instead missed some meals. Stanley's weight went to 315 pounds and Williams publicly targeted him with a barrage of fat jokes: "Stanley thinks a balanced meal is a Big Mac in each hand." "Whoever said no man is an island never saw Stanley in a swimming pool." And so on. Stanley was not amused.

If Stanley and Shaquille O'Neal had not become such good friends at LSU, what happened next would have been almost cruel. A year after drafting Stanley, the Magic had the first overall pick in the 1992 NBA draft and selected O'Neal, by then twice an All-American and once the national collegiate player of the year. Having O'Neal meant that Stanley was expendable. He was traded to the Los Angeles Clippers—long considered one of the worst franchises in all of American sports—and it was there that he would spend the next five years.

They were five more years of high hopes dashed by a combination of high living and debilitating injuries. One year, Stanley ruptured his right Achilles' tendon; the next year, his left. Then he had disk problems in his back. NBA insiders and journalists consistently noted that Stanley seemed to be out of shape. His lack of discipline continued to be a problem. He kept boozing. He smoked pot. His handling of money was horrendous. Stanley averaged almost $3 million a year in salary—plus bonuses and other income for endorsements and appearances—but he always found new ways to separate himself from his riches. That would continue for his entire eight-year, five-team NBA career.

"I've done everything that you can imagine," Stanley says. "I've owned five houses and twenty-two cars—everything from a Bentley to a Mustang. I've owned yachts, boats, jet skis. You name it, I've had it. Don't have it no more!"

He laughs. It is the same deep-belly laugh that has always been with him. It lights up his face and instantly transforms him into the biggest kid in the world. Stanley has never lost the ability to laugh at himself, laugh at the situations he gets himself into, laugh at just about anything or anyone he encounters on his outsized journey of the improbable. It is another of the qualities that has always made him so endearing to so many people.

As an NBA player in Los Angeles—the self-proclaimed entertainment capital of the world—Stanley mixed and mingled with high-profile celebrities. Rap music always being a go-to source of energy for him, Stanley enjoys mentioning that he used to hang out with Snoop Dogg, Dr. Dre, and even the great Tupac Shakur. He also had numerous acquaintances who were gang members. Despite the intense rivalry of the Bloods and the Crips, Stanley had friends in both gangs.

The ability to pin down details related to all of Stanley's expensive holdings and habits has been lost to time. But the story of a luxurious house he owned in Los Angeles says a lot about both his long-ago lifestyle and his enduring personality. Late in his time with the Clippers, Roberts had seven people living with him, living *off* him, at that house. When Stanley tired of the constant company and wanted to be alone, he did not kick out his live-ins; he just rented an apartment and moved out of his own residence. Stanley was concerned that the others wouldn't have anywhere else to go. Alas, his so-called friends did not turn out to be exactly who Stanley thought they were.

People in that house were not the only moochers who found Stanley to be an easy target—someone who way too often led blindly with his heart instead of boldly with his head. Stanley also lost a considerable chunk of change after opening a sporting-goods store with a partner who turned out to be not so much of a partner. He dumped funds into several failed attempts in the music business: small rap and R&B labels that never quite made it. And he simply gave away piles of money—sometimes in the form of what were benevolently called "loans"—to people both in Los Angeles and back home in South Carolina.

"I had a lot of fake friends," Stanley says. "Like Puff Daddy says, more money, more problems. The more money I made, the more problems I had."

Stanley nonetheless takes full responsibility for every bad decision he made. He owns his actions. Reflecting on his wildest NBA days, Stanley is both calm and comfortable when he offers this: "I did some very stupid things."

He still had shining moments that could never be taken away.

One of his favorites came late in his rookie season, the night of Saturday, March 21, 1992. Stanley and his Orlando Magic teammates, entering Chicago Stadium with an anemic record of 16–51, worst in the Eastern Conference, were not expected to do much against the reigning NBA champion Bulls. Michael Jordan and company were on an eight-game winning streak and number-nine figured to be a given.

All went according to form through three quarters, the Bulls coasting toward victory, and they went up by 20 points early in the fourth. As Jordan would later put it, the Bulls then fell asleep. But there was another way to describe what happened: the Magic simply went on a tear—and Stanley was the man down the stretch. He had four powerful dunks in the final five minutes. He finished with 18 points and 9 rebounds. The final score was a stunner: 111–108 for the Magic.

Walking off the court, Jordan told Stanley something he would never forget: "If you play like that every game, you will *own* the NBA." Twenty years later, Stanley thinks back to that statement and blurts out one of his own: "I wish I could've listened!" Then he laughs a big laugh, his usual deep-belly release of both air and positive energy, and he's ready to talk about something else.

His final years of professional basketball were not pretty.

In 1997, the Minnesota Timberwolves made a trade with the Clippers to acquire Stanley. His scoring dropped. His interest in playing diminished. The Timberwolves released him after one season.

Stanley had a limited stint with the Houston Rockets in early 1999 and another with the Philadelphia 76ers later that year. Then all the madness finally caught up with him. He was again battling injuries. This time it was a bad shoulder that had required surgery and a back strain. But the knockout blow came on November 24, 1999, when Stanley was banned from the NBA for a positive drug test. The league had instituted new policies to curtail the use of illegal drugs, and Stanley's expulsion was the first under the stricter rules. The NBA announced that he had tested positive for an "amphetamine-based designer drug." Stanley would later identify it as Ecstasy. Whatever it was, he was banned from the league for at least two years. After that, he could apply for reinstatement, but by then he'd be widely labeled as damaged goods: an almost-thirty-two-year-old has-been with a battered body and a tainted past.

Things got worse.

Stanley was by now the father of four children with four different mothers, and he sometimes came up short with his financial support. In Florida, he was arrested after an argument with the mother of one of his children. The charges were later dropped. But this was not Stanley's only brush with the law.

In late 2000, he was arrested in Houston for possession of cocaine, a charge that would land him in jail for more than a month and would eventually get him five years of probation. Still, he was not able to avoid trouble. He was again arrested—again for possession of cocaine—this time in Fresno, California. He would now be on probation in two states.

"This drug thing, it's a beast," Stanley says. "I always knew better, but I still got into the drugs . . . kept getting into the drugs."

After landing him in jail, after taking him in and out of several rehabilitation and counseling programs, the beast finally took him to a place he could define only as rock bottom. Stanley asked himself—more than once—the most pain-filled question imaginable: Did he even want to live anymore? Fortunately, he kept thinking of his children, kept telling himself he still had too much left to do in this world, and he was always able to push away his darkest thoughts.

It was during this time—jobless, directionless, damn near hopeless—that Stanley had "Makaveli" tattooed down his right forearm in black, script letters. The name came from Tupac, who had used it as a pseudonym for the final album he recorded before his death in 1996. It was Tupac's tribute to Italian Renaissance philosopher Niccolo Machiavelli, who was at least rumored to have faked his own death. Tupac had been drawn to the story of Machiavelli and fascinated by his writings. Stanley felt a connection of his own: "It was the thing about faking his death. I felt like doing that sometimes—just to get away from everything. Just to disappear and get away from everything."

Deep down, Stanley knew that his emotional fantasy was a nonstarter. Although a man his size might be able to run, it would be virtually impossible for him to hide.

The NBA reinstated Stanley on January 16, 2003. The 76ers still owned his playing rights but no longer wanted him. Neither did any other team in the league. Wanting to stay in basketball—even if he had to take giant steps down in both stature and salary—Stanley signed on with the Harlem Globetrotters.

The Trotters were soon in Louisiana for a game against a college all-star team—part of the 2003 Final Four weekend during which a new NCAA champion would be crowned in New Orleans. Dale Brown went to see Stanley at his hotel.

After twenty-five years at LSU, Brown had been out of coaching for six years—retired—but he'd never stopped caring about his players. After all that Stanley had been through, Brown still considered him one of the most likable guys he'd ever known. Still, there was a persistent frustration Brown had never managed to shake. He felt that he had failed with Stanley—had never really been able to motivate him during his time at LSU. Brown considered it the biggest individual failure of his career.

"What could I have done differently?" he asked Stanley.

Stanley hated that his coach—one of the greatest motivators he'd ever known—felt burdened by such a question.

"There really wasn't anything else you could have done," Stanley said. "I just didn't believe in myself. I mean, I was blessed with talent, so many gifts from God. And then I didn't use them the way I should have. That's not on you. That's on me."

There were tears of regret that day at the hotel. As Stanley's eyes leaked, there was also the comfort of clarity.

His last chance in the NBA came from the Toronto Raptors. They called the first week of 2004. Stanley went to Toronto for a workout. But the Raptors did not sign him. Their general manager, Glen Grunwald, told reporters Stanley needed to be in better shape. And—with that—his NBA days were done.

He had played in 300 games, starting more than half of them, during his eight seasons. He had averaged 8.5 points and 5.2 rebounds per game. But those were not the numbers people would always talk about. They would talk about his weight. And they would talk about the most staggering figure of all: the amount of money Stanley had blown through. It is impossible to put an exact number on it. Stanley has at different times estimated it was anywhere from $30 million to $45 million—and now says it was probably in the low end of that range.

His longtime agent, Oscar Shoenfelt, says something close to $20 million in salaries alone "could be about right" but that would not include contract bonuses and other income (about which he declines to discuss specifics).

Whatever the figure, one thing was clear when Stanley returned from that tryout in Toronto to his adopted hometown of Houston. He was borderline broke. A large symbol of his fiscal condition stood back in South Carolina—straight across the street from the trailer in which his mom still lived. It was a vacant, incomplete house Stanley had long before started building for her but had never been able to finish. His vision had been grander than his ability to execute it—his will larger than his wallet.

One final stretch of basketball—with a team in Puerto Rico—resulted in one more injury. Stanley had knee surgery and again returned to Houston. This time, in 2004, he was forever done playing professional ball. From Spain to all those NBA teams to the Globetrotters to Puerto Rico . . . from 1990 to 2004 . . . so many ups and downs along the way . . . such a wild variety of experiences. And now it was over. It was time for other things.

Stanley sold cars at a dealership for a while. After that, he took a job making deliveries for a courier service. Then he started working in commercial construction. All went well enough for him while laboring—as a foreman—on an office building. Then Stanley suffered an elbow injury and got into a dispute related to workers' compensation. His employer let him go.

Stanley kept wondering about his future. Without basketball, what would he do for the rest of his life? How would he earn a living?

He also used this time to concentrate on his present. He got clean. He got sober. And he truly dedicated himself to staying that way.

What Dale Brown most wanted for Stanley was the same thing he wanted for any of his former players still without a college degree. He wanted him back in school. From the time Brown left coaching in 1997, he had used a three-ring binder to organize contact information and updates on the lives of all 160 ex-Tigers he would always consider his own. The first section in the white binder was marked *Academics*.

"Everything starts with education," Brown says. "All of my guys who graduated, they're all successful. They have jobs. Their marriages are more likely to last. And so on. Martin Luther King said it best: 'Education sets you free.' And that's exactly what I've always wanted for anyone who ever played for me."

In early 2005, the typed pages and scribbled notes in Brown's binder showed that 103 former players had graduated. Fifty-seven had not. Brown was in Houston one weekend and went to see Stanley. They talked about all sorts of things. More than once, though, Brown locked in on the idea of Stanley returning to LSU as a student. It was something he'd already been pushing for a while. Stanley hemmed and hawed. Maybe he would think about it.

Stanley's oldest child, his daughter Stanecia, later hit him with a tough question: "Why do you expect me to go to college when you didn't finish?" She was mostly messing with her dad. (Stanecia is now twenty-one and thriving as a junior at the University of South Alabama.) But there was also a serious undertone to her playful challenge. Stanecia's query and Brown's persistence gave Stanley a lot to think about.

"Nothing was really working out for me in the job market," Stanley says. "With the past that I had, and with no degree, I didn't have a lot of options. The only jobs I could really get were manual labor. But my body was beat up. I had no real skill or craft. So I had to make a decision."

The decision did not take days or weeks. It took months.

Stanley finally convinced himself there was only one thing to do: *Let me go back to school and try to find myself.*

He was headed back to LSU—back to his past in search of a future.

Nobody said it would be easy. The course credits he had earned in the late 1980s no longer counted—"academic bankruptcy" being the term an LSU administrator used when explaining to Stanley that the passage of so much time had rendered those credits worthless. In the fall of 2007, he had to start all over again.

Stanley would pay his tuition primarily with loans and part-time jobs—along with some assistance from an NCAA program designed to support former athletes returning to school. Dale Brown would later help with the rent on a campus apartment. In the beginning, though, Stanley wanted to do as much as possible on his own.

He spent his first semester living with former LSU teammate Wayne Sims and his family. Stanley did not have a car. So he usually took a bus to school. He was the only seven-foot-tall, thirty-seven-year-old freshman on campus.

Focused on Stanley's size—and failing to consider his age—a fellow student once asked him if he was on the LSU basketball team (meaning the *current* team). "Uh, no," Stanley said. "I'm probably old enough to be your father!" Stanley got a kick out of that.

He was not nearly as amused by his classes. Algebra was one of the first. After so many years away from any math lessons, all those formulas and equations might as well have been written in Chinese. And it was not only math that initially made him wonder if returning to school had been a good decision. It was *everything*. So much had changed since Stanley had last been a student. In the 1980s, he had taken a typing class. Now such a class did not even exist. And everyone did most of their work on computers. Taking an *online* class? Last time Stanley was in school, nobody could have imagined such a thing—or even known what it would one day mean.

Stanley was initially afraid of all that he had taken on: "It was a culture shock." Plus, he learned that he had dyslexia. Nobody had ever before detected that. The diagnosis came as a jolt. It also gave him hope. By addressing his reading disability—working both with academic counselors and on his own—Stanley would have a chance to do better than he ever had in school.

Nothing seemed to help much in that first semester. After finishing it with a 1.75 grade point average, Stanley decided to take some time off to regroup. As frustrated as he was, he easily could have quit altogether. But something was different this time. He was different. Stanley was determined not to fail.

His next semester, fall of 2008, Stanley dedicated himself like never before—and it showed. His 3.25 GPA was the best he'd ever done in college. He knew he still had a long way to go. He was also undeniably headed in the right direction. Stanley was beaming.

He decided to major in sport administration.

Classmates enjoyed his easygoing, jolly nature. Teachers valued his abundance of real-world experiences and appreciated his willingness to share so much of himself with others.

"What stands out about Stanley is that he's so personable, very engaging," says Dee Jacobsen, coordinator of the undergraduate sport administration program, who served as Stanley's adviser and also taught him in a few classes. "Stanley is what we would call a non-traditional student. Our students are mainly eighteen to twenty-four years old. But Stanley worked and blended well with all of them. I always knew I could count on him to start a good discussion in class."

Stanley was the only student in any of his classes to be featured in a commercial for a local car dealership. He was the only one who football coach Les Miles asked to address his team about all he'd been through. He was the only one whose name popped up on the scoreboard during an LSU basketball game as the answer to a trivia question—something about that 1990 Loyola Marymount game in which he shot a perfect ten-for-ten from the floor. Stanley was the only one who often drew stares—his massive dimensions had a way of doing that—and sometimes signed autographs.

Then there was the time Shaquille O'Neal showed up on campus and called out his name with great love and respect. It was the evening of Thursday, September 8, 2011. Three months earlier, O'Neal had announced his retirement after nineteen years in the NBA, and now he was at LSU for the unveiling of a replica statue that would forever honor him: 900 pounds of bronze Shaq—a dunking Shaq—greeting visitors in front of the basketball practice facility. It was the first time a statue of any LSU athlete had been permanently placed on campus.

"I'm humbled," O'Neal told reporters after the unveiling ceremony. "There's a lot of great players that came through this university—a lot that were greater than me. Pistol Pete. Bob Pettit. Stanley Roberts. Guys like that. So I'm just honored that they chose me to build a statue of."

Stanley had attended a VIP reception with O'Neal prior to the unveiling and had enjoyed seeing his old buddy so happy at the public ceremony. But he was not around when O'Neal threw his name into that lofty trio along with Pete Maravich and Pettit (both of whom were included in the NBA's 1996 list of the fifty greatest players in league history). It was a few days later when Stanley first heard about that.

He laughed his big laugh. He smiled his big smile.

He questioned whether his name really should have been mentioned in that context.

"I don't know about that, but I appreciate it," Stanley said. "Me and Shaq, at LSU, we were close from Day One. We got to hang out quite a bit. I always remember one night we were just sitting in his dorm room and talking. He told me all the things he wanted to accomplish. He was only a freshman, but he already knew. He said he was going to graduate. He was going to be a great NBA player. He was going to be a rapper. And he ended up doing everything he said. Shaq had a mindset. When he set a goal, he was going to achieve it."

It was a good thing Stanley had finally developed a sturdy mindset of his own. He needed it to confront the final challenge on his path to graduation. The first week of August, Stanley went to a cardiologist for routine testing that was recommended due to an earlier issue. The doctor detected major blockages in three coronary arteries—meaning the blood flow in Stanley's heart was terribly insufficient. Triple bypass surgery was immediately required.

This was an issue way more important than any class assignment or academic exam.

It was a matter of life and death.

Everyone Stanley knew—his academic advisers and Dale Brown included—strongly suggested that he withdraw for the fall semester. Granted, it was supposed to be the final semester of his monumental journey to a college degree. But nobody thought he could pull it off while recovering from such a major surgery. Everyone wanted him to skip a semester and push back his graduation to the spring of next year.

Stanley was nonetheless determined to stay on schedule. He requested special permission to take his final economics course as an independent study. His appeal was granted—and Stanley opted to stay in school. His first month after surgery was primarily spent in bed and doing physical rehabilitation, so he had a lot of catching up to do with his school work. But now he had the heart—literally and figuratively—to finish the job.

When his final grades came in, when he knew he had actually made it across the finish line, Stanley soaked in the combination of joy and relief, and he treated himself to a grand conclusion: *This is the biggest thing I've ever accomplished.*

He now gets to formalize his accomplishment by participating in LSU's winter graduation ceremonies: the 279th commencement exercises in school history. Wearing his purple cap and gown, Stanley is about to walk across a stage in the Carl Maddox Field House and grip a diploma with his name on it.

Dale Brown watches from a seat in the front row. Next to him is Wanda Carrier, Brown's longtime secretary in the LSU basketball office, now administrative assistant to athletic director Joe Alleva. On the other side of Carrier is Wayne Sims, Stanley's old teammate with whom he lived when he first returned to school. Sitting nearby, in a wheelchair, is Stanley's most beloved witness of all: his mom, sixty-three-year-old Isabella Davis, not feeling so great with hip and knee ailments that have long plagued her, but in from South Carolina for an occasion she never would have missed.

Stanley is one of fifty-four students graduating with a Bachelor of Science degree in sport administration. Each owns a personal story of triumph leading to this day. Stanley's just took the longest to write. The narrative was a bit more complicated than most.

His name is called—"Stanley Corvet Roberts"—and a chorus of cheers washes over him. It is the loudest response of the morning.

Clearly, Stanley has collected many fans who never saw him dribble or dunk a basketball.

His smile is bigger than ever as he crosses the stage, and that pain in his ankle is gone, at least for now, because he is pretty much floating. Stanley is floating as he reaches with his left hand and takes hold of his diploma . . . floating as he takes the final steps in a journey that began nearly a quarter-century ago.

"Bravo!" Dale Brown says. "What a moment!"

When Stanley descends from the stage, he goes straight to his mother, leans down to her wheelchair, and kisses her on the cheek.

"I love you," Isabella Davis whispers to her son.

The look on Stanley's face says almost everything he could possibly say. His glow announces both his joy of the moment and his love—for a lifetime—of his mother. But there is one critical message that cannot be seen on his face. The message is buried beneath his gown. It is carried in the form of a tattoo—his favorite of the many decorating his body—this one stretching like a billboard high across his back.

The tattoo is bold both in size and declaration: *Only God Can Judge Me.*

Stanley Roberts now lives in Baton Rouge and works in the human resources department of CB&I. He is also an assistant basketball coach at Ascension Christian High School in nearby Gonzales.

The Gift of Being Remembered

February 22, 2013

He is only a few minutes away now—about to make the familiar turn off Old Scenic Highway in Zachary, Louisiana, and head down a quiet, country road to deliver the news to his old friend. But Buddy Wicker has already waited so long for this—years—and now he simply can't contain himself. His left hand stays on the steering wheel of his gray Silverado pickup truck while his right hand reaches for the cell phone. At 11:10 in the morning, Wicker calls the home of Frank Brian, soon to be ninety years old, a man once known as "Flash" because of his speed on a basketball court.

"Frank, it's a done deal," Wicker says into the phone. "We're in."

Brian needs no explanation. He knows that the "we" is really only him. And he knows exactly what it means to be in.

"This is the best news I've heard in a long time," Brian says. "Cuz"—he calls just about everyone he knows by his abbreviation for cousin—"I don't know how I can thank you."

Brian has good reason to be grateful. He has just been given a gift of remarkable magnitude, something that cannot be bought in a store or wrapped in a box. It is the gift of being remembered.

Frank Sands Brian was born May 1, 1923, the same year Calvin Coolidge became President of the United States, Yankee Stadium first opened in New York, and Louis Armstrong made his first recording.

In rural Louisiana, basketball was not a priority. Brian was introduced to the game when his father nailed "a little hoop" on a pecan tree outside their farmhouse. Zachary High School—fifteen minutes north of Baton Rouge—did not even have a gymnasium until his senior year there. Prior to that, Brian and his teammates played their home basketball games outdoors . . . on dirt.

"If it rained, we didn't play," Brian recalls, laughing at the memory. "But it was a good court. We even had lights on it. There were no bleachers. People would just stand around and watch. But it was a lot better than most of the courts at other schools. Some of those dirt courts, we'd have to run the hogs off of them before we could play the game."

Seriously? Hogs?

"I'm telling you how it was," Brian says. "Boy, things have really changed since then, you know it? Yes, sir."

Buddy Wicker and Frank Brian have been friends for close to forty years. They met playing golf. And it was only in recent years—when Brian could no longer handle the outings—that they stopped playing together. Wicker is a former school teacher who manages rental properties in Baton Rouge. Brian is a retired cattle rancher who also owned a livestock auction company. His fourth wife, Liz, is in her mid-fifties and works as a personnel supervisor at a Baton Rouge chemical plant, so he has plenty of time to visit with friends.

Wicker is also younger than Brian, by two full decades, but they have shared a lot through the years—their love of basketball, for one thing. Wicker always knew that Brian had long ago played for LSU. He also knew that his friend was one of the original players when the National Basketball Association (NBA) was formed in 1949. Then—while visiting with Brian one day about ten years ago—Wicker noticed some dusty, old scrapbooks someone had pulled out from under a bed in the guest room.

"Mind if I look?" Wicker asked.

"Oh, it's just some stuff my mother used to cut out of the newspapers," Brian said. He was mildly embarrassed because she had often underlined his name in the clippings—and sometimes not only once per article, but every time it appeared.

Wicker flipped through the yellowed pages for a few minutes before coming across something he could hardly believe. Looking up at his friend, Wicker was equally shocked and awed: "Damn, Frank, you played in the first NBA All-Star Game?"

"Well, yes, I did," Brian answered, almost sheepishly, as if his mother had still been around to grab a pen and had just underlined his name again.

That inaugural All-Star Game—played in the Boston Garden on March 2, 1951—was a wonderful memory. Brian ran the court that night with some of the best-known basketball players in the history of the game, including George Mikan and Bob Cousy. But it was nothing Brian would ever introduce into conversation without being asked about it.

Wicker just sat there for a minute, stunned. Then he went back to reading.

The path from that dirt court in Zachary to the hardwood floors of the NBA was no straight line. In his first year on the LSU varsity, listed as a six-foot, 162-pound forward during the 1942–43 season, Brian averaged 14 points per game and was the only Tiger named to the All-Southeastern

Conference team. The "handsome, black-haired Brian"—so called by The Associated Press—also excelled as a sprinter once the basketball season ended. In one track meet, he even defeated LSU sports legend Alvin Dark, also a basketball teammate, in the 220-yard dash. Brian was a fun-loving member of the Sigma Nu fraternity, and he was known to get along quite well with the coeds. Life was good.

Then Uncle Sam called for him.

With the demands of World War II pulling students from across the nation, Brian was inducted into the U.S. Army and told to report for basic training in May 1943. He became a medical and laboratory technician, and his assignments took him to Army installations in Arkansas, Oklahoma, Missouri, and New Jersey. At Fort Dix—in Jersey—he attained the rank of master sergeant. Being in the military was a major adjustment for Brian, as it was for so many young men at the time, but the biggest changes came in his personal life. On February 27, 1944, Brian got married at age twenty. A year and a half later, his first child, Barbara Lee Brian, was born.

Frank Brian never could have imagined being a college basketball star, husband, and dad—not all at the same time—but those were his shared roles once he was released from the Army. In the fall of 1946, after missing three years of school, he returned to LSU and rejoined the Tigers. Local newspapers ran photos of him riding a bicycle on campus, with little Barbara Lee sitting in a metal basket perched above the front tire. One of the photo captions referred to "flashy Bengal" Frank Brian. Another tagged him with a much loftier title: "candidate for All-America" at the position of forward.

If anything, Brian had only improved while gone, playing on several military teams and getting stronger. He was now a well-muscled 175 pounds, a weight he would have no problem maintaining by eating plenty of his favorite Louisiana foods, especially country ham and grits.

Fans enjoyed Brian's fast-paced, high-flying style of play. Local scribes sometimes seemed almost breathless as they banged away on their manual typewriters during the 1946–47 season.

One newspaper story began by celebrating Brian as the "curly-topped, 23-year-old father . . . whose basketball feats to date have surpassed any individual performance seen in this locale for many years." It went on to say: "Using his speed to the greatest possible advantage . . . Brian gains momentum on fast breaks, leaps high in the air within shooting range of the basket, and passes or shoots at will, depending upon the position of teammates and the defense set up by opponents. His ability to execute these split-second decisions while hovering in midair is one of the most amazing feats of physical coordination ever witnessed in these parts at least since Superman became the idol of comic-reading kids."

Brian averaged more than sixteen points a game while leading LSU to a record of 17–4 (making the Tigers a combined 35–8 in the two years he played varsity). He was again named to the All-SEC team. And he learned about professional basketball—specifically about a collection of teams known as the National Basketball League (NBL).

"I had no idea I could be paid to play," Brian says. "But a lot of people started calling to let me know about that. When they wanted to pay me, I thought, well, these people are crazy. I mean, pay me to do something I already loved to do?"

The corners of his mouth break into a gentle smile. Sixty-six years later, Frank Brian still finds it hard to imagine the measure of good fortune that came his way in the spring of 1947.

Brian still had a year of college basketball eligibility and a bunch of classes left to earn a degree, but several professional teams wanted to sign him, and he had a family to support. The Anderson Packers, in basketball-crazy Indiana, made it an easy decision. "They said if I signed, they would give me the top salary in the league," Brian recalls. "Whatever the top guy was getting, they would match it. Well, it turned out that George Mikan was getting $7,500. So they paid me $7,500. That seems awful low nowadays, but I was tickled to death that I was going to make that much money for five months. At the time, I really had only two things in mind—taking care of my family and saving up enough money to buy a ranch."

The Packers were lucky to get Brian. He moved from forward to guard in the NBL, but playing a new position did nothing to diminish his production. In his first two years with the Packers, he led the team in scoring and was twice named an NBL All-Star. In his second year—the 1948–49 season—Brian and the Packers won the NBL title by sweeping the Oshkosh (Wisconsin) All-Stars in the championship series. The third and final game of that series also turned out to be the last NBL game ever played. During the summer of 1949, NBL leaders met with owners of another professional league, the Basketball Association of America, and decided on a merger.

The NBA was born.

In its first season, 1949–50, Brian was the league's third-leading scorer, at 17.8 points per game, trailing only George Mikan of the Minneapolis Lakers (27.4) and Alex Groza of the Indianapolis Olympians (23.4). The Anderson Packers folded after that season, but Brian joined the Tri-Cities Blackhawks (now the Atlanta Hawks) and never missed a beat.

He was on the Blackhawks when he was selected for that first NBA All-Star Game. Playing before a crowd of 10,094, Brian scored 14 points, making him the second-leading scorer on the West squad. Still, his team lost, which was too bad: members of the winning team got $100 each.

Brian was traded to the Fort Wayne Pistons (now the Detroit Pistons) before the start of his third NBA season, and he was once again selected for the All-Star Game. On February 11, 1952, back in the Boston Garden for the second year in a row, Brian had thirteen points, seven rebounds, and four assists. "He was a hard player to guard," says Bob Cousy, now eighty-four and relaxing in Florida. "He was just so fast, quick as could be."

Brian and Cousy are among only four men who played in the first two NBA All-Star Games and are still alive. Frank Brian is the oldest of the four.

"Hey, I'm living on borrowed time!" he says. "But when I really stop and think about it—boy, I am lucky. I feel awful lucky to have had a life this long."

The closest Brian came to winning an NBA title was in 1955 with the Pistons. It was the first season the league used a shot clock—allowing an offense only twenty-four seconds per possession—in order to eliminate stalling and to generally speed up the game. The change added excitement throughout the season. But nothing was more dramatic than the climax of the playoffs. With the Pistons and the Syracuse Nationals tied at three games apiece, the NBA championship series was not decided until the closing seconds of the seventh and final game. By the thinnest of margins—92–91—Syracuse won both the game and the league title.

Brian and the Pistons made it back to the NBA Finals in 1956. But they again lost—this time in five games to the Philadelphia Warriors. Brian played only part of the next season, and then he was done. After ten years of professional basketball, eight of them as a high-profile NBA pioneer, Frank Brian headed home to Louisiana. He was ready for life on the farm—ready to concentrate on his cows.

In 1986, Brian was inducted into the Louisiana Sports Hall of Fame. Four years later, the leaders of Zachary High School welcomed him into their Hall of Fame as well. Nobody representing the LSU Athletic Hall of Fame ever called. But Brian never gave that much thought—and why would he? He had never been one of those ex-jocks who had to keep grasping at past glory in order to feel whole. The thought of collecting another honor for his long-ago feats of athleticism had nothing to do with preparing cattle for sale. Life moved on—and Brian was perfectly content.

But that was before his friend Buddy Wicker came across those bulging scrapbooks.

It was also before LSU celebrated the one-hundredth birthday of its basketball program—from 1909 to 2009—by naming an All-Century Team. On Saturday, January 31, 2009, an all-time "Sweet Sixteen" of players, determined by the combined voting of fans and a selection committee, was announced at halftime of a home game against Arkansas. Some of the choices—Bob Pettit, Pete Maravich, Rudy Macklin, Shaquille O'Neal—were so obvious that voting was merely a formality. If there were a Mount Rushmore of LSU basketball, the faces of those four men would be staring out from stone. And some of the other picks were almost as easy to make. But Buddy Wicker—watching from the stands of the almost-filled Pete Maravich Assembly Center—did not focus so much on the players who *were* selected. He was way more concerned about one who was not. Heading home after the game, he could not shake a single thought: *How in the world did they not include Frank Brian?*

Brian would later offer his friend a simple explanation: "Hey, I've been gone so long, nobody knows who Frank Brian was. You know, forty or fifty years pass, and people forget about you." Actually, more than *sixty* years had passed since Brian played for LSU.

Precision aside, though, the passage of time was explanation enough for Brian, and he told his friend not to worry about any honorary basketball team. Of course, as well as Brian knew Wicker, he should have known that telling him not to worry about something he really cared about was the equivalent of shouting "Stop!" at a speeding bullet and expecting it to start flying in reverse.

How to air his frustration? How to remind people of his forgotten friend?

Wicker wrote a letter to the editor of the *Baton Rouge Advocate* in which he defined the All-Century Team as "flawed" because "the early years of LSU basketball" were not adequately represented—and specifically because Brian was snubbed. Wicker was pleased when the letter was published.

Then he learned of another way in which his friend had been left out. Someone told him that Brian had never been inducted into the LSU Hall of Fame. Wicker could hardly believe it—and his amazement was only heightened when he found out why Brian had never even been considered for the honor: He had never graduated from LSU, or from any other college, and the LSU Hall of Fame had a rule requiring a degree for induction.

"Really?" Wicker wanted to know. "I mean, the guy accomplishes everything he did in basketball, he spends more than three years serving his nation during World War II, he ultimately chooses to take care of his wife and their baby daughter instead of finishing school—and then they want to keep him out of the Hall of Fame because of a rule like that?"

Wicker went to Brian and said he wanted to take up his cause.

"You don't need to do that," Brian told him.

But Wicker was insistent.

Brian had only one request: "Cuz, just don't make anybody angry, OK? I don't mind if you talk to some people over there, but LSU has always been very special to me. The last thing I'd want to do is make anybody angry over something like this."

Wicker started with phone calls to a few people who either worked at LSU or were somehow connected to its athletic department. He introduced them to the story of a man whom he felt should have required no introduction—calling it an "injustice" that Brian was not in the Hall of Fame—but his pitch was consistently rejected.

Nobody questioned whether Brian's athletic achievements were worthy of consideration, but that rule about having a college degree was generally viewed as an impenetrable wall: solid as rock and equally unforgiving. Exhibit 'A' was Pete Maravich. He was a big enough figure in school history that the campus basketball arena had been named for him; absent a degree, however, he had never been inducted into the LSU Hall of Fame. Exhibit 'B' was Shaquille O'Neal. After leaving school early to enter the 1992 NBA draft, the former All-American had become one of the best-known and most successful athletes in any sport. Still, it was not until late 2000—after completing his bachelor's degree by taking correspondence courses—that Shaq was finally welcomed into the LSU Hall of Fame.

Wicker was undaunted. After all, the U.S. Army had never pulled Maravich or O'Neal out of college. Wicker figured that reasonable people might be open to an exception for a man who'd given some of the best years of his life to serving his nation during World War II. After months of talking up his man to anyone who would listen, Wicker wrote a letter—dated November 9, 2010—to officially nominate Brian for the LSU Hall of Fame.

Peter Finney of the New Orleans *Times-Picayune*, the widely admired sage of Louisiana sports journalism, followed with a letter of his own. Finney wrote that he would put Brian's name "very high" on a list of the top ten basketball players in LSU history. He stated that Brian "did enough to merit being a slam dunk for admittance" to the hall of fame.

Finney closed with this: "I remember Frank Brian as a virtuoso performer who dominated his era. To me, an LSU Hall of Fame without him is incomplete."

Wicker pleaded his case to Trent Johnson, then the LSU basketball coach, and Johnson invited Brian to watch his team practice one day, but he also made it clear that he lacked the clout to get anyone elected to anything.

Wicker also got a brief audience with Shaquille O'Neal, at a Baton Rouge book signing when the big man was promoting his autobiography, but as kind as Shaq was when told about Brian, that encounter also went nowhere.

Wicker tried LSU athletic director Joe Alleva. He called on former LSU basketball coach Dale Brown. He just kept contacting anyone even tangentially associated with LSU sports who might be willing to support his lobbying efforts.

Everywhere Wicker went, he was armed with a 336-page "book" of old articles, photographs, and assorted clippings related to Brian's basketball career. This was not a book in the traditional sense; it had never actually been published. Wicker just visited a Kinko's whenever he needed a few more copies.

Jaws dropped as people learned about Frank Brian. A good number of longtime LSU sports insiders were amazed that they'd never even heard of the man. But nothing ever really changed. Brian still lacked a degree—and the LSU Hall of Fame still had its rule about that.

Billy Cannon, one of the most prominent athletes in LSU history, came up with an idea. The 1959 Heisman Trophy winner, now seventy-five, wanted to arrange a meeting to see if there was anything he could do. He and Brian were friends, and Cannon knew Wicker as well, so he wanted to help. Cannon called Herb Vincent, a senior associate athletic director he'd long known, and a lunch was scheduled for the LSU Faculty Club. In addition to Cannon and Wicker, several other Brian supporters filled the table, including Joe Dean, the early-1950s LSU basketball star who served as athletic director from 1987 through 2000.

Vincent explained that the only way to get Brian in the Hall of Fame would be by appealing to the LSU Athletic Council for a special waiver of the degree requirement. Only with that preliminary step could the separate Hall of Fame Committee even consider the nomination of Brian. Vincent wanted to be supportive. But he also stressed that getting a waiver would not be easy.

Soon thereafter, Wicker made a cold call to Bill DeMastes, an LSU English professor then in his first year as the school's Faculty Athletics Representative. It was in that role that he also served as chairman of the Athletic Council. Not knowing Wicker and never having heard of Frank Brian, the first thing DeMastes thought was: *How am I going to get off the phone?* But Wicker quickly turned him. "That was the amazing thing about Buddy," DeMastes says. "He somehow made me feel like I had known him forever. His enthusiasm came across right away, and he just kept talking, so I figured I might as well listen for a little longer."

Days later—this was last November—Wicker and DeMastes met for lunch at The Chimes, a popular restaurant just outside the North Gates of campus. Wicker had a copy of his Frank Brian book for DeMastes. And he pummeled the professor with his usual talking points about all that Brian had accomplished as a basketball player. *Very impressive*, DeMastes thought. *It's probably still a long shot that the council will eliminate the degree requirement for him. But this is a case that needs to be considered.* He was especially moved by the fact that Brian had been called from college to serve in the military. DeMastes wondered if those lost years would be enough for the council to justify an exception.

One hundred and twenty-three men and women, primarily athletes and coaches but also a few other contributors, have been inducted into the LSU Hall of Fame since the first election of members in 1937. Herb Vincent did some research and found that at least three former athletes—Glenn "Slats" Hardin in 1937, Joe Bill Adcock in 1978, and Alvin Dark in 1981—had somehow been admitted without a degree. He could not find any records providing the reasons for those aberrations. But their existence alone gave Wicker three threads of hope yesterday afternoon as he took an elevator to the sixth floor of the LSU Athletic Administration Building. For the first time since Wicker and DeMastes had shared lunch three months earlier, the Athletic Council was meeting, and the matter of Frank Brian was included as "new business" on the agenda.

Before the start of the meeting, Jack Andonie, a retired doctor from Metairie and influential member of the council, pulled out an old magazine he wanted others to see. The 1948 edition of *Basketball Illustrated* featured Brian on the cover—and it clearly represented another thread of hope for Wicker. If Andonie were not in favor of a vote for Brian, he certainly would not have gone on eBay and bought a magazine to pass around.

Huddled in a corner of the room, several council members chatted about an amazing tidbit they had just picked up from someone who had been researching Brian's career: the fact that he had known Jim Thorpe, one of the most famous athletes ever, back in the 1940s. All these years later, how many people can say that of the iconic multi-sport star and Olympic champion who was born in 1888 and died in 1953? It was nothing that would affect the upcoming vote, but those council members were intrigued.

Once the meeting began, it was quickly apparent that most of those in attendance supported a waiver for Brian. During fifteen minutes of discussion, the primary issue was that chunk of years Brian devoted to the Army. Athletic director Joe Alleva and Andonie—the man with the magazine—were among those who cited the importance of that military service.

Still, there was a snag. A two-thirds' majority—nine of thirteen voting members of the council—was needed to grant the waiver. But four members were absent and one abstained from voting. That left eight "yes" votes—one short of the requirement. DeMastes asked if everyone was OK with putting the matter on hold until he could contact the missing members to see if they wanted to vote. Everyone was in favor of that. And that was how it happened that the vote was not final until this morning.

DeMastes called Wicker with the good news.

Wicker headed straight to Brian's home to deliver it.

But he couldn't wait to get there. After several years of relentlessly asking total strangers to care about Brian the way he did, several years of working the telephone and pounding the pavement for Brian to be honored in what he deemed to be appropriate fashion, Wicker simply couldn't wait.

With his ninetieth birthday fast approaching—it is sixty-eight days away—Brian can't help but wonder sometimes: *Is it really possible that so many years have passed since those days of playing LSU basketball? Since World War II? Since those nascent days of the NBA?*

His scrapbooks remain packed away in the guest room. His memories of games long gone remain the same no matter what anyone else knows—or does not know—about them. He never asked anyone for the gift of being remembered, but it sure means a lot to him now.

Opening the front door of his house for Wicker, Brian hardly knows what to say. The men shake hands. They smile. They laugh.

"We got it done," Wicker says.

Actually, one step remains: a vote by the Hall of Fame Committee. But Alleva has made it clear that getting the waiver was really the only obstacle. Details aside, it is time to celebrate.

Brian's brown eyes lock on Wicker, and the man once known as Flash says: "I just wish there were some way to really express what I'm feeling. You're a good friend, Cuz."

Frank Brian was inducted into the LSU Athletic Hall of Fame on September 13, 2013. He called it one of the best things that had ever happened to him. Now ninety-two years old, Brian still lives in Zachary and enjoys following LSU basketball.

Rally Corn

April 19, 2013

As the LSU baseball team keeps collecting victories—the second-ranked Tigers have won a remarkable thirty-five of thirty-eight games—an unusual contributor sits silently in the dugout.

It is a can of corn.

Its label offers standard instructions for storage and preparation. None of that matters to the Tigers. To them, the only relevant instructions were delivered by a Louisiana-based television star who happens to be a fan.

The corn was a gift from Jase Robertson, who lives in West Monroe, but is nationally known thanks to the reach of reality TV. Robertson is featured on "Duck Dynasty," a popular A&E show that follows his family and its business, Duck Commander, which markets duck calls and other hunting gear.

On Sunday, March 3, Robertson threw out the ceremonial first pitch before LSU played Nicholls State at Alex Box Stadium. Wearing a camouflage outfit and black boots, he was quite a sight as he walked to the mound. Robertson also wore a black beanie, but the cap was no match for his piles of long, unruly brown hair. For anyone familiar with the TV show, it was all that wild hair, along with his oversized shaggy beard, that instantly identified him.

Robertson threw a decent ball to backup catcher Chris Chinea. He offered high-fives to LSU players. Then—standing at the top of the dugout steps—he gathered the team for a pep talk. That was when he held up his gift for all to see: a 29-ounce can of "Golden Sweet" whole kernel corn.

"We had no idea what was going on," says first baseman Mason Katz, the senior slugger who is leading the Southeastern Conference with 60 runs batted in.

Robertson started with a hunting lesson. He said that corn was the best "duck call" in the world, spreading it on the ground being the best way to bait a field and attract ducks. He also stressed that it was illegal to do so. With that in mind, Robertson suggested another purpose for the corn. He wanted the Tigers to use it for good luck.

His logic required a creative game of connect-the-dots: Nebraska is one of the top corn-producing states. Omaha is in Nebraska. The College World Series is in Omaha. And that is where LSU wants to finish its season by winning a national championship.

With a black Sharpie, Robertson wrote on the top of the can: "Back to Omaha!!"

He signed his name.

Then he issued oral instructions: *Keep this with you for the rest of the season. Take it with you when you go to Omaha. Then—once you win that national championship—all of you sign the can and bring it back to me.*

The phrase "can of corn" has a long history in baseball, but it traditionally means something very different: an easy-to-catch fly ball. The Tigers were breaking new ground. This was the birth of Rally Corn.

A year after adopting a stuffed animal they named Mouton the Rally Monkey—and then coming up just one game short of making the 2012 College World Series—the Tigers were eager to embrace whatever help they could get.

Senior Joey Bourgeois, one of the best relief pitchers on the team, quickly volunteered for a role he never could have seen coming: keeper of the corn.

"I just knew I'd do a good job taking care of it," Bourgeois says.

The corn generally stays in his locker.

When the Tigers play at home, Bourgeois carries the can into the dugout and places it in the helmet rack—always on its own shelf.

"Every time we come to bat, we see it, and it reminds us what we're working towards," freshman shortstop Alex Bregman says. "That can of corn represents everything we're trying to do."

Katz sees it as a reminder that personal goals are not important—that only "the ultimate team goal" of winning the national championship matters.

Some of the players do more than just look at the can. They also give it a quick touch for good luck.

"It has a little magic to it," Bregman says. And he is certainly in a position to know—carrying a .424 batting average and tied for most hits in the nation (67).

"Sometimes I'm just touching that can of corn and hoping it'll give me a spark," freshman outfielder Mark Laird says.

When the Tigers play on the road, Bourgeois packs the corn in his travel bag and finds a good spot for it in the team's temporary dugout. He's committed only one error. The evening of Tuesday, March 26, right before playing Tulane in New Orleans, Bourgeois realized he had forgotten the corn. He panicked. *What if we don't get the job done without the corn?* Much to his relief, LSU won in a 14–1 blowout. The keeper of the corn was off the hook.

Bourgeois promises that the corn will not miss another game.

Head baseball coach Paul Mainieri gets a good laugh out of the whole thing.

"I'm not a believer in superstition, but my attitude is, why take a chance?" he says. "If having a can of corn in our dugout gives our players any added confidence, for whatever warped reason there might be, then I'm all for it."

The LSU baseball team and its can of corn both made it to the 2013 College World Series. Neither of them won a game there. Joey Bourgeois, now a Xerox sales representative in Baton Rouge, still has the corn. The can sits on an entertainment center in his bedroom. Bourgeois says he will one day put it in a display case with the cleats and glove he used in Omaha—a permanent reminder of all the fun he had playing college baseball.

Tigers Roar at Red, Rock & Blue

June 28, 2013

The last time former LSU baseball star Ryan Theriot took his cuts in a ballgame, he was playing for the San Francisco Giants in the fourth and final game of the 2012 World Series against the Detroit Tigers. With the score tied at three and the drama of extra innings unfolding at Comerica Park in Detroit, Theriot opened the tenth inning with a single. Three batters later, he slid across home plate with the Series-winning run and then unleashed a barrage of celebratory screams into the chilly October night. It was a storybook ending to a twelve-year career in professional baseball.

Things are much different as Theriot settles into the batter's box this time. Eight months removed from both the glory and the stress of Major League Baseball—now retired and back home in Louisiana—Theriot is enjoying a hot Friday evening at Cypress Mounds Baseball Complex in Baton Rouge. He is wearing baggy shorts, a blue softball jersey, and an easy smile that says it all: *Hey, no big thing, we're only here for a good time and a great cause.*

So what if Theriot hasn't played softball since phys. ed. class in middle school? This game is filled with folks who are not exactly world-class wizards of the softball diamond. That is the whole idea of the annual "Celebrity/Sorta Celebrity Softball Game" organized by WAFB-TV sportscaster Jacques Doucet. He brings in a bunch of people known for doing other things—many of them high-profile LSU sports figures—and puts on an entertaining slow-pitch game to raise money and awareness for U.S. military personnel and their families.

The pitcher about to deliver the ball is Gordy Rush of the LSU Sports Radio Network. The catcher is LSU women's basketball coach Nikki Caldwell. The first baseman is former LSU basketball star Ricky Blanton—now a forty-seven-year-old owner of an insurance agency.

In the third-base dugout, Baton Rouge Mayor Kip Holden claps with encouragement for Theriot. Former LSU quarterback Jarrett Lee also stands in support of their teammate—watching from just in front of the seated Curious George "rally monkey" he brought to the game for whatever power it might offer.

Theriot is ready now.

Rush under-hands a meatball of a pitch. Theriot locks in on it. He swings with great might but pops the ball up, harmlessly, to the left side of the infield. Third baseman Warren Morris—yes, *that* Warren Morris, the former LSU baseball player who hit a walk-off home run to win the 1996 College World Series—yields to the call of shortstop Jason Williams (an All-American on that same championship team). Williams easily makes the catch.

Theriot is frustrated.

Returning to the dugout, he pauses to address his coach, local ESPN radio host Matt Moscona: "I was trying to go deep."

Looking entirely serious, Moscona responds with only this: "Dude, next time you gotta touch the rally monkey!"

Doucet has a perfect record so far. Three straight years he has coached his Red team to victory against Moscona's Blue squad. That made for plenty of light-hearted smack talking as the fourth-annual game was promoted the last few weeks.

"This year, we're taking you down!" Moscona warned Doucet when their official draft of players went live one afternoon on his radio show.

There was even "heated" discussion about how the absence of former LSU pitching great Ben McDonald—the only pitcher the Red team has ever used but unable to make it this year—might affect the outcome of the game.

Doucet was not fazed by such talk. Late yesterday, he fired a shot in the form of a publicly available tweet to Moscona—"Look what I'm going to win again Friday! #Dynasty"—along with a photo of the "Celebrity/Sorta Celebrity" trophy.

In truth, however, the thirty-six-year-old Doucet does not really care much about winning or losing.

"Those days are long gone," he says. "Now it's all about who we're able to get to play in the game, crowd turnout, how much money we raise, and then, of course, just wanting everyone—players and spectators—to enjoy the whole event. Those are the biggest things."

With that in mind, Doucet's favorite part of the game has nothing to do with pitching or hitting or fielding. It is the team introductions—when longtime LSU baseball publicist and stadium announcer Bill Franques employs his voice of authority to offer a biographical nugget or two on each player.

"Just looking at all those people here in one place, and then everyone in the stands applauding for them as their names are called, it's almost a little surreal for me," Doucet says. "I mean, you plan, you plan, you plan, you envision it, and then when it actually unfolds in front of your eyes—*Wow, this is pretty cool.*"

Team Blue gets off to a good start.

In the first inning, thirty-nine-year-old David Dellucci, a Baton

Rouge native who played thirteen years of Major League Baseball, blasts a two-run homer to right. The score is 2–0.

In the second inning, the Blues benefit from some bad pitching by Gordy Rush, who is quickly proving he is no Ben McDonald. First, Rush hits former LSU basketball player Garrett Temple—now with the Washington Wizards—with a pitch. Even in this game of slow-pitch, Temple gets a free trip to first base for that. Then, with two outs and bases loaded, Rush forces in a run by hitting former LSU football receiver Rueben Randle (now with the New York Giants). The Blues are up 3–0.

The Reds yank Rush from the mound before the bottom of the third inning, moving Jason Williams from shortstop to pitcher. But no pitching change can eliminate the universal rule that just about anything can happen on a field of play.

Proof of this truism is delivered by one of the most popular players in recent years of LSU football, Australian punter Brad Wing, now a rookie with the Philadelphia Eagles, who is playing in the first softball game of his life. With two outs and former LSU football receiver Terrence Toliver (now with the Chicago Bears) on second base, Wing approaches the plate. Actually, not knowing much about the rules of the game, he starts by standing *on* the plate before being corrected and backing off a bit.

Wing's lack of expertise bodes well for the Red team. But nobody in the field knows about yesterday's stealth outing. Wing, never having swung a baseball or softball bat and hoping to avoid embarrassment, made a special trip to Walmart. He bought a softball, took it to his old high school, Parkview Baptist, and had a friend throw him pitches while he hacked away with a borrowed bat. Wing by no means perfected the science of hitting—smooth he is not—but he nonetheless knocks a solid single to right field. Toliver scores and the lead is 4–0.

Wing is still bubbling when he returns to the dugout. "That was fun," he says. "Pretty exciting." Then the full measure of his surprisingly successful debut grabs hold of him: "Hopefully I don't have to bat again, so I can just end on a good one."

Maybe a thousand people are here to watch. Members of the military sang the national anthem and lined up on the mound for the ceremonial first pitch. The Pelican Broadcasting Network will televise its coverage of the game multiple times the next few weekends.

Doucet never could have imagined any of this when he and a few high school buddies built a softball field behind his family home in the small town of Maurice, Louisiana, just outside Lafayette. This was in the early 1990s, and Doucet had been inspired by the movie *Field of Dreams*, in which Kevin Costner builds a baseball field behind his Iowa farmhouse and thereby opens the way to a beautiful father-son story of hope and healing.

Doucet was not seeking anything so dramatic. He was only looking to have fun with his friends. Off he went to a local hardware store for lumber and chicken wire to construct an outfield fence. Doucet and company cleared brush. They created base paths and made a place for home plate just in front of a big tree. They set up wooden benches for the teams.

"Jacques had a vision, and he was just so persistent," says Taylor Begnaud, his best friend since kindergarten. "It was definitely a group effort. But Jacques was the one always driving us to get it done. The rest of us would have been perfectly happy just hanging out and having a good time."

Soon after the field was finished, young Doucet wanted to create an event as well. He had always enjoyed "putting things on," as he says, whether that meant hosting a neighborhood Super Bowl party or just an informal night of loud music and silliness with friends (always going heavy on hard rock from the late 1980s). So why not put together a little softball tournament?

In 1994—the summer after Doucet and Begnaud graduated from high school—the inaugural "Doucet/Begnaud Invitational" was played with four teams. The tournament went through a couple of stops and starts through the years. It eventually outgrew the field behind the Doucet residence. Then came the biggest changes: In 2006, at the urging of Begnaud, by then an Army veteran who had served in Kuwait, the tournament became a fundraiser for military-related charities (with proceeds now split by "The Blue Star Mothers of Louisiana" and "Support Our War Heroes"). In 2010, with the goal of reaching a broader audience and maximizing impact, Doucet and Begnaud moved the whole operation to Baton Rouge, where they could leverage Doucet's exposure as a local TV guy and his relationships with area sports figures.

What started as a one-day gathering of teens is now a full weekend of competition and concerts for people of all ages. The softball tournament remains what Doucet calls "the backbone" of it all, but adult kickball and youth baseball tournaments are also included—with the combined number of teams (131) at an all-time high this year.

The overall event is called Red, Rock & Blue. And the "Celebrity/Sorta Celebrity" game has grown into a wonderful opening act.

In the fourth inning, Doucet transitions from cordial host to scrappy contributor, putting the Red team on the scoreboard with an RBI single. Blue still leads 4–1. But Red is showing signs of life.

Pitcher Jason Williams continues to silence the bats of the Blue team. And his squad finally turns into the Big Red Machine of years past—scoring two runs in the fifth inning and four more in the sixth.

Nobody has a bigger moment than former LSU basketball star Brandon Bass (now a power forward with the Boston Celtics). When Bass last played in the "Celebrity/Sorta Celebrity" game—two years ago—he struck out three times in a row. All he did was swing and miss! Now he shines with a well-hit single. His confidence is soaring. "Next year I'm going for a home run," Bass says. "I finally feel like I can really play."

Joe Horn, one of the most prolific receivers in New Orleans Saints history, is quick to congratulate Bass. Horn is a vocal leader in the Red dugout, urging on teammates and celebrating big plays as if some sort of legitimate championship hangs in the balance.

"It's such a blessing just to be out here and to play in a game like this," he says. "I love the cause—doing something to give back to the troops. I love the competition and the camaraderie. I love everything about it."

With seven unanswered runs, Horn's Red team is now ahead 7–4.

Doucet is always aiming for entertainment value. And so he has members of the Alex Box Stadium grounds crew here to drag the infield dirt before the seventh inning. Anyone familiar with LSU baseball knows what this means. The downsized crew of four soon stops working and starts dancing. This time, its tortured yet terrific routine is choreographed to an old 'N Sync song, "Bye Bye Bye," which is blaring over the sound system.

The performance stirs the crowd, but it fails to awaken the bats of the Blue team.

For the fourth consecutive inning, the Blues put a big zero on the scoreboard.

The Red team explodes for four more runs in the top of the eighth—stretching its lead to 11–4—and that should pretty much do it.

Mayor Holden is not ready to concede, though. He gathers his teammates for a pep talk before the bottom of the eighth. With tone both steady and sincere, he says: "All of us have to concentrate on exactly what our job is."

The Blue team responds by adding two more scoreless innings to its string of futility—the closing act being an ugly strikeout by former LSU football All-American Ben Wilkerson (a dominant center on the 2003 national championship team)—and the game is over.

Final score: 11–4. The Red team—even without Ben McDonald—is victorious for the fourth straight year.

The trash talking will only heighten in advance of next year's game. For now, though, everyone is focused only on the good time and the great cause of the evening. Everyone is much more interested in the same core concept that once motivated Doucet in the solitude of a back yard: the magic of bringing people together through sports.

Celebrities and sorta celebrities line up to exchange hugs and handshakes and laughter—lots of laughter as they're already rehashing highlights and lowlights of the game.

Fans join in to get pictures and autographs.

Two decades after Doucet built his personal field of dreams, nobody is in a hurry to leave this one.

Thanks to the work of Jacques Doucet, Red, Rock & Blue has continued to grow each year. In addition to lifting the spirits of military families and bringing together all sorts of folks affiliated with LSU sports, the annual event has grossed a total of more than $500,000.

Kimbeaux

July 31, 2013

There was a time when leaving town meant something entirely different. It meant that Kimberlyn Duncan—then an overwhelmed college freshman—was about to give up. In the fall of 2009, she was ready to dump her dream of being an LSU sprinter and head home to Texas.

Classes were not the problem. She was doing well in school, as she always had. But failure kept finding her on the practice track. She could not drive out of the starting blocks with the form and power her coaches wanted to see; could not lift her knees the right way once up and running; could not keep up with her teammates during conditioning drills; could not seem to do *anything* that met expectations.

"Kim, that's not what I asked you to do, not even close to what I just showed you." Those dreaded words from head coach Dennis Shaver were spoken so many times that they never really stopped playing on her internal sound track, endlessly assaulting whatever confidence remained.

Was she just not good enough to be part of an elite track-and-field program? Duncan had not forgotten that no other school had even offered her an athletic scholarship. Maybe all those other coaches—every other coach in America—had been right to ignore her.

Sometimes the tears flowed before she called home. Other times it was not until getting her mom on the phone and rehashing everything—yet again—that Duncan's eyes started leaking. Either way, the calls were frequent, often three, four, or five times a day, and the message became consistent: "I'm done, Mom. I can't do this anymore. I'm ready to leave. I'm ready to come home."

So much for the dream she had chased since middle school—the dream about running for the one team that always seemed to dominate whenever she was able to catch a track meet on television. Duncan would just pack her belongings, return to her parents and little sister in Katy, Texas, and figure out something else to do.

But her parents had other things in mind—things such as perseverance and faith.

"Just hang in there," her mother, Schrylean, kept telling her. "There's obviously something those coaches see in you that you don't see in yourself. That's why they wanted you in the first place, and that's why they're always staying on you the way they do."

Ultimately, Duncan decided to stay in Baton Rouge, which proved fortunate for all involved. Otherwise, she never would have achieved one of the most remarkable strings of individual championships in the history of collegiate track and field. She never would have become one of the most decorated athletes—in any sport—ever to wear the purple and gold of LSU.

To a casual spectator, sprinting might appear to be one of the least complicated activities in any sport. The first person from here to there wins. Simple as that. For participants and coaches, however, proper preparation and execution are anything but simple—and the analysis of both never seems to end. Olympic champion Carl Lewis once put it this way: "If someone outside our little world ever observed the way we spend hours on end dissecting something as simple as running from point A to point B, he'd almost have to conclude we're nuts. But that's us. That's the world in which we live."

As a college neophyte, Duncan saw it as a foreign world. She had been running track since seventh grade. Her senior year at Cypress Springs High School, months after signing a letter of intent to attend LSU, she became Texas Class 5A state champion at 200 meters. But being at LSU—getting acclimated to one of the top track programs in the nation—was something else altogether. She had never been exposed to such rigorous training. Her running mechanics had never been picked apart with such attention to detail.

Coach Shaver kept telling her she was just "scooting" across the track instead of applying sufficient force to the ground with her feet. He repeatedly reminded her to exaggerate her knee lift: "Higher, Kim, higher, like you're about to hit yourself in the chest." He felt that Duncan had "good frequency" with her turnover, meaning her legs were moving fast from one step to the next, but he was not satisfied with the length of her strides. They were too short. And those were only the main issues related to running at full speed. Shaver also thought Duncan had a flawed start—she was just "popping up" out of the blocks instead of really driving out of them—and a "fairly weak" acceleration phase en route to top speed.

As rough as all of that looked to a longtime technician, the good news was that everything Shaver observed could be overcome with hard work. He believed that most of Duncan's mechanical issues were attributable to her lack of power. She was slender—five-foot-nine, 130 pounds, with limbs that just kept going—and had never done any serious training with weights. Now was the time to start a full regimen of strength exercises.

The bad news—as weeks turned into months and months into a full semester—was that Duncan continued to feel lost. She found it impossible to detect any real improvement. She generally trailed most of her teammates during training sessions. As Duncan now says of those early days on campus: "I knew that the road to success wasn't going to be easy. But it felt like I was on a road that wasn't going anywhere."

Her initial races did not brighten her outlook.

Running the 60-meter dash in the 2010 Purple Tiger indoor meet at LSU, Duncan placed seventh out of eight finalists. A week later, at the New Mexico Invitational, she dropped to last place in the 60 final. Duncan also ran the 200-meter dash at that meet in Albuquerque, finishing fourth, but with a relatively slow time of 24.24 seconds. Next up was the Tyson Invitational in Arkansas. Duncan's 60 time of 7.50 seconds was twenty-seventh best in the qualifying round—meaning she failed to advance. Her 23.86 in the 200 was better than she had done in New Mexico, but facing a much higher level of competition, her time was only fourteenth best in the field.

It was nothing unusual for a freshman to face early difficulties with collegiate competition. But Duncan had a tough time seeing the big picture. She saw herself only flailing against the downward pull of defeat.

She started to rationalize: *I guess I'm just glad to be at LSU. I'm never going to make it to the top. But at least I'm going to be here with some of the stars.*

"No!" her mom kept telling her. "You're going to *be* one of the stars!"

Duncan was hesitant to discuss her constant doubts with her coaches. Still, they knew she was struggling. One of the assistant coaches, Marvin Gibson, pulled her aside one day and told her: "We didn't bring you here for nothing. You're going to be great. You just have to keep pushing."

Ade Alleyne-Forte, a year ahead of Duncan and already an All-American as a member of the LSU men's 4 x 400-meter relay team, also did his best to encourage her when she was down. More than once, Duncan went to him with the same refrain: "Ade, I'm just trying to get this training right." Alleyne-Forte looked at her—a friend he viewed as shy and soft-spoken—and offered this: "Kim, you don't see it, but you're good. You need to see it yourself."

She tried to keep that thought with her.

Duncan also held tight to the advice she got from senior All-American Samantha Henry, one of the most accomplished sprinters in school history. Once, when Duncan was stressed out, Henry told her she needed to do two things. The first—"calm down"—was a simple but challenging thought for someone so consumed by anxiety. The second—"just keep praying"—was much more natural for someone who had always been deeply spiritual.

There was no "light switch" moment when a clear path to success was suddenly flipped on and illuminated—no single moment when Duncan felt the twin weights of doubt and disappointment lifted from her lean frame. Improvement came in small pieces. It came with trial and error. It came with repetition and resolve.

Duncan got stronger.

Her running form got better.

She finally started to feel comfortable at LSU—even stopped all her talk about leaving Baton Rouge and heading home.

Duncan's first significant breakthrough came late in her freshman year—April 2010—when she won two races in the LSU Alumni Gold meet. The first victory came as a member of the Lady Tigers 4 x 100-meter relay team. The second came by running her best time ever up to that point—22.96 seconds—in the 200. So what if it was wind-aided and therefore would not officially count as her personal record? Duncan had long before set a goal of going under 23 seconds by the time she finished at LSU. She could hardly believe it when she saw the time: *Did I really just do that?*

Coach Shaver was both happy for her and inquisitive.

"How'd you feel?" he asked Duncan.

"Good!" she said.

"What'd you do different?"

Duncan just shrugged and told him the truth: "I don't know."

She was not yet capable of really analyzing how she ran a race. But the lack of detailed understanding did not diminish the combination of joy and relief washing over her. More important than any step-by-step analysis was an overall conclusion she could finally allow herself to process: *OK, you can actually run fast!*

Duncan was named Southeastern Conference female freshman of the week.

It was her first collegiate honor—the first tangible hint that any athletic glory might one day belong to her.

Running second leg on LSU's 4 x 100 relay team, Duncan became an All-American at the end of her freshman year. Then—as a sophomore—she started collecting national championships.

The first came on March 11, 2011, at the NCAA Indoor Championships in College Station, Texas. Duncan won her signature event—the 200—with a time of 22.85 seconds. She was both stunned and thrilled: "I had tons of emotions. I knew I was happy. But I didn't know if I wanted to cry or what." She did not cry. She did have two powerful thoughts that would keep her emotional tank filled for a while. First: *Wow, I'm finally getting what I'm supposed to do*. Then: *Whoa, now I'll be expected to win another championship when we go outdoors*.

Duncan did that and more. When the NCAA Outdoor Championships were held that June in Des Moines, Iowa, she not only won a race.

She took over the meet—transforming the Drake Stadium track into a personal stage and delivering a staggering series of performances. In the 100-meter dash, Duncan ran a personal best of 11.09 seconds and was national runner-up to Oklahoma's Candyce McGrone, who beat her by a mere hundredth of a second. Next was the 4 x 100 relay. Duncan anchored the Lady Tigers to the gold medal in a season-best time of 42.64 seconds. Then came the 200-meter dash and her attempt to achieve the indoor-outdoor double. Duncan ran another personal best to win that race and a second-straight national title. Her time of 22.24 seconds also set a stadium record.

When all the running and jumping and throwing were done at those NCAA championships, Duncan had collected more individual points—20.5—than any other athlete in the meet. She also might have established a record for understatement when she soon thereafter told an interviewer: "I am a much more mature and confident person today than I was just one year ago."

As a teammate and friend, Brieanna Kennedy, a year older than Duncan, had thoroughly enjoyed watching her progression from overwhelmed freshman to super sophomore. Kennedy, one of the best hammer throwers in Lady Tiger history, also enjoyed watching as a fan.

"I was always in such awe of Kim," Kennedy says. "Not in a creepy way. I was just in awe of the type of person she was—the way she interacted with people, the whole way she carried herself. She was probably the most humble person I knew. But she was always having fun, too, always laughing, always down for a good time."

Then there was her look.

"Always so stylish," Kennedy says. "That sleek, short haircut, bangs across her forehead. Her fingernails—always nice and long, always intricately detailed. Those hoop earrings. She was always wearing those big, big hoops—that was her thing. Oh, and then she would throw on her high heels whenever she felt like it. Nobody could rock the heels like Kim."

Kennedy had never known anyone who could at once be so humble and so stylish. She'd also never imagined that someone could be that way and then also be so remarkably focused and effective once she stepped on the track . . . temporarily replacing her soft and welcoming countenance with a mask of intensity—her game face—and then crushing pretty much anyone who lined up against her.

With all of that in mind, Kennedy decided that Duncan needed a nickname. It would have to reflect both style and power. It would have to incorporate a touch of Louisiana but still be one of a kind—unique—just like her friend.

The name came to her one night when she and Duncan were hanging out with a bunch of teammates at an off-campus apartment: *Kimbeaux*. It had the sound and power of Rambo—the tough-guy movie character played by Sylvester Stallone. It had a touch of Louisiana—the Cajun *eaux* being employed the same way it is in *Geaux* Tigers. And it was both stylish and unique. Who had ever seen such a name?

"You need to get a trademark for it," Kennedy told Duncan. "I'm telling you, when you're famous, this is going to be a big thing."

"Kimbeaux?" Duncan said.

"Yeah, girl, that's you now! You're Kimbeaux!"

Duncan just laughed.

But the name stuck. She loved having it.

Kimbeaux never looked back.

As a junior, she was the most dominant collegiate sprinter in the nation. Indoors and outdoors, she repeated as national champion at 200 meters, becoming the first woman in NCAA history to win back-to-back indoor and outdoor titles in the event. She also kept getting better in both the 60-meter dash and the 100, running a personal best of 10.96 seconds to set the SEC Championships meet record and then placing second in the NCAA Championships for the second straight year.

Even her biggest disappointment of the year was a sign of good things to come. On June 30, 2012, competing at the U.S. Olympic Trials in a 200-meter final filled with professional stars, Duncan's fourth-place finish made her the best-performing collegian but left her one spot short of qualifying for the American team. Her time of 22.34 seconds meant that she missed being in the 2012 London Olympics by twelve hundredths of a second.

Duncan was later named 2012 winner of The Bowerman Trophy—track-and-field's equivalent of football's Heisman—as the most outstanding collegiate female athlete in her sport.

This year she just kept adding to her resume. Two more NCAA titles in the 200—indoor and outdoor—gave Kimbeaux an astounding six straight national championships in her best event. That made her the only sprinter in NCAA history—male or female—to sweep indoor and outdoor titles three years in a row. She even saved her best for last. Her wind-aided time of 22.04 seconds in her final collegiate race—huge, gold, hoop earrings flying with her every step of the way—was the fastest she had ever run the 200. It matched the fastest 200 run under any conditions in collegiate history.

A track-and-field enthusiast could spend hours making lists of all that Duncan accomplished—races won, records broken, awards accumulated—as a Lady Tiger. But only a few numbers are needed to translate the scope of her achievements for anyone not familiar with the minutiae of the sport.

Seven times—six in the 200 and once on a relay team—she was an NCAA champion.

Twelve times she won SEC titles.

Fourteen times she was an All-American.

Not bad for someone who initially spent so much time thinking she was not even good enough to be on the team.

Coach Shaver has a strong case when he labels Duncan "maybe one of the greatest athletes—in any sport—we've ever had on our campus." Track and field being what it is, a "minor" sport deep in the shadows of football and the other "major" LSU sports, he is also well aware that most people in town have never heard of Kimbeaux.

Shaver ponders a never-going-to-happen hypothetical question: *What if track and field got the same type of attention as football and basketball—where would that leave Duncan in the overall context of LSU sports history?*

"Kim would be iconic," Shaver says. "She would be right up there with the all-time LSU greats. Billy Cannon, Shaquille O'Neal, anyone you want to name—Kim would be right up there with them."

Last month, Duncan made her debut as a professional athlete, running as a Nike-sponsored sprinter at the U.S. Outdoor Track and Field Championships in Des Moines. It was a huge opening competition for someone just out of college, as the national championships also served as the American qualifying meet for the upcoming IAAF World Championships in Moscow (the sport's premier event in this non-Olympic year).

Watching Duncan run in Iowa, Shaver saw a very different sprinter than the one who first showed up at LSU. Kimbeaux carried herself with such confidence—a quiet confidence, but nonetheless palpable. Physically, she was also much stronger now. And her running mechanics were the best they had ever been—legs firing so efficiently, arms pumping with consistent form and power, open hands slicing the air like human blades.

Warming up for the 200-meter final on Sunday, June 23, Duncan had the look of track royalty. Then she went to work in Lane 6—next to reigning Olympic champion Allyson Felix in Lane 5—and earned a crown. Felix led most of the way. But Duncan held form the best and took control in the final fifty meters. She finished first with a time of 21.80 seconds (ahead of Felix's 21.85). Duncan didn't care that her time was wind-aided. It was the fastest she had ever run. She had just defeated the Olympic champion to claim her first national title as a professional. She would soon be running for Team USA in the World Championships.

Kimbeaux had a single word to describe how she felt: "Overjoyed!"

Four years removed from all those stress-filled phone calls of her freshman year—all those days spent on the brink of quitting LSU and going home—Duncan is not merely talking about leaving Baton Rouge. She is actually doing it.

Her mother and sister have been in town to help with the big pack: cleaning out her off-campus apartment and hauling her belongings to a storage unit. Duncan will return in the fall. As a professional sprinter, she will continue to train with Shaver.

For now, though, it is time to leave. At 4:20 on a steamy Wednesday afternoon, the Duncan ladies settle into Schrylean's black Kia Sportage. They are heading home to Texas, where, in two days, Kimberlyn will celebrate her twenty-second birthday.

"I can't wait," she says. "All I want to do is relax—go out to eat with the family, watch a few movies at the house."

Duncan will also get in her final two workouts of the week. This is no time to deviate from her training schedule—not with the best sprinters on the planet soon to share a track with her in the biggest meet of her life. After a few days at home, Duncan will fly to Russia for the World Championships, her first opportunity to represent the United States on such a grand stage.

Wearing the red, white, and blue of Team USA will be quite a thrill for a young lady once dressed in doubt more than anything else. Duncan will also be wrapped in a collection of syllables she never would have assigned to herself during her early days at LSU. It is a simple but powerful statement she stumbled across on Pinterest and happily claimed as her own: "I'm going to succeed because I'm crazy enough to think I can."

Kimberlyn Duncan won her opening race in the 2013 World Championships and advanced to the 200-meter semifinals, but she failed to qualify for the final. In 2014, she placed second in the U.S. national championships. Duncan now lives and trains in Los Angeles. Her primary goal is to make the U.S. Olympic team for the 2016 Summer Games in Rio de Janeiro, Brazil.

Legends

August 31, 2013

Other than the one impossible-to-ignore icon towering over West 33rd Street between Fifth and Sixth Avenues—the Empire State Building is tough to miss—the rest of the block could be pretty much any other block in Midtown Manhattan. There is a Starbucks, a deli, a drugstore, an upscale clothing store, a downscale souvenir shop, lots of office space, a parking garage, a couple of pubs, and an "adult boutique" named Empire Erotica. None of it is anything unusual for New York.

But wait. There is also an oversized Mike the Tiger—a nine-foot-tall, air-filled "balloon" version of the LSU mascot—standing on the sidewalk outside a sports bar called Legends. Mike is wearing a purple football jersey with "LSU" in bold, white letters across the chest, his right hand proudly raised with the index finger pointing skyward in standard "We're Number One" fashion.

Countless city slickers stream past Mike without knowing or caring what he represents and oblivious to the fact that the 2013 LSU football season begins tonight. Why would they care that the twelfth-ranked Tigers are about to play twentieth-ranked Texas Christian University (TCU) in the Cowboys Classic at AT&T Stadium in Texas? New Yorkers being New Yorkers, they are busy with other things.

But a growing number of folks inside the bar—hundreds of men and women sporting lots of purple and gold—know exactly why Mike is standing sentry by the door. They have all come for the same reason. For an LSU fan in New York City, there is only one place to be on a football Saturday night: packed into Legends right along with everyone else screaming "Tiger Bait!" at the forty television screens scattered throughout three floors of never-ending athletics (broadcast variety) and ever-flowing alcohol (including Hurricanes and Louisiana-brewed Abita beer whenever LSU plays).

Tonight's game will be nationally televised by ESPN. But Legends always picks up TV coverage of the Tigers no matter who is carrying the game. Year-round, the bar stays decorated with LSU football photos, banners, and other memorabilia. The game-day menu features Louisiana specialties such as "gator or boudin sliders" and gumbo. And the Golden Band from Tigerland fills the joint with all the right music—courtesy of an iPod—at all the right times.

"Every year, we try to put in a few more upgrades, anything that will add to the overall atmosphere," says forty-five-year-old Noel Firth, co-owner of Legends and the man who has transformed the place into Tiger Stadium North. "We just want everyone to feel like they're back at home."

This is quite a statement coming from an Irish cop who grew up in the Bronx and spent most of his adult life as a New York City police officer. Firth has come to really enjoy and appreciate the people of Louisiana.

Half an hour before the opening kickoff of the season—and half a nation away from Arlington, Texas, where the real action will occur—Tim Gaiennie approaches his regular spot at a back corner of the main bar to perform a little action of his own. He connects a cord from his iPod to a wall-mounted control panel. He switches a button on the panel. And—just like that—he is master of the Legends sound system:

a thirty-four-year-old architectural design manager who doubles as New York-area chapter president of the LSU Alumni Association and triples as a barroom blend of "band director" and deejay.

Gaiennie begins by playing "Pregame Salute," a longtime LSU standard, and the Legends crowd responds with a burst of cheering, screaming, and all-around excitement that basically translates to this: *Man, that off-season was way too long! We're ready for some football!* Gaiennie plays a few other band songs, including "Hey Fightin' Tigers" and "Tiger Rag," the knowing crowd closing out the latter piece with well-timed shouts of "T-I-G-E-R-S . . . TIGERS!"

"I do all the music exactly the way they do it in Tiger Stadium," Gaiennie says. "I was in the band back in the late nineties"—a clarinet player—"so I have it all down."

In addition to the official LSU tunes, he also plays "Louisiana Saturday Night" by Alabama (the country band . . . not the football team). And—with kickoff fast approaching—he squeezes in one more favorite for fans of the "home" team: "Callin' Baton Rouge" by Garth Brooks. The folks at Legends, filling all thirty tables and booths on the main floor, and already standing three-deep at the sixty-foot-long bar, have been musically lifted into full-frenzy status.

Gaiennie has to hustle now. It is 9:10 p.m. in New York—8:10 at the stadium in Texas—and the game is about to begin. Gaiennie flips a switch on that panel behind the bar, and the sound system reverts to ESPN audio: "Thirty-four wins in the last three years." It is play-by-play man Brad Nessler talking about LSU head coach Les Miles and his Tigers.

Jaden Oberkrom of TCU kicks off to open the game. LSU returner Odell Beckham Jr. gathers in the ball and takes a knee deep in the end zone. The LSU offense—led by senior quarterback Zach Mettenberger—will start the season at its own twenty-five-yard line.

Legends is buzzing.

As a member of the New York Police Department, Firth directly experienced the horrors of the 9/11 terrorist attacks. On September 11, 2001, he went from one hospital to another, tracking bodies in emergency rooms. The next day, he saw for himself what remained of the World Trade Center and felt total shock and disbelief. Firth was assigned to a makeshift bereavement center at the Lexington Avenue Armory. He also spent weeks digging through debris at a Staten Island landfill. Dump trucks kept bringing it from ground zero and countless investigators—Firth among them—kept digging for evidence.

There were still times after that when Firth was able to enjoy his job as a sergeant. And he later worked as a bodyguard for a private firm. But he also knew that he wanted to try something entirely different. He decided to open a restaurant with a lot of bar space and lots of TVs—a place that most people would just call a sports bar. Firth retired from the police department, took out a bank loan, and went to work on Legends. The doors opened in the fall of 2008.

"It's been a lot of fun," Firth says.

And the people of a foreign land—foreign to him—have had a lot to do with that.

A few weeks after opening Legends, he heard that some people from Louisiana were looking for somewhere to get together and cheer for their favorite football team. Members of the LSU alumni group had been gathering for games at another bar, but they wanted a bigger space and the comfort of a "home" bar that really wanted them. Firth and Gaiennie met. Legends and the alumni group seemed to be a good fit. And so on October 25, 2008, about twenty LSU alums showed up at the new bar to watch a Saturday afternoon game being played in Baton Rouge: the LSU Tigers hosting the Georgia Bulldogs.

Things have evolved dramatically since then.

"Now, whenever LSU plays, we average about four hundred people," Firth says. "It's turned into a real party atmosphere. And you should see this place for the Alabama game. The line to get in goes all the way down the street. The whole scene is pretty wild. I mean, *wild*. I never knew people could be so passionate about college football."

TCU is not Alabama. But a season opener between two ranked teams is still a big deal to everyone here. This is clear from the reaction at Legends, less than six minutes into the first quarter, when LSU kicker Colby Delahoussaye boots a 23-yard field goal for the first points of the game. There is clapping and shouting and high-fiving. Bottles and glasses are lifted in celebration. There is chanting: "L-S-U! L-S-U! L-S-U!"

Gaiennie fills the air with band music—"Fight for LSU"—and the crowd responds with renewed energy. But it's nothing compared to what comes next. With a commercial showing on the TV broadcast, Gaiennie picks up the tempo, blasting Jay-Z and Alicia Keys—"Empire State of Mind"—and the place goes wild.

In New York, concrete jungle where dreams are made of.
There's nothing you can't do.
Now you're in New York.
These streets will make you feel brand new.
The lights will inspire you.
Let's hear it for New York, New York, New York.

There is dancing and general merriment throughout. There is also an unlikely juxtaposition in play: a fired-up collection of Louisianians partying to a lyrical celebration of the Big Apple. Most of these folks now call themselves New Yorkers. Others are just visiting. Either way, they are all now united as one—one loud and festive melting pot of support for the Fighting Tigers.

"This is amazing," says Jodi LeBlanc, a forty-year-old registered nurse who lives in Denham Springs, Louisiana, but is spending the weekend with a home-state friend now residing in Brooklyn. "This is the second-best place to watch an LSU game. Obviously, the best is Tiger Stadium. But this is next. I *love* this place."

Colonel Michael Edmonson loves it, too. The Superintendent of Louisiana State Police is sitting with his wife and a couple of friends at a high-top table in the front section of the main floor. He's wearing blue jeans, a white polo shirt, and running shoes instead of his familiar police uniform. There is nowhere he would rather be.

Edmonson discovered Legends while in town on business the year it opened, and he's been coming back—once a season—ever since. He and Firth met the first time he came in. The bond of law-enforcement "brotherhood" gave them a starting point. And they became good friends.

As much as Edmonson enjoys being with Firth at Legends, it was his own chance to play host that meant the most to him. Until last year, Firth had never been to a college football game, at LSU or anywhere else. Edmonson finally got him to visit Baton Rouge for one—and it was a huge game: top-ranked Alabama (with a record of 8–0) against fifth-ranked LSU (7–1) the night of Saturday, November 3, in Tiger Stadium.

Before his 2008 promotion to head the state police, Edmonson served as a personal game-day guard for LSU football coaches from Jerry Stovall to Les Miles. His insider's access to the LSU program—combined with the status of his current position—allowed him to provide Firth with an extraordinary weekend. "Southern Hospitality" is the title Firth later gave it in his photo album commemorating the occasion.

He got a tour of the LSU locker room. He learned what real Southern college football tailgating is and then stood by the door of a team bus as Miles exited for the walk down Victory Hill. He touched the "WIN!" bar on the way to the field and stood on the LSU sideline to watch pregame warm-ups—taking a break from the action only so he could pose for photos with cheerleaders. Once the game started, Edmonson and Firth watched it from the LSU chancellor's suite.

"Not bad for my first college game ever," Firth says.

The only negative was the late-game turn of events that stunned the LSU crowd into silence and agony. With less than a minute to play—and LSU leading 17–14—Alabama running back T.J. Yeldon caught a screen pass from AJ McCarron and went twenty-eight yards for the winning touchdown. Only fifty-one seconds remained. And—once that time was gone—so too was any chance LSU might have had at a national championship.

Disappointment aside, Firth had such a good weekend that he went home with a suggestion for one of his four children, Taryn, then a high school senior still undecided on what college to attend: "You really ought to think about LSU."

Taryn is now a freshman there.

While her dad is in Manhattan entertaining the head of Louisiana State Police, she is enjoying her Saturday night in Baton Rouge—a native New Yorker watching the football game at an LSU fraternity party.

Geaux figure.

Tonight's game is a good one.

LSU takes a 16–10 lead into halftime.

The third quarter ends with a wider margin for the Tigers: 30–17.

TCU then closes the gap with a touchdown and a field goal in the fourth quarter. With 7:35 to play, the Tigers and the Horned Frogs are locked in a 30–27 battle.

The Legends crowd has gone from confident to antsy. Three times in the first half the Tigers had to settle for short field-goals after reaching the red zone but failing to get a touchdown. Were those missed opportunities for more points now going to cost them the game?

"Time to finish this!" a male voice declares from amid the throng at the center of the main bar.

"Let's go, Tigers!" comes the high-volume response of a woman standing nearby.

In Texas, LSU kick returner Odell Beckham Jr. fields the ball a couple of yards into the end zone and charges out with it . . . running . . . dodging tacklers . . . still going . . . all the way to the TCU twenty-five-yard line before he's finally taken down.

"A big boost for LSU when they needed it," analyst Todd Blackledge says on the TV broadcast. The Legends crowd is back at full force—lots of cheering and shouting. But the Tigers still have work to do.

Running back Terrence Magee gets nothing on a first-down run. He gets the ball again and gains five yards up the middle. There is grumbling at Legends. *Please, not another field goal. We have to get in the end zone*. On third-and-five from the twenty, Zach Mettenberger connects with receiver Jarvis Landry for a short gain in traffic over the middle. But Landry breaks free from the safety covering him, stiff arms another defensive back at the five . . . and he's in for a touchdown.

Legends is again euphoria central.

This time, soon after Gaiennie cranks up his music, the revelry is highlighted by the shaking and twisting of a woman who has climbed atop the main bar and transformed it into her personal dance floor. She is thirty-year-old Tara Mitnick, a former LSU soccer player and now global brand manager for a New York-based fashion business. With Mardi Gras beads hanging from her neck and her left hand gripping a Bud Light bottle, Mitnick could just as easily be back in Louisiana as she pumps her right arm in the air to celebrate. One of her friends, standing on a bar stool in front of her, is more restrained in her dance moves but equally excited that LSU now has a 10-point lead with only 6:09 remaining in the game.

When the women return to floor level, a middle-aged man leans in and tells them, "It's a shame you guys don't have any fun when you're here."

Mitnick replies without hesitation: "We *always* have fun!"

The score holds. LSU closes out the season opener with a 37–27 victory.

It is 12:45 in the morning—New York time—when the teams in Texas shake hands and head off the field.

Legends is a happy place.

Outside, on the sidewalk, Mike the Tiger shines brightly under city lights.

Compared to the famous landmark he's facing across the street, Mike is merely a speck in the concrete jungle. For now, though, he's getting more attention than the Empire State Building. People leaving Legends can't get enough of plastic-and-air Mike—the combination of school loyalty and liquid encouragement leading to some creative poses as they take pictures with their favorite mascot.

This Mike will never sound off for them the way live Mike will sometimes roar back on campus in Baton Rouge. But at least they can put their arms around this one. They can put their arms around him and feel a little bit closer to home.

Things People Save

October 17, 2013

The Jack and Priscilla Andonie Museum houses a vast collection of LSU sports memorabilia. The game ball used when LSU became the first American school to play intercollegiate football on foreign soil, defeating the University of Havana, in Cuba, on Christmas in 1907 . . . Olympic medals won by hurdler Glenn "Slats" Hardin in 1932 (silver) and 1936 (gold) . . . basketball Hall of Famer Bob Pettit's LSU warm-up jacket and pants from 1954 . . . one of Pete Maravich's signature "floppy socks" from the 1970s . . . a Shaquille O'Neal size-22 game shoe . . . the bat Warren Morris used to hit the winning home run in the championship game of the 1996 College World Series . . . and so much more. It is all on display—hundreds of items—at the campus sports museum.

But countless pieces of LSU sports history have never made it into the Andonie Museum or any other public repository. They can be found only in the privacy of homes and offices. So I've been asking people in and around Baton Rouge: What—if anything—have you saved that might have a good story attached to it? Here are some of my favorites: half a dozen stories about things LSU athletes and fans have saved—and one about a special keepsake that got away.

Poster Boy

Before the existence of websites, the proliferation of sports-talk radio, and the seemingly endless coverage by ESPN and other cable TV networks, big-time college football players were promoted the old-fashioned way. In-house public relations folks known as Sports Information Directors generally did two things to publicize star athletes: scheduled them for as many interviews as possible and circulated all manner of printed materials trumpeting their greatness.

And so it was that LSU quarterback Tommy Hodson got a poster.

After stellar seasons as a redshirt freshman and sophomore—twice being named All-Southeastern Conference while leading the Tigers to the Sugar Bowl in 1986 and to the Gator Bowl in 1987 (when LSU finished with a record of 10–1–1)—Hodson entered his junior year as a preseason All-American. But the LSU brass had an even loftier title in mind for the humble kid from little Mathews, Louisiana, down on Bayou Lafourche: Heisman Trophy winner.

The idea was to at least push Hodson into the Heisman conversation as a junior—with the hope that he might actually have a chance of winning the award as a senior. In addition to aggressive contact with regional and national media members, initial plans called for bumper stickers, billboards, and posters. Lots of posters.

LSU staffers selected an action photo from the previous season—Hodson unleashing a pass against Ohio State—and they splashed his name in big, gold letters (4 inches tall) across the top of the posters. Below "HODSON" and off to the right, they placed a single word—"Heisman"—in smaller letters. Fifteen thousand copies were made, but LSU fans quickly gobbled up the free posters, so more were printed.

As things turned out, Hodson never became a serious Heisman contender. (The award went to Barry Sanders of Oklahoma State in 1988 and Andre Ware of Houston in 1989.) But Hodson set numerous LSU records that still stand, including most career passing yards (9,115), touchdown passes (69), and wins by a starting quarterback (31). He went on to play six seasons in the NFL. And—a quarter-century after the launch of that "Hodson for Heisman" campaign—he has a short stack of posters packed away in the attic of his Baton Rouge home.

"Thanks to my mom!" Hodson says with a laugh. "About five or six years ago, she was cleaning out all the stuff she'd saved from when I was playing, and she dumped it all on me!"

Shoe Story

The call came the night of Tuesday, February 9, 1993, when the Michael Jordan-led Chicago Bulls—in the midst of a three-year reign as NBA champions—needed to temporarily fill the roster spot of an injured player. Coach Phil Jackson wanted former LSU star Ricky Blanton, a twenty-six-year-old forward then playing for the Sioux Falls Skyforce of the minor-league Continental Basketball Association. Blanton had earlier played professionally in Italy and had also been in preseason training camp with the Bulls, but he had never played in a regular-season NBA game, so he was thrilled about getting a shot at the big time. Off he rushed to Indianapolis, where the Bulls had a game against Reggie Miller and the Pacers just hours after his arrival.

There was only one problem. Riding the team bus from a hotel to Market Square Arena, Blanton realized he did not have any shoes he could wear. All he had was a pair of white-and-blue Nikes from the Skyforce, and they wouldn't work with the red and black of a Bulls uniform. What to do? Once in the locker room, Blanton went to longtime Bulls equipment man John "Ligs" Ligmanowski and asked for help.

"What size you wear?" Ligs asked.

"Fourteen," Blanton said.

"Well, MJ"—as in Michael Jordan—"might be able to help you out."

Blanton momentarily froze: *Uh, how's this gonna work? I'm gonna have to ask him, or you will?* Although hesitant to do so, Blanton ended up asking Jordan if he had an extra pair of shoes he could use, and the most famous player on the planet immediately put him at ease.

"No problem," Jordan said.

Reaching into his locker, he grabbed a new pair of his personal Air Jordans—a pristine combination of white, red, and black, punctuated by Jordan's familiar number 23 on the backs of them—and gifted them to his newest teammate. So what if the shoes were a size too small and Blanton had to squeeze into them? He had no choice.

Blanton lasted only ten days with the Bulls, playing a total of thirteen minutes in two of five games they had during that stretch. But he got to score the only three NBA baskets of his career. He got to collect the memories of a lifetime by playing with one of the greatest teams in the history of basketball. And he still has the one pair of shoes he wore every step of the way.

Twenty years after his stint with the Bulls, Blanton, now in the insurance business and a radio analyst for LSU basketball games, says: "I don't know what possessed me to keep the shoes. But I'm glad I did." They sit on the floor of a hallway closet in his Baton Rouge home. He has never put them out on display. But he's never wanted to get rid of them, either.

A Piece of That Night

When Jay Dardenne was a young boy in the 1960s, his love of LSU sports could practically be classified as genetic. He went to countless football and basketball games—and became enthralled by all things purple and gold—because his dad was a longtime ticket-taker at both Tiger Stadium and the John M. Parker Agricultural Center (the old "Cow Palace" in which the basketball team played). Later, as an LSU freshman, Jay became a regular in the Tiger Stadium student section. He was thrilled to be there when magic happened the night of Saturday, November 4, 1972. With 0:00 on the game clock, quarterback Bert Jones completed a 10-yard touchdown pass to running back Brad Davis, and the extra point both defeated rival Ole Miss (17–16) and extended an LSU winning streak to eleven games. Four decades later, that touchdown remains one of the most dramatic moments in the history of LSU football.

"I'll never forget it," says Dardenne, now fifty-nine and lieutenant governor of Louisiana. "The student section went wild. Nobody got hurt—not that I know of—but everybody was suddenly pushed forward. If I was in row P when the surge started, I was in row L or M when it was done."

Part of the reason Dardenne will never forget it is that he keeps a piece of that night prominently displayed on a wall in the second-floor study of his Baton Rouge home. Protected behind glass in a gold-colored frame, it is a white number 48 jersey—what's left of it anyway—worn by Brad Davis during that game. Tearaway jerseys were still allowed then, and this one has nine ugly holes in the back alone, along with a badly ripped "V" in the purple "DAVIS" above the 48. Other than that, the jersey is a pure gem. Dardenne bought it at auction in the 1980s—"for a couple hundred bucks or something like that"—while hosting the local portion of a Jerry Lewis Telethon.

The lieutenant governor has long been an avid collector of sports memorabilia. His study contains enough sports items to double as a museum. But none of them means more to him than the Davis jersey and everything it represents. "My first season in Tiger Stadium as a student," Dardenne says. "And what a night!"

Power and Glory

Without speaking a word, Jim Taylor's guest bedroom—more a sports shrine than a resting place—tells a remarkable tale of power and glory. The power was in his legs: from 1958 through 1967, Taylor used them as a hard-charging fullback to attack NFL defenses while carrying a football. The glory was highlighted by his 1976 induction into the Pro Football Hall of Fame: he was the first of Vince Lombardi's legendary Green Bay Packers to be so honored. Not bad for a Baton Rouge native and former LSU All-American who, when selected in the second round of the 1958 NFL draft, had no idea where Green Bay was—or that Wisconsin even had a professional football team. Taylor's initial contract with the Packers gave him a $1,000 signing bonus and a first-year salary of $9,500.

At age seventy-eight, Taylor could now pick a single item from the guest room of his Baton Rouge home and sell it for more. In a corner, protected in a wood-and-glass display case, sits the almost-3-foot-high trophy he got as the NFL's Most Valuable Player in 1962. Next to it is a replica of his bust displayed at the Hall of Fame in Canton, Ohio. Dozens of framed items fill the walls. Facing each other on opposite sides of the room are one of his original green jerseys (number 31) from the Packers and the first of four *Sports Illustrated* covers on which he was featured (this one dated September 10, 1962).

"I guess I've saved a few things," Taylor says.

A *few?*

The room houses commemorative footballs, helmets, and signed posters from Hall of Fame events. There are football trading cards and photos galore, paintings, and more trophies—all of them celebrating the first man to gain more than a thousand yards rushing in each of five consecutive NFL seasons (1960 through 1964).

"A lot of old, good memories," Taylor says.

After nine years with the Packers—including four NFL championships and culminating with a victory in Super Bowl I on January 15, 1967—Taylor spent one year with his home-state New Orleans Saints (their inaugural season) before retiring as a player.

Standing with Taylor and his wife, Helen, at the end of a personal tour of the guest bedroom, I ask him: "All these years later, what does all this stuff mean to you? What do you think about when you're in here by yourself?"

"Oh, I guess I just look back at it all, and I reflect," Taylor says. "I just enjoyed competing. That was always the name of my game—*competing*."

The Power of 54

Mikie Mahtook entered the championship round of the 2009 College World Series with the same father-son inspiration he always carried into a ballpark. Although his dad was forever gone, the victim of a heart attack when Mikie was only four, the LSU center fielder wanted to honor his memory by doing something special for him. Whatever it might be—getting a key hit or perhaps making a big play in the outfield—the freshman standout would be doing it with Mikie Sr. on his mind.

Mahtook had limited but specific memories of his dad. He remembered Mikie Sr. being there when he played with his toy soldiers. He remembered jumping into his parents' bed and lying down between his mom and dad whenever he felt like it. And he would never forget the evening of June 21, 1994. That was when his dad collapsed while playing tennis and died at the age of thirty-two.

In addition to the memories, Mahtook had learned about his dad from family and friends. So many people in their hometown of Lafayette, Louisiana, had stories about Mikie Sr.—and virtually everyone knew he had played football for the LSU Tigers. Michael A. "Mikie" Mahtook wore jersey number 54 as a linebacker in the early 1980s.

Growing up without his father, Mikie Jr. loved hearing LSU football stories, and he came to view that number 54 as an indelible symbol of his dad. It became a powerful reminder of his belief that Mikie Sr. was always somehow watching out for him.

Mahtook loved that his mom, Mary Ann, had gotten a phone number ending in 54. He once drove past a bank, noticed a sign lighting up to indicate a temperature of 54 degrees, and his whole day was made. But that was nothing compared to the incident with his meal money. Six weeks into his first season at LSU, riding a team bus to the Baton Rouge airport for his first weekend trip as a starter for the Tigers, Mahtook nervously wondered whether he would perform up to expectations. Then he opened an envelope containing his school-provided per diem and was amazed to find exactly $54. He called his mom and told her: "Don't worry. I'm going to be OK."

It was nothing unusual, then, that Mahtook wanted the power of 54 with him at the College World Series. He used a black Sharpie to write "54" on his cleats and purple to put it on his batting gloves. He wrote his dad's number on a small piece of cloth and taped it to the inside of his game jersey.

All was set for the opening game of the best-of-three national championship series: LSU against Texas at Rosenblatt Stadium in Omaha, Nebraska. Mahtook even chuckled to himself about the number of wins the Tigers had already collected that year—54!—before taking the field against the Longhorns.

But the night of Monday, June 22, 2009, did not start well for him. Three times in a row Mahtook struck out. Then—with the Tigers trailing 6–4—he grounded into a double play that ended their half of the eighth inning. Less than a month after being named MVP of the Southeastern Conference tournament, Mahtook was now crushed by the thought that he was letting down his team.

The Tigers were not done, though. With two runs in the ninth, they pushed the game into extra innings—and the score was still tied at six when Mahtook dug in to bat in the top of the eleventh inning. With two outs, LSU had men on first and third. Mahtook had played in pressure-packed situations throughout the season, but none matched the magnitude of this one.

He took a fastball for a strike. He swung at another and missed it. Then he was late getting around on a third straight fastball, just managing to foul it off. Mahtook—hitting a healthy .323 for the season—was clearly having a tough time. Texas pitcher Brandon Workman went to a curveball next, but it was outside and in the dirt, and Mahtook stayed away from it. With the count now 1-2, Workman returned to his fastball, Mahtook again swung late, and the result was another foul ball.

Locked in a battle that was equal parts mental and physical, Mahtook stepped out of the batter's box to gather himself. He put his head down and did something that he almost never did during a game. He asked for help from above. Not from God . . . but from old number 54.

"Daddy, please help me," Mahtook said in the silence of his mind. "I need you. Please let me come through. I need something good here."

As much as Mahtook had struggled all night, he felt an unusual calmness as he settled back into his hitting stance. Workman threw a curveball that failed to drop as low as he wanted it. Mahtook ripped a single into center field to score DJ LeMahieu from third—the game-winning hit in a dramatic 7–6 LSU victory.

Two nights later—after Texas had tied the series by winning game two—Mahtook got another game-winning RBI as LSU defeated the Longhorns 11–4 in the third and final game. The Tigers were national champions. Mahtook packed away a few items that he would always keep in the family: his cleats, batting gloves, and a game jersey. All of them adorned with his favorite number. All of them permanent reminders of the night that he and his dad came through together with the biggest hit of his All-American collegiate career.

Mahtook—now playing professionally in the Tampa Bay Rays organization (last season with the Double-A Montgomery Biscuits)—has never again experienced anything like that transcendent moment in Omaha. But he is still scribbling "54" on his batting gloves and cleats. He is still playing for the man who once showed him how to line up his toy soldiers.

Chinese Bandit

The old football helmet resting atop a bookshelf in the home-office of Gus Kinchen needs no explanation. The Kinchens of Baton Rouge have always been a football family. But the pointy-topped coolie hat sitting next to the helmet? It is an unusual form of headgear to keep on display—a lid most often associated with Chinese laborers and in this case adorned with purple "LSU" letters.

But what a story it tells.

The tale begins more than half a century ago—in 1955—when LSU hired a thirty-year-old football coach named Paul Dietzel. Young Dietzel had a sign painted for the entrance to the LSU practice field, optimistically welcoming his charges to "The Proving Grounds." But after winning only eleven of thirty games in three years under Dietzel, the only thing proven by the LSU Tigers was their own mediocrity. More of the same was predicted for 1958. A preseason poll of sportswriters placed LSU eighth in the twelve-team Southeastern Conference. Tiger Stadium held 67,510 seats, but expectations were so low that tickets were printed for only 30,000 of them. There were grumblings that Dietzel had to go.

Then everything changed for the better.

The turning point was Dietzel's decision to break his squad into three permanent units and play an unusual style of platoon football. The eleven best players would play about the first half of each quarter on both offense and defense. Two backup units—one on offense, the other on defense—would split the remaining playing time. This would allow the best players to stay fresher. It would also boost team morale because more players would actually get to play.

The new system brought immediate success. Winning game after game was itself a surprise. But the most unexpected outcome was the stellar performance of the least talented of the three units: the defensive specialists who came to be known as the Chinese Bandits. The name came from a popular comic strip, Terry and the Pirates, in which artist Milton Caniff had characterized Chinese bandits as the meanest and most vicious people in the world. That was exactly what Dietzel wanted in his defensive unit. Gus Kinchen played right end for the Bandits and quickly became a leader.

"Bless his heart, he didn't have any speed and he wasn't very big," teammate Don "Scooter" Purvis would later say. "But Gus was one of the best technique players you'd ever see. He had the savvy and the know-how. He was never out of position—always covering his assignment. And he was just an excellent leader."

Three things happened as LSU continued winning: The Tigers kept climbing the national rankings. School officials scrambled to print more tickets. And the Chinese Bandits kept gaining popularity.

Fans simply loved the Bandits—and the Chinese theme started popping up everywhere. Thousands of people wore straw coolie hats to the games. The LSU cheerleaders unfurled a large banner with "So Lau Yah" ("Hold That Line") written in Chinese characters. A Memphis disc jockey wrote a Chinese Bandit chant that the LSU band put to music and played in the stadium.

Players on the other two units got plenty of attention, too, especially do-it-all halfback Billy Cannon, who would win the Heisman Trophy the following year. But the Bandits were often front and center when it came to fan frenzy and media coverage. *Sports Illustrated* and *Life* magazine ran prominent feature stories on them—the former declaring the defensive specialists "the darlings of the South" and the latter including a large color photo of them wearing wicked-looking Chinese masks. After the tenth and final regular-season game, in which LSU clobbered Tulane, 62–0, to remain undefeated and lock up the national championship (then decided before bowl games), Associated Press writer W.B. Ragsdale Jr. said of the Bandits: "This is possibly the most publicized substitute team in college football history and probably the proudest."

LSU went on to defeat Clemson, 7–0, in the Sugar Bowl. For the season, LSU had given up fewer than five points per game, outscoring its opponents by a stunning margin of 282 to 53. At the end of 1958, the Tigers were named AP "Team of the Year" not only for college football but for the whole of American sports, beating out the New York Yankees of Mickey Mantle and the Baltimore Colts of Johnny Unitas.

Five and a half decades later, seventy-five-year-old Gus Kinchen sees his old coolie hat as much more than a dust collector. It is also a symbol of one of the most amazing seasons in the history of LSU sports—and of the wonderful platform that being an original Chinese Bandit provided Kinchen for so many years thereafter. He credits that platform for his first job (with IBM) out of school. He credits it for his many years of work with the Fellowship of Christian Athletes, for whom he served as area director until 2009. And there have been countless expressions of thanks and appreciation from LSU fans who still embrace the wonderment of that long-ago perfect season.

"I'm grateful for all the memories, so many pleasant memories," Kinchen says now. "But when I look back, I don't really see the games.

I see all the people I got to meet. I see so many relationships that have always stayed such a big part of my life. I look at that coolie hat, and that's all I really see now—people and relationships."

The One that Got Away

Before playing football for LSU in 1999 and 2000, quarterback Josh Booty spent five years as a professional baseball player—and he even got a championship ring when the Florida Marlins won the 1997 World Series. Playing third base, Booty appeared in only four Major League games that year—none in the playoffs—after a late-season call-up from minor-league ball. But his timely visit to the bigs yielded a hunk of jewelry that would always be an impressive conversation piece. Or so he thought.

In February 2002—Booty was by then an NFL quarterback with the Cleveland Browns—he went to New Orleans for Super Bowl weekend. His team was not playing. (The New England Patriots and St. Louis Rams were.) But Booty wanted to meet up with friends and have a good time. One of his buddies who made the trip was Kevin Millar, a baseball friend who had completed four Major League seasons but without ever reaching the playoffs.

Millar had a brilliant idea one night in New Orleans. Heading out to a celebrity-filled Super Bowl party—and "trying to be cool for the ladies" (his words)—he asked Booty if he could wear his World Series ring. Booty just laughed and handed it over. "No big deal," he says now. "Millar was my boy, my best friend in baseball, so why not let him have some fun with it?"

Deep into a long night of partying, Booty and Millar found themselves in Harrah's Casino, in the company of several other NFL quarterbacks, and the football players ended up in a just-for-fun debate about which one of them was the best athlete.

"All of us were talking junk, just messing around, might have been a few drinks involved," Booty says. "And I finally had to go with my strongest stuff. *Hey, I'm the only two-sport athlete, and I have a ring. Any of y'all have a ring? Show them my ring, Millar!*"

Millar glanced down at his hand and immediately realized what he had done.

He dashed away—in a panic—back toward the men's room he had visited only a few minutes earlier. He went straight for the counter on which he had rested the ring while washing his hands . . . the counter on which he had *forgotten* the ring when he exited the room. As much as Millar wanted to see that oversized ring shining up at him, it was nowhere to be found.

Security was called. But nothing could really be done. The ring was gone.

Booty—now thirty-eight and living in Dallas—has never again seen it.

Jay Dardenne is now campaigning to be governor of Louisiana.

Mikie Mahtook made his Major League debut with the Tampa Bay Rays on April 10, 2015. Five days later, in his third at-bat with the Rays, he got his first hit as a big leaguer: a two-run homer against the Toronto Blue Jays.

Lunch with the Belles

November 22, 2013

Football has afforded Randall "Blue" Gay a generous collection of glorious moments. As a small but scrappy defensive back, he played on the 2003 LSU team that won the BCS national championship, and he played on winning Super Bowl teams with the 2004 New England Patriots and the 2009 New Orleans Saints. But Gay has never experienced anything like this: an indoor parade through the 70,000-square-foot exhibition hall of the Baton Rouge River Center . . . a shiny "Grand Marshall" sash ceremoniously draped across his chest . . . lots of women excitedly calling out to him as he rides with his wife and two young sons (ages five and nine) in a dressed-up golf cart.

"We love you, Blue," comes a high-pitched shout from the crowd.

"Love you, too," Gay reciprocates.

He smiles broadly. And he keeps tossing Mardi Gras beads toward the open hands of appreciative women. Of course, the beads are exclusively purple and gold, allowing them to blend right in with just about everything else here. Clothing? Lots of purple and gold. Banners and table decorations? Purple and gold. Items for sale at the twenty-one vendor booths? All things purple and gold: from sandals to soaps, from blouses to beer coolers, from jewelry to mousepads—and so much more. Communal spirit? Love purple! Live gold!

Welcome to the unique universe of the Bengal Belles, a high-energy, fun-loving group of female LSU football fans best known for festive luncheons that double as pep rallies and triple as fundraisers. This is the sixth and final luncheon of the 2013 season, which means it is Senior Day. Tomorrow in Tiger Stadium, the eighteenth-ranked LSU football team will battle Heisman Trophy winner Johnny Manziel and his ninth-ranked Texas A&M Aggies. For now, though, quarterback Zach Mettenberger and nine other LSU seniors will face only the warmth and support of some eight hundred women—and a smattering of men ("Bengal Beaus")—all of whom are eager to celebrate and thank them for the whole of their collegiate careers.

The event-opening Parade of Dignitaries is led by a scaled-down version of the Golden Band from Tigerland (ninety members including Golden Girls). *Daaa Daa Daaa Da!* Those four opening notes are certainly familiar to all the "dignitaries" riding in ten golf carts behind the band. In addition to Gay, they include: LSU athletic director Joe Alleva and his wife, Annie, a member of the Bengal Belles board; Kathy Miles, wife of LSU football coach Les Miles; LSU baseball coach Paul Mainieri and his wife, Karen; LSU track-and-field coach Dennis Shaver; Hilary Tuttle, reigning Miss LSU; and two other students, Alex Cagnola and Emma Arceneaux, king and queen of the 2013 Homecoming Court.

Women of all ages and sizes stand three and four deep as the parade passes by along the perimeter of the mammoth hall. This being Louisiana, they are not the least bit shy about shouting for beads and acting silly along a parade route. Mike the Tiger and a contingent of LSU cheerleaders are also adding energy to the proceedings. And Belle, the resplendently dressed mascot of the Bengal Belles, is darting all over, dainty parasol held aloft, her furry mask giving the false impression that she just removed herself from a Broadway production of *Cats*.

Gay—in his third year of retirement from the National Football League and his second year of law school at nearby Southern University—can hardly believe the scene. Riding in the back of the lead cart, the thirty-one-year-old Brusly, Louisiana, native is waving at fans, aiming beads as best he can, and loving every second of it.

"My first indoor parade!" Gay says. "Definitely didn't have this when I was at LSU. It's amazing to see how much this whole organization has grown. Same nice people. The ladies were always so nice to us. But now the Bengal Belles are just so big. This is like, wow!"

Even Aimee Simon—the leading force behind it all, a five-foot-two, high-octane grandmother who has always liked to think big—never foresaw anything nearly this grand in her initial vision.

The year was 1996. Head coach Gerry DiNardo was reviving the LSU football program—bringing back the magic, as he used to say—after the dismal four-year coaching tenure of predecessor Curley Hallman. DiNardo was not only starting to win on the field (with a first-season record of 7–4–1 in 1995). He was also building his program by way of savvy marketing—and one of his earliest creations was a booster group named the Tiger Gridiron Club.

Simon was one of the first women—one of the *only* women—to attend Gridiron Club lunches during DiNardo's inaugural season. It was there that she met the coach's wife, and Terri DiNardo eventually had a question for her: "Do you think we could start a group like this for women?" Years earlier, when Gerry was an assistant coach at the University of Colorado, Terri had enjoyed a weekly women's lunch at which coaches showed game videos to teach female fans about the X's and O's of football. Anywhere from fifty to a hundred women attended.

"You think that would work here?" the first lady of LSU football wanted to know.

"Absolutely," Simon said.

And with that they were on their way to becoming co-creators of the Bengal Belles. Simon, then a dental hygienist, took on the role of president. She enlisted the help of her two best friends, fellow Baton Rouge residents Machita Eyre and Carolyn Hebert. Still, Terri DiNardo had no idea what to expect. One day, when Simon, Eyre, and Hebert were brainstorming with her in the kitchen of her home, Terri asked: "Do you think we'll be able to get fifty women to our first meeting?"

On Thursday, September 5, 1996, two days before the LSU season opener in Tiger Stadium, two *hundred* and fifty women filed into the Lod Cook Alumni Center for the first Bengal Belles luncheon. Local businessman Norman Deumite, an avid supporter of LSU athletics who gave the Belles their first $1,000 to cover start-up costs, stood at the door and handed out roses. Gerry DiNardo was the keynote speaker, and his assistant coaches also attended, along with team captains Ben Bordelon and Allen Stansberry.

The Belles later got involved with more than just hosting lunches during the DiNardo years. After Vanderbilt coach Rod Dowhower caused a stir by refusing to let LSU wear its traditional white jerseys for a game in Tiger Stadium—instead exercising a visiting coach's right to select uniform colors . . . and he wanted white jerseys for *his* team—the Belles created a "White Out Vandy" campaign and encouraged all LSU fans to wear white shirts to the game. (LSU recorded both a "white out" and a shutout that night. Final score: 35–0 for the home team.) The Belles also put on a "Stampede to the Stadium" 5K race in support of the LSU Library. They organized a "Ghosts of Past Seasons" Halloween-week dinner to honor LSU football legends. And there were other special events.

"We were always doing something new and different," Terri DiNardo would later recall. "We were just like this force to be reckoned with. I mean, give Aimee Simon an idea, and it would just be done."

When things eventually went south for Gerry DiNardo and his Tigers—with eight straight losses leading to his dismissal late in the 1999 season—Terri had one last request for Simon. "Please keep the

Bengal Belles going," she said. "Coaches are going to come and go. But this is an organization for LSU. It is an organization for all the women who are passionate about football. The organization always needs to go on."

Fourteen years later, as Simon approaches the podium on a stage in the River Center—the Parade of Dignitaries complete—it's hard to imagine anyone else as president of the Belles. With the eighteenth year of the group drawing to a close, Aimee Simon is the only president it has had. The sixty-three-year-old mother of three and grandmother of three—a self-described workaholic—long ago quit her job in a dental office (after twenty-seven years as a hygienist) to concentrate on her volunteer work with the Belles. Her husband, Chip, a prominent endodontist and lifelong LSU fan, was more than OK with that. He, too, is all in when it comes to supporting the Tigers.

"Woooooo!" is the first thing Aimee says—unleashes, really—into a microphone at the podium. She is just so excited to be here.

Sticking with standard procedure—standard for her—Simon's outfit alone is enough to announce that it is "game day" for the Belles. Her wild ensembles are always built around LSU colors or tiger-striped patterns. And they are always punctuated by one of her signature hats: some sort of look-at-me lid guaranteed to be the only one like it in the room. Purple is her color today. Purple jacket with sequins splashed all over it. Purple hat and feathery growth climbing up one side of it. Purple on her earrings. Purple peeking out from the silver of a heavy necklace. Purple polish on all her nails—yes, all twenty of them, fingers and toes. She could be a plum.

Simon makes brief opening remarks and introduces the dignitaries onto the stage. She asks for a moment of silence in memory of Joe Dean, the former LSU athletic director who died last weekend at the age of eighty-three. Then she calls everyone to action, telling guests that the buffet lines are opening: "So enjoy your food." Simon does not say to enjoy it quickly. But maybe she should. Another parade—this one featuring today's top-billed honorees—will start in fifteen minutes.

For Simon, it has never been enough to make good on what Terri DiNardo asked of her—to just keep the Belles going. She has always been determined to keep them *growing*. And she has certainly done that. When the luncheons got too big for the alumni center, the Belles began using downtown hotels. Then—a few years ago—they outgrew the hotels and moved to the River Center. The Belles now have eight hundred and two members (more than double the current membership of the male-dominated Gridiron Club).

Still, size is only one reason athletic director Joe Alleva makes the blanket statement that "there is nothing like the Bengal Belles anywhere else in the country." He is also talking about impact. By way of membership dues and luncheon fees, raffles and auctions, special events and sponsorships, the Belles have raised more than a million dollars in support of LSU athletics, with most of the money going to the Cox Communications Academic Center for Student-Athletes. And Alleva is talking about passion. These women are mighty passionate about football—and about their commitment to having a good time.

In a town that knows no communal love greater than its affection for the football Tigers, the Bengal Belles offer the intoxication of proximity: up-close-and-personal visits with LSU players and coaches normally seen by most fans only on television or from afar in a giant stadium. The Belles are the only open-to-the-public organization with the regular participation of players and coaches at its events.

And what a show the players put on!

There is plenty of football talk when emcee Gordy Rush—an LSU football alum and longtime radio broadcaster—gets them on stage at the luncheons. But the players also feel free to just be themselves. They share personal tidbits, take all-in-fun jabs at teammates and coaches, and generally ham it up in ways they never would at a press conference or in just about any other public forum.

Where else would the star running back open up about having cried when he watched *Titanic* and then act out a dramatic scene from the movie? That's what Jeremy Hill did at a luncheon early this season. It was the same day fullback Connor Neighbors was asked to share a secret with the Belles—something even his teammates didn't know about him—and he said: "Well, only a select few know, but I used to tap dance back in the day!" Next thing the ladies knew, the thick bruiser was tapping out a few moves for them, and they responded as if he'd just scored a last-second touchdown to defeat Alabama.

There have been many other memorable nuggets this season. Among them: Tight ends DeSean Smith and Dillon Gordon squaring off in a playful arm-wrestling battle on the podium. Long snapper Reid Ferguson and kicker Colby Delahoussaye competing in what Rush called an "Aussie off" as they did their best imitations of Australian punter Jamie Keehn's accent. Freshman quarterback Anthony Jennings going deep ("Lean on Me") and big-boy defensive tackle Anthony "The Freak" Johnson going soft and sensitive ("All My Life") while singing solos for the ladies. Zach Mettenberger confiding in the Belles that he has always had "like a huge fear of birds" ever since one got into his childhood home—Mettenberger was seven at the time—and even flew around in his bedroom for a while.

"As a player, the best thing about going to the Bengal Belles is just the ability to put smiles on people's faces," says junior Jarvis Landry, one of the most productive wide receivers in school history. "The women are very energetic, very lively. The spirit of LSU definitely lives within all of them. And that's what makes the lunches so great. We get to make all those women smile. And we get to give them more idea of who we really are as people—the people behind the facemasks."

The band is marching again. The golf carts are rolling. The women are back on their feet—standing and waving pom-poms and crowding close to enjoy the main event of the day.

The Parade of Seniors is in full force.

Riding in the lead cart, Mettenberger has not been targeted with such energy since the last time a defensive lineman locked in on him. Of course, that was all about wanting to crush him into the ground. This is about smothering him only with admiration and appreciation. "Wave to us!" a middle-aged woman calls out to the star quarterback. Mettenberger offers a hand to both the air and her recording-it-all cell phone. Then he goes back to throwing beads and miniature tigers. In addition to an endless supply of beads, the players have also been armed with little stuffed-tigers to shower upon fans. Toward the end of the parade, Mettenberger notices Kathy Miles standing in the crowd—she has missed only one Belles luncheon in nine years—and he exchanges smiles with the wife of his head coach. Then he sees that ten-year-old Macy Miles, the baby of the family, youngest of four children, is also there. Mettenberger floats a tiger to her. Macy gathers it in—and she glows.

She is not the only one.

Plenty of adults are also shining with joy.

With music blaring and spirits high, one thing is certain: This is not the place to lament any shortcomings of an LSU season marked by inconsistent performance. The Tigers winning only three of six Southeastern Conference games so far? Losing their last two to unranked Ole Miss and in a blowout to archrival Alabama? A shaky defense that has disappointed way too many times? Those are issues for another day. These Belles are interested only in living out the words of their mission statement by offering their "unconditional and unwavering support" to the players.

"True fans, that's what we have here," says Lee Ann Howard, a retired science teacher who lives in Plaquemine and has been active with the Belles since their inception. "We're always going to love our Tigers. And how great is this? I mean, where else can you go and have this kind of camaraderie?"

That is one word for it. When the parade ends and the players gather by stairs to the stage, linebacker Lamin Barrow has another description for what he has just experienced: "Pandemonium!"

It takes a few minutes for everyone to settle back down at their tables. Then the players are introduced onto the stage. Each will have a turn with a hand-held microphone. Gordy Rush is ready for them.

He starts with routine questions: What is your favorite memory as an LSU Tiger? What life lessons will you take away from your coaches? What would you like to do—as a career—after football?

But the brief "interviews" do not stay routine for long. Defensive tackle A'Trey-U Jones belts out an abbreviated version of "Amazing Grace" (getting applause for his courage as much as his talent). Wide receiver James Wright is asked to show off his argyle socks—and happily does so. Defensive back Tre' Sullivan offers a few questionable dance moves.

There is even an exchange concerning Mettenberger's choice of footwear to go with his loose-fitting pants and untucked, white button-down shirt. One of the most prolific quarterbacks in school history is wearing soft, fluffy-topped, brown moccasins—most people would just call them slippers—over white socks.

Rush to Mettenberger: "Before we get on some serious talk . . . you're rocking the moccasins down here. Talk to me about this look."

Mettenberger (sheepishly): "I mean, it's all about comfort."

The crowd laughs. Rush shakes his head in disbelief. Then he gathers himself.

He asks Mettenberger what it has meant to him to have the success he has had at LSU. Mettenberger turns reflective. He sighs. With his head down and speech slowed—seemingly by emotion—the Georgia native starts by saying: "Growing up, I definitely never thought I'd be here in Baton Rouge. But I'm sure proud to call myself a Tiger now." He talks about the way his coaches and "everybody in this community" have helped him grow both as a football player and as a man: "There's a lot of people that need to be thanked for that." And—with those heartfelt words—he pretty much owns the room.

When Rush and Mettenberger finish—completing the player interviews—Simon returns to the podium to close the program. She has sponsors to thank and housekeeping items to announce. More than anything, though, she wants to share her excitement as she introduces the two-part grand finale of Senior Day: the traditional singing of the LSU alma mater and then "our second line" parade.

The singing is weak as the players stand side-by-side on the stage, arms draped over one another's shoulders, swaying back and forth to the music, just as they do on the field after victories. The second line that follows—with plenty of colorful umbrellas for the players and their parents—is disconnected and directionless. It never really goes anywhere beyond the front of the stage, quickly disintegrating into nothing more than a collection of hugs and handshakes and picture-taking.

But so what?

None of this is about perfection.

Eighteen years after Terri DiNardo and Aimee Simon first met, it is only about togetherness. It is about having a good time for a good cause. It is about the magical bonds between a team and a town.

The Marine Sergeant

February 2, 2014

With all the media attention leading up to Super Bowl XLVIII—the Seattle Seahawks playing the Denver Broncos this evening in New Jersey—a two-year-old video clip has gotten lots of airtime. It has been included in multiple TV feature stories. One of the network pieces is still circulating by way of social media.

The brief clip shows a short-haired U.S. Marine standing behind a podium on stage at Radio City Music Hall in New York. He is not big—five-foot-ten, 170 pounds—but Sergeant Luke Boyd is nonetheless impressive. He looks sharp in his Dress Blue Bravos, the left breast of his crisp uniform adorned with a colorful collection of badges and ribbons. Boyd has served in Afghanistan. He is officially a "tactical data systems technician"—someone who specializes in ground-to-air communications. He is also an expert shooter with both a pistol and a rifle.

For this moment in the video, however, his heart jumping with excitement, Boyd is a football fan before anything else. He is one of several military representatives the National Football League is honoring at its annual draft—a ceremonial "thank you" to all Americans in the armed forces—and he's been given the opportunity to announce one of the draft choices. Leaning into a microphone, Boyd reads from a large card: "With the seventy-fifth pick in the two thousand and twelve NFL draft, the Seattle Seahawks select . . . Russell Wilson. Quarterback. Wisconsin."

The video is back in play for good reason. It helps tell the story of Wilson's meteoric rise from questionable third-round pick—some critics called him too short for the NFL—to his current status as Seattle's starting quarterback and one of the premier young players in the league. Wilson's growing tale of the improbable will now match him against star quarterback Peyton Manning on the biggest stage in football.

But there is another remarkable story connected to that draft video. It belongs to the Marine sergeant. While the Seahawks and Broncos prepare for the opening kickoff at the Meadowlands in New Jersey, Luke Boyd settles into a window booth of a crowded sports bar to watch the Super Bowl on television. This is in Baton Rouge, where Boyd now resides with his wife and baby daughter. He is attending LSU as part of a highly selective program that allows him to remain on active duty and work toward becoming an officer while the Marine Corps pays for his education. But that alone is not what makes him unique.

In addition to being a Marine and a family man, Boyd is an LSU football player—a twenty-seven-year-old wide receiver who is both the oldest member of the team and the only one ever deployed to serve his nation in war. And here is the most enchanting aspect of the whole narrative: He never would have become a Tiger without that one memorable day—April 27, 2012—at the NFL draft. It is a story that begins with the charm of serendipity.

Prior to announcing that momentous draft pick by the Seahawks, Boyd waited backstage at Radio City and visited with a few former NFL stars also participating in the draft. Among them was Willie Roaf, the onetime New Orleans Saints offensive lineman who had recently been elected to the Pro Football Hall of Fame. The six-foot-five, 320-pound Roaf happened to notice that Boyd's cell phone was in a case decorated with an LSU logo. Boyd was not yet attending the state university but had plans to enroll. "I'm a Louisiana Tech boy," Roaf told the Marine. "We don't like LSU!" He then went from playful jab to important information: "You know Les Miles is here, huh?"

Boyd did not wait long to ask an NFL staffer if he would take him to meet the LSU football coach. Miles and the Marine were soon shaking hands in a curtained-off hospitality area reserved for players and special guests. As a longtime LSU football fan, someone who as a teen had always used the Tigers when playing college football video games, Boyd was thrilled to take a picture with Miles. But the significance of a posed photo was nothing compared to the content of their conversation.

Boyd told Miles he was a big LSU football fan—and that he also *played* football. He had been selected to attend the draft after being named most valuable player in a Marine Corps league while based at Camp Pendleton in Southern California. Years earlier, he had also played a season of college football at Fairleigh Dickinson University in New Jersey. Boyd went on to tell Miles that he was preparing to be an LSU student—he was set to start there in January 2013—and then he calmly said: "I'd really like to play for your team. Would it be possible to get a tryout?"

Miles initially responded with humor, saying that perhaps Boyd's background—specifically his combat training—could help his Tigers on the football field: "Hey, if we need a guy to take anyone out, you'll be our guy." Boyd chuckled. Then Miles turned serious, offering both kindness and sincere encouragement. How else could he treat such a respectful young man covered in the dignity of Dress Blues? He gave Boyd the name of the proper "coach" to contact back in the LSU football office—Sam Nader, actually the assistant athletic director for football operations—and told him to send video of his game highlights.

Boyd could hardly believe his good fortune. He also knew that pretty much anyone could make a phone call and put together a video. He had no idea if anything would ever come of it.

Luke Boyd had already traveled an unconventional path.

As a young boy growing up in Stafford, Virginia, a child of divorce who no longer had any contact with his dad, he had three constants in his life. He had his mom, Dianna Jenkins, who worked a variety of jobs—delivering pizza and cleaning houses among them—and was very much devoted to him. He had his one-year-older brother, Jared, with whom he was always close. And he had a dream: He wanted to be a professional football player. He wanted someday to be just like his idol, Emmitt Smith, star running back of the Dallas Cowboys.

As time went on, Luke progressing from youth football to the varsity at Colonial Forge High School, his dream slipped from fond hope to fanciful vision. He had neither the size nor the talent for any realistic shot at ever playing in the NFL. But he still held tight to his love of football. He loved everything about it—everything from the action and excitement of the game itself to the strenuous challenges of preparation and the camaraderie of being on a team.

So he decided to keep playing in college. Although Division III Fairleigh Dickinson had never had much of a football program—and the 2005 team was not expected to be anything special—Boyd just wanted to enjoy the game for as long as he could. He lasted only a year at the New Jersey school, however, as he and his high school sweetheart, Tina Porter, came to feel that being together was more important than anything else.

Porter had been attending the Savannah College of Art and Design in Georgia, but she was ready for a change and decided to transfer to LSU. In August 2006, Boyd came to Louisiana with her, also wanting to enroll at LSU, but he failed to get the financial aid he sought and could not afford tuition. While Porter studied graphic design and began competing as a long-distance runner for the LSU track and cross country teams, Boyd took night classes at Baton Rouge Community College and worked days as a mover for United Van Lines. It was his first of several jobs during the next two years. He also laid floors and did other interior work for a construction company, became a residential real-estate agent, and did some landscaping—all of which led him to life-changing clarity. Boyd wanted to do something with greater meaning and purpose—something that would give him more direction.

His girlfriend came from a family of Marines and had long encouraged him to join the Corps. His own brother had become a Marine. In April 2008, Boyd walked into a Marine recruiting office on Jefferson Highway in Baton Rouge. Nobody there needed to sell him on anything. He was ready to enlist.

A month later, Boyd was at boot camp on Parris Island in South Carolina.

Two years after that, by then married to Tina, he was deployed to Afghanistan. Boyd spent six months there—from September 2010 until March 2011—working with a unit that set up operating bases. The rules of engagement and importance of success were drastically different than they'd been for him half a decade earlier—his fun-filled days on a football field replaced by the ugly realities of war—but proper preparation and teamwork were again critical to everything he did.

It was after returning from Afghanistan that Boyd started playing in the Marine football league. "Not the highest level of athletic talent I've ever seen, but it was really competitive," he says. "For me, it was just so great to be playing football again."

Of course, when his selection as league MVP yielded his trip to the

NFL draft—and then being there unexpectedly afforded him an audience with Les Miles—the importance of his time playing Marine football was retroactively elevated to huge.

Once enrolled at LSU—in pursuit of a degree in construction management—Boyd called Sam Nader in the football office. Unable to reach Nader on the phone, Boyd just showed up at the office one day—dressed in Marine uniform—and asked for him. After almost four decades on the LSU staff, Nader had met countless young men wanting to try out for the team without having been recruited. But he'd never before been approached by a uniformed military man asking to be a walk-on. They had a good talk. When Nader asked about a highlight video, Boyd said he was still working on that and would soon get it to him.

Fortunately, there was plenty of footage available from his games. Boyd put together a six-minute package: forty plays showing him as a wide receiver on offense, a free safety on defense, and in a variety of roles on special teams. That little bundle of energy wrapped in jersey number 4 was all over the field. Grabbing passes out of the air! Blocking with all his might! Making interceptions! Scoring touchdowns! Boyd had no idea what the coaches would think of his video. He just sent it to Nader and figured he'd soon find out.

There was one other matter to address. The LSU compliance office needed to make sure Boyd would be eligible to join the team. Nobody in the athletic department could recall ever having an active-duty military man on the football roster—not in recent times—so everyone wanted to be cautious in gathering all the necessary information before clearing him to play. Three months passed before Nader finally called Boyd to inform him that all was good. Boyd was home with his wife and their beautiful baby—blue-eyed little Natalie, then eight months old—when he took the call.

"Are you still interested in playing?" Nader said.

"Absolutely," Boyd said.

"Well, we have a spot for you. We'd love for you to come out."

The rest of the conversation—details—was forever lost to the explosion of childlike joy that immediately overwhelmed Boyd. The thought of playing football again—for any team—was enough to fill him with excitement. But this was so much bigger than just playing football again. He was going to be an LSU Tiger!

As soon as he got off the phone, he darted outside and ran around his yard in wild celebration. "A happy dance," Boyd would later call it. Watching her husband—laughing both at him and for him—Tina did not need any explanation of what had just happened on the phone. She knew him well enough to know.

When Boyd was done in the yard, he did some more dancing in the house, running up and down a hallway, banging on walls, screaming as if he'd just won the biggest jackpot ever known to man.

"Yes!" Boyd shouted. "Hell, yeah!"

The 2013 LSU football season was soon to begin—and Sergeant Luke Boyd would be wearing jersey number 15 for his favorite team in the world.

Surreal is the label he puts on some of his favorite early moments as a Tiger.

Being fitted for his helmet and shoulder pads: "I was in uniform—Marine uniform—when I got to the equipment room," Boyd says. "I took off my shirt to be fitted, so I was standing there in my trousers, and it just didn't feel real. It was like I was watching myself in a movie or something. But it was actually happening, too. I was living it."

The first time he approached his Tiger Stadium locker to dress for a game: "It's hard to put into words how exciting that was. It was a dream that I never thought would come true. The first thing I did—very sneakily, not really wanting anyone else to see me doing it—I took a picture of my jersey hanging in my locker. And then I sent it to my wife. We were texting back and forth."

The first time Tina saw him on television during a game: It was the night of Saturday, September 14, 2013. LSU was playing Kent State in Tiger Stadium. Tina, by then a professional photographer, was watching at home—on ESPNU—with baby Natalie by her side. All of a sudden, she saw her husband talking to teammate Odell Beckham Jr. on the sideline. Tina posted a screen shot of that on Instagram with a message saying "We saw daddy on TV" and several hashtags including #soproud and #livinghisdream.

"Those first few weeks, there were so many amazing things to take in," Boyd says. "To most of the guys on the team, I was 'the Marine' or 'the older guy.' But at the same time, I was almost like a little kid, getting to be on the inside of something so special that I'd always followed and looked up to from the outside."

Tina had to remind him more than once: "You're not a fan now. You're a player."

He was the only LSU player whose days often began by leading 5:30 a.m. physical training sessions—"PT"—for a group of ROTC students across town at Southern University. It was one of Boyd's obligations that came with attending school as part of the Marine Corps Enlisted Commissioning Education Program.

He was the only LSU player who meticulously folded and stored every item in his football locker with the care of a well-trained military man.

He was the only player whose teammates called him "Sarge"—even though Marines generally frown upon abbreviating the rank of sergeant that way. (Boyd did not want to squelch the enthusiasm of his new civilian friends by correcting them.)

He was the only player repeatedly asked by teammates about killing people.

Offensive lineman Jonah Austin, in his third year at LSU, was among the first to inquire. Before practice one day, he approached Boyd in the locker room with a straightforward question about his time in Afghanistan: "I got to ask you, bro, you ever killed anybody?"

Boyd answered the same way he always did when anyone outside the military asked him about that: "We did some work out there."

Austin did not know what to make of that. Other teammates were equally baffled when they asked similar questions and got the same answer. That was precisely the way Boyd wanted to leave it—intentionally vague. Speaking softly but firmly, he says, "Some things don't need to be talked about."

Boyd knew that being a first-year walk-on came with limits. He never made the regular-season travel squad—dressing only for home games and the post-season Outback Bowl (for which almost everyone on the roster was allowed to travel). He never expected to play in a game—and never did. He knew that any on-field contributions would be made only during practice.

As a member of the scout team, his primary job was to help LSU's starting defense prepare for games by lining up against it and mimicking the offense of each upcoming opponent. In football parlance, it is known as giving "a good look" for the defense to practice against. Boyd embraced the role with great enthusiasm and energy. His approach was consistent: "Every single practice, I practice like it's a game."

Teammates and coaches saw that—and respected it—from the day he arrived.

"Everybody on the team loves him," says kicker Colby Delahoussaye, whose locker in the Football Operations Center is next to Boyd's. "He's so humble. He's always looking to do for others instead of for himself. And I've never seen him in a bad mood. He's always smiling."

Leon Wright, a graduate assistant who works with the scout team, quickly identified Boyd as "a go-to guy" for whenever he needed someone to run extra plays. "He's one of the hardest workers we have," Wright says. "He's tough. He has good speed. And he does a great job for us."

It is highly unusual, if not unique, for a football player to think of having a "best game of the season" without actually playing in it. Boyd had one. It was the November 23 victory—34–10—over ninth-ranked Texas A&M. All week leading up to that game, he had worked in practice against freshman cornerback Rashard Robinson, helping prepare him to face one of the most talented wide receivers in the nation, six-foot-five Mike Evans, the favorite target of quarterback Johnny Manziel. Then Robinson pretty much shut down Evans in Tiger Stadium, holding him to three catches for only thirteen yards when covering him.

Boyd celebrated—a lot of jumping up and down and cheering—every time Robinson successfully defended a play. "That was definitely my highlight of the season, the most self-fulfilling personal excitement I felt," he says. "I'm certainly not saying I was the reason Rashard did so well, but I knew I at least had a hand in it."

Robinson greatly appreciated all that Boyd did for him.

"Going against him in practice, it's really a humbling experience, just to see how much he cares and always wants to help me get better," Robinson says. "He really helps me a lot with my fundamentals and my techniques. And he's always encouraging me. Luke is just a great person to be around."

Boyd hopes to get in some games next season.

"The likelihood of me getting a whole lot of playing time is not very realistic," he concedes. "But I'm trying to get on special teams. That would be my best opportunity to get on the field."

He'd like to be a holder for field goals and extra points.

He'd love to get a chance to be on the kickoff coverage team.

For now, though, Boyd is most interested in watching the player he announced into the National Football League. It is late in the fourth quarter of the Super Bowl. The Seahawks have dominated the Broncos from start to finish—leading 43–8 with time winding down—and Russell Wilson has had the greatest football day of his life. Two years after Marine Sergeant Luke Boyd called out his name at Radio City Music Hall, Wilson is about to be the winning quarterback in the Super Bowl.

The sergeant is living a dream at what he considers the pinnacle of college football. Wilson is one of the hottest young athletes in all of American sports.

"Pretty amazing," Boyd says. "I mean, the story just keeps getting better."

Luke Boyd never got in a game as he concluded his two-year stint as an LSU walk-on during the 2014 season. He did, however, celebrate a personal milestone in Tiger Stadium before the season started. On July 1, 2014, Boyd was promoted to staff sergeant. With friends, family, and a small group of Marines in attendance, the promotion ceremony was held in a stadium suite overlooking the field.

Tweet Dreams of Omaha

June 3, 2014

The LSU locker room at TD Ameritrade Park was not a happy place. The baseball Tigers had just been eliminated from the 2013 College World Series in the worst possible way—immediate back-to-back losses, the dreaded "two and barbecue"—and against a backdrop filled only with promise. With a record of 57–9, already having tied the school mark for wins in a season, the Tigers had stormed into Omaha, Nebraska, longtime home of the CWS, as the top-ranked team in the nation. Then this: a 2–1 loss to UCLA and—two days later—a 4–2 nightmare against North Carolina. Late in the afternoon of Tuesday, June 18, the sting of defeat ruled the locker room. There were tears. There were hugs. There was the harsh reality that this band of brothers—with All-Americans Mason Katz and Raph Rhymes among the departing seniors—would never compete together again.

Sitting alone at a locker, freshman shortstop Alex Bregman felt the abrupt sadness of it all washing over him, and he also felt the weight of his own disappointing performance. Like the overall team, he had done nothing but shine throughout most of the season. Heading to Omaha, Bregman led the team in batting average (.380) and the entire Southeastern Conference in hits (104). He had already been named national freshman of the year by both *Collegiate Baseball* and the National Collegiate Baseball Writers Association. None of that helped him in the

CWS. In the eighth inning against UCLA, Bregman made a fielding error that allowed the winning run to score. And he went hitless, a combined 0-for-8, in both games.

What to do with his failure? How to respond?

He certainly wouldn't just sit there and mope. No, Bregman being Bregman, he had to take his failure and somehow convert it into fuel. Still wearing his white number 30 jersey and his usual abundance of eye black—now smudged and faded—he reached into a travel bag for his iPhone. He went straight to Twitter and used his thumbs to tap out a single thought: *Road to Omaha starts tomorrow.*

Bregman wanted the world to know that he was ready to battle again. It was also a note to himself. At 5:35 p.m. only twenty-six minutes removed from the inglorious ending of his otherwise fabulous season—Bregman sent out his tweet.

He was soon named winner of the Brooks Wallace Award as national shortstop of the year, which was consistent with his first-team selections to multiple All-America teams. But Bregman had not only been wildly productive as a hitter and fielder. He had also been prolific as a tweeter.

He tweeted an assortment of personal and team notes, some purely factual, others intentionally playful. More than anything, though, his tweets—short messages of up to 140 characters at a time—offered a steady stream of motivational material.

Persistence is way more important than perfection . . .

Fall 7 times, get up 8.

Limits and fears only exist in the mind #DareToBeGreat

Never let the odds keep you from what you know in your heart you were meant to do

Force success . . . No other option

Two weeks before playing in his first LSU game—the 2013 season opener against Maryland—Bregman had tweeted a picture he'd just taken in Alex Box Stadium. It showed the giant scoreboard and the white-faced clock mounted above it, the glow of illumination making the circular timepiece look almost like an extra moon against the black sky. Bregman had just completed one of his signature late-night practice sessions—he could never field enough ground balls or take enough swings—and now he wanted to share what otherwise would have remained a private moment. At 11:26 on a Friday night, he tweeted four words with his picture: *They sleep Tigers grind!*

As relentless as Bregman had always been on a baseball field, he was equally consistent with the full-speed-ahead tenor of his tweets.

You learn the most from your failure . . . Baseball is so great because you get to go out and play again the next day.

A champion is someone who gets up when he can't

Success is made from hanging on after others have let go.

While browsing on Twitter one day—just curious to see how some LSU athletes used social media—I happened upon all of this Bregman material. His seemingly endless stack of tweets captured my attention. But it was that one post-elimination tweet from the locker room at the College World Series—the stunning immediacy of it—that intrigued me the most.

I had watched enough LSU baseball to know that Bregman, at five-foot-eleven and not quite 190 pounds, played with passion and hustle. I had heard countless stories about him being the baseball equivalent of a gym rat—unusually driven toward greatness . . . always working at the game that owned him. But now I wanted to know more.

What made this young man tick?

What made him the way he was?

And I wondered what he would do for an encore: How would he follow up on one of the most impressive freshman seasons in the long and storied history of LSU baseball?

I decided to follow Bregman—both on Twitter (@ABREG_1) and in the real world—as he and his teammates tried to navigate a path back to Omaha. Then I would write about him.

Much to my good fortune, Bregman agreed to go along with my idea, meeting with me every now and then—usually over lunch or dinner—for lengthy interviews that quickly progressed into the comfortable conversation of friendship. He also shared his family and some of his friends with me.

None of us could have predicted the challenges—both on and off the field—that would come to define Bregman's sophomore season. But the challenges added depth and meaning. After all, absent the furnace of adversity, how does a young man really grow? How does he ever get a chance to exhibit his full measure?

I'd walk through hell in a gasoline suit to play baseball. It is an old Pete Rose quote that Bregman once tweeted. But the words just as easily could have originated with him.

His love of the game is a family thing.

It started, long before Alex was born, with his paternal grandfather. After serving in the U.S. Coast Guard, Stanley Irwin Bregman had a distinguished career in his hometown of Washington, D.C. Starting in the 1950s, he served in numerous political roles supporting high-level Democrats including Adlai Stevenson, Hubert Humphrey, and Walter Mondale. He also formed a law firm that specialized in government relations. For a sports-loving guy, though, none of that could match the joy of his position with the Washington Senators. As general counsel of the old Major League Baseball organization—now the Texas Rangers—it was Bregman who in 1969 negotiated the hiring of the great Ted Williams as manager of the team. The Senators lasted only three more years before departing to Texas, but it was a thrilling time for Ben and Sam Bregman, the schoolboy sons of the team lawyer. They often visited the RFK Stadium clubhouse, where they talked to the ballplayers and dreamed of someday being just like them. The boys also got to know one of the most famous men in baseball history, and Ted Williams even knew their names. He gave the boys bats and team jackets and—best of all—he gifted them with his time and kindness. Sam Bregman, now fifty, still has a black-and-white photo Williams signed for him more than forty years ago. "To Sammy," it is inscribed. "Your pal . . . Ted Williams." The photo has never lost its magical power. With a mere glance at it, Sam is carried across time and space to the innocence of childhood and the unsullied simplicity of believing in heroes.

There is one other baseball-related possession—if a painful memory can be labeled that way—that has never lost its hold on Sam. It is the story of his decision to stop playing his favorite game. In the fall of 1981, Sam followed his older brother to the University of New Mexico, where Ben was on scholarship as a second baseman. Sam joined the team as a non-scholarship, walk-on player hoping to work his way into the lineup, and he got off to a good start with an impressive home run in an early-fall game. His father was even there—visiting from D.C.—to see it. Sam was thrilled that his dad witnessed his first collegiate homer. Then things went downhill. Sam had a tough time hitting anything but fastballs. He was not included on the travel team for the spring season. So he quit. There was no "Oh, I'll just work harder to make this happen" or "You keep watching me, coach! I'll show you what I can do!" There was only this: "I'm done." Thirty-two years later—now a prominent attorney with a lovely wife and three thriving children—Sam offers a harsh assessment of his decision to quit at New Mexico: "Biggest mistake of my life . . . biggest regret of my life. It still hurts to think that I didn't give it my all."

Alex Bregman has heard about this for as long as he can remember. He's heard about it because Sam is his dad. With blood flowing in a straight line from Stan to Sam to first child Alex, the love of baseball was just as much a part of the passing down as the plasma and platelets.

A family photo shows little three-year-old Alex with Stan—Alex then called him Zayde, Yiddish for grandfather—at a minor-league baseball game in the Bregmans' adopted hometown of Albuquerque. A giant tub of popcorn, about the size of Alex's head, shares a ballpark seat with him. Grandson and grandfather are both gripping the tub, and the boy's smile says it all: *What could be better than this?*

Alex started playing tee ball when he was four. He collected baseball cards, piles of them, learning the names and positions of all the best big leaguers. He became a bat boy for the University of New Mexico Lobos. He immersed himself in the online world of fantasy baseball, once managing a dozen teams at the same time. Then there was the matter of naming the family dogs. The discussion with his parents was never about whether the brother-sister pair of Labrador retrievers would be named after baseball players. It was only about which players to choose. The male was ultimately named Koufax, as in pitching legend Sandy Koufax of the old Brooklyn and Los Angeles Dodgers. Gender discrepancy notwithstanding, the female was named Jeter, in honor of longtime New York Yankee shortstop Derek Jeter.

Baseball also gave Alex something of a childhood mantra that still echoes in his mind: *Bang that ball! Bang that ball!* It started with Zayde shouting that to his grandson during his early days of tee ball—Stan had by then moved to New Mexico as well—and it never really stopped. Straight through Alex's high school years, Stan almost never missed a game, and his favorite words of encouragement always stayed the same: *Bang that ball! Bang that ball!*

Six days after being eliminated from the College World Series, Alex Bregman was back in a baseball uniform, but wearing red, white, and blue instead of LSU's purple and gold. He would spend the next month playing for the USA Baseball Collegiate National Team. His first game was in Fayetteville, North Carolina, the evening of Monday, June 24, 2013. Batting third against the Fayetteville SwampDogs of the Coastal Plain League, Bregman lined a first-inning double into right centerfield to knock in the first run of the game. He followed that with singles in his next two at-bats. So much for his silence at the plate in Omaha. Everything was back to normal.

Team USA went on to win twenty of its twenty-three games. All three losses came in a five-game series against the Japanese national team (in Japan). But the tour ended with a stellar string of victories—a five-game sweep of highly regarded Cuba—and Bregman's overall summer production looked a lot like his output as an LSU freshman. He led Team USA in hits (twenty-six) and total bases (thirty-five) while batting .361 and still tweeting like a champion.

The will to succeed . . .

Adversity causes some to break, others to break records.

You try to break me down Imma go harder . . . #FutureIsNow

The game-worn USA jersey Bregman packed away as a keepsake carried the same number 30 he had selected at LSU. The number had special meaning to him. It represented every Major League Baseball team—all thirty in existence—that failed to pick him in the first round of the 2012 MLB draft that took place after his senior season in high school. "The thirty teams that messed up," Bregman came to call them.

There were reasons he was passed over. Prime among them was an injury at the most inopportune time: a badly broken middle-finger on his right hand—his throwing hand—that forced him to miss all but a few games that year. There was still plenty of talk about him being selected high in the draft. After all, Bregman had long been known to professional scouts. They certainly heard about him in 2010, when he was named USA Baseball player of the year after leading the sixteen-and-under national team to a gold medal in the Pan American Championships. In 2011, as a high school junior, he then hit a whopping .678 and set a New Mexico single-season record with nineteen home runs.

As the 2012 draft approached, Bregman was clear with the Major League scouts who called. He repeatedly told them the same thing he had told LSU coach Paul Mainieri: If he was picked in the first round, he would sign to play pro ball; if he was taken any lower than that, he would stick with his commitment to attend college and play for the Tigers. Several teams still tried to entice him after the first round. The Arizona Diamondbacks were the most aggressive. What if they took him in the second round but still offered something at least approaching first-round money—maybe a signing bonus of $800,000 or so? What if they could pay him closer to a million dollars? As much as Bregman was tempted to accept, he was also determined to stay the course. "It was not easy," he says. "But I wanted to be a man of my word."

The Boston Red Sox eventually selected Bregman in the twenty-ninth round, just in case something happened to change his mind. Nothing did. But Bregman still exited the process with two gifts. One was the knowledge that he was wanted: "Even though I knew I wasn't going, it was still pretty cool to get drafted." The other was a jersey number—his new number 30—that would serve as a constant reminder and tangible motivator.

All of this became relevant again in July 2013, the month before Bregman returned to LSU for his sophomore year, when Mason Katz texted him about changing his uniform number. Katz, by then playing minor-league ball in the St. Louis Cardinals organization, wanted to bequeath his number 8 to Bregman, just as earlier LSU star Mikie Mahtook had passed it down to Katz. Much like jersey number 18 for the LSU football team, number 8 had become a jersey of great distinction for LSU baseball. It stood for hard work and dedication to the team. It stood for leadership.

Bregman had to choose: Stick with the 30 that had been so good to him—the symbolic number that had served him so well—or switch to the 8 and all that it represented? To him, it was an easy decision. Bregman would wear the new number. He thanked Katz. The change was finalized during a phone call from Coach Mainieri. Then Bregman tweeted out the news: *It's an honor to be able to put on the #8 jersey next year. #tigahs*

When Bregman got back to Baton Rouge, he moved into a three-bedroom, off-campus condo with two teammates. He and Aaron Nola, the reigning SEC pitcher of the year, one of the best pitchers in LSU history, already knew each other from the year before. But Bregman and Henri Faucheux (pronounced *on-REE FOH-shay*) had never met. After spending the previous year at an Alabama community college, Faucheux—a Louisiana native, raised in LaPlace—was new to LSU. He quickly learned about Bregman.

Number one: He was totally locked in on baseball. "*Relentless* probably doesn't say enough to describe him," Faucheux says. "He just outworks everybody here—probably outworks everybody in the whole country."

Number two: Cleanliness was not a priority. "Great guy . . . good roommate," Faucheux says. "He'd do anything for you. But, man, you can definitely tell his mom's been cleaning up for him his whole life. Washing clothes? Not his forte. Doing dishes? Not his thing."

Tired of seeing dirty clothes everywhere—and aggravated by seeing Bregman wearing things he had "borrowed" from him without asking—Nola eventually showed Bregman how to use the washer and dryer. Then Faucheux schooled him on the basics of the dishwasher. Still, almost two weeks after Bregman moved in, his roommates were stunned to see him actually pulling clean glasses and plates from it. Nola was impressed enough that he decided to document the occasion, taking a picture of Bregman in action and tweeting it out with a message: @ABREG_1 *unloading the dishwasher for his first time*. (Female fans might have enjoyed that he was shirtless. Most guys were more interested in the poster Bregman had picked out to hang above the kitchen sink: an attention-grabbing bikini shot of *Sports Illustrated* swimsuit model Kate Upton.)

Nola and Faucheux would have other minor roommate-issues with Bregman. He'd play his rap music too loud. He'd mess with the thermostat and then fail to put it back the way it was, transforming the place into an icebox. He'd leave without turning off lights. One time, Bregman cooked eggs at about 1:00 in the morning, and a while later, Nola realized that he hadn't bothered to turn off the stove. "What are you doing?" Nola exclaimed. "You're going to burn the house down!"

Mostly, though, Bregman and his roommates had a good time together. They'd watch movies. They'd go out in a small boat on the pond behind their condo. They'd select targets out by the water and shoot at them with a pellet gun. They'd compete in card games and on PlayStation. Faucheux would play his guitar—mostly country music—and Bregman would sing as best he could. (As Faucheux puts it: "He's no George Strait. He's no Tim McGraw." But they always laughed and enjoyed themselves.)

One thing the roommates did not do as a trio was go on an out-of-town fishing trip. Nola and Faucheux had the whole thing planned. They were going with their dads for a three-day getaway to Venice,

Louisiana, and they wanted Bregman to join them. He initially leaned toward going—or at least that's what he was saying—but as the long weekend approached, Bregman could not talk himself into it. Going fishing would mean time away from baseball: no batting cages . . . no ground balls to field. "He didn't really say it directly, but we all knew why he wasn't going," Nola says. "I mean, Alex can't spend a single day away from Alex Box Stadium." As Nola, Faucheux, and their dads had a nice, relaxing time in Venice, Bregman just kept doing his thing in Baton Rouge. This was in early November. The start of LSU baseball season was still more than three months away.

No need for an alarm clock, let your passion wake you up
Refuse to be stopped and you won't be.
If what you did yesterday seems big, you haven't done anything today.
There are no shortcuts to any place worth going.
#dreamchasin
#OnAMission

His drive is a family thing, too.

Alex's father was a hard-charging prosecutor before going into private practice as a defense attorney. Sam Bregman served on the Albuquerque City Council in the mid-1990s. He later ran for mayor and for Congress—losing both times—but he never stopped advocating for causes. Last year, he was elected chairman of the Democratic Party of New Mexico, and he pledged to fight like a "pit bull" for his causes. Two of his biggest legislative pushes have been to increase funding for early-childhood education and to raise the state minimum wage to at least $10 an hour.

Alex's mother was valedictorian of her high school class in Brentwood, New York, a Long Island girl who was equal parts perky cheerleader and overachieving student. The parts were equal because she knew only one way to do things: all in. Jackie Bregman graduated magna cum laude from the Touro College Jacob D. Fuchsberg Law Center in New York. She practiced law for a while. And now she operates her own real estate brokerage. *Competitive* is one of the first words Alex uses to describe his mom. When he was a young boy, Jackie taught him how to play chess but never intentionally let him win. He claimed victory only when he eventually figured out—on his own—how to beat her. Jackie has never lost her intensity. Two years ago, when asked to support an Alzheimer's Association fundraiser by participating in a dance contest, she was not about to just go through the motions. She took dance lessons, practiced for hours, and performed with gusto. Jackie's cha-cha made her champion of the gala.

The source of Alex's drive? His work ethic? His love of competition?

Sam offers this: "Alex has always seen two parents working our tails off."

It made sense, then, when Sam once saw young Alex dive to catch a football—on pavement—in the cul-de-sac at the end of their street. It made sense that the boy could not just leisurely toss a baseball every once in a while against the wall behind the family home. Alex had to keep throwing the ball, throwing it, throwing it—day after day after day—until he finally busted right through the cinder block. Sam thought that was great. It meant that his son had good aim—he kept hitting his spot!

As Alex navigated the world of youth baseball, Sam often looked back at his own playing experiences. That meant reflecting on the decision to quit his college team. Whenever he thought about that, his heart would tell him, yes, he was indeed taking the right approach with Alex. Sam never spent much time telling his son how to throw, how to field, how to hit. He was much more interested in three other essentials.

Hustle.

Attitude.

Effort.

"Oh, my God," Alex says. "That's all I ever heard about. Hustle. Attitude. Effort. Those were the only things that mattered. Part of that was me always being one of the smallest kids. I always had to find ways to set myself apart. But, really, it was just my dad being my dad. He'd never really say anything to me if I didn't get a hit, didn't make a good play, or whatever. But, man, if I ever even thought about not hustling, not having a good attitude, not giving the right effort . . ."

In 2008, the summer before starting high school, Alex went to a baseball camp at the University of New Mexico. The first day of camp, New Mexico coach Ray Birmingham stood before some fifty boys and talked to them about one of the most important decisions they would ever make. At some point in their lives, no matter what paths they chose, they would have to decide if they truly wanted to be great. "People either decide to be average or decide to be great," Birmingham told them. "Deciding to be great isn't easy. You're either in or you're out. There's no in-between. You have to decide that you'll do everything needed to be great. And if you ever have to start explaining things—why you didn't do something you know you need to be doing—then you're out. Simple as that." When Birmingham finished speaking, the boys started breaking into groups to do drills, but Alex had something he wanted to do first. He went straight up to Birmingham and told him: "I want to play in the big leagues." The boy was announcing his decision to be great.

"This was an eighth-grader, going into ninth, and he said it with such conviction," Birmingham recalls. "It just gave me chills, and then I watched him in the camp. He definitely walked the walk. That fire he had, that determination, you could *feel* it."

You're either in or you're out. Bregman was in.

"That speech was huge for me," he says. "That's when I started really busting my butt."

As time went on, Bregman not only increased his efforts. He also elevated his ultimate target. Sure, greatness was a fine distinction and would more than suffice for most people. Not for him. Somewhere along the way, Bregman decided that his goal was to be the best baseball player on the planet—the best who ever lived. And he actually had the courage—the audacity—to say those words aloud in the company of other people. This was not braggadocio. It was a straightforward statement that might help others toward understanding why he did so many things that he did . . . why he *lived* the game of baseball instead of just playing it.

Bregman's motivational tweets kept flowing throughout the months leading up to the 2014 season.

Confidence is a stain you can't wipe off

The man who has no imagination has no wings. #DreamBIG

Good things come to those who wait. . . . Great things come to those who get off their butt and figure out a way to get the job done.

Allergic to Average

Taking that road less traveled. . . . . #ALLin

And there were many others.

Bregman also shared plenty of playful material.

Taking a jab at one of his best friends on the team, freshman Jarret DeHart, about his lack of speed, Bregman announced to the Twitterverse: *If @JartDeHart raced a pregnant woman, he'd come in third.*

Before the LSU football team played archrival Alabama, Bregman offered a list of ten things better than 'Bama. Among them: final exams, cold sores, Justin Bieber, and prison.

For anyone who might be interested in a glimpse of the silliness that sometimes takes place in team-only areas of Alex Box Stadium—in this case it was the players' lounge—Bregman tweeted a Vine video showing a game of "Sting Pong" he and teammate Danny Zardon played. Wearing no shirts, Bregman and Zardon took turns smacking Ping-Pong balls into each other's bare backs. The idea was to see who could inflict the most pain and who could take it the best. Not the most highbrow form of competition ever conducted on a college campus—but they had a good time with it.

On Friday, January 31, two weeks before its season opener, the LSU baseball team held its annual media day. It is hard to imagine another collegiate baseball program drawing close to fifty journalists for such a gathering, but at LSU this was business as usual. The Tigers were ranked as high as number two (by *USA Today*) in the national preseason polls, but the specific expectations of a given year hardly mattered. For eighteen straight seasons, LSU had led the NCAA in baseball attendance, and Tiger fans were always eager for news about their team.

After a buffet lunch in the Champions Club at Alex Box Stadium, Paul Mainieri stood behind a podium and took questions. One of the first was about Bregman, who would again hit third for LSU. With the departures of Raph Rhymes and Mason Katz—who had "protected" Bregman by hitting behind him the season before—was the coach now worried about teams being able to pitch around his star shortstop? After a quick chuckle, Mainieri said, "Yeah, I'm worried about them pitching around Bregman, because I'd like to see him swing that bat as often as he can." It was an indirect way of saying what everyone in the room already knew. For the 2014 Tigers to get where they wanted to go, Bregman would have to lead the offensive charge.

When Mainieri finished, the media folks went outside to the field, where all the players and assistant coaches were available for interviews. Bregman, sitting in the LSU dugout, was a priority stop for anyone covering the team. TV cameras rolled. Writers scribbled in notebooks. Recorders captured every word.

Was Bregman ready for the season opener? "Definitely," he said. "I can't wait. I'm ready to compete, ready to get this thing going."

After his big year as a freshman—and now being one of the team leaders—did he feel more pressure than he did last season? "Yeah, I think there's more pressure on me," Bregman said. "But I love that. I want the pressure. I want to be that guy up in the ninth inning when we need a hit to win the game."

What was the goal this year? Getting back to Omaha? "Getting back to Omaha, but also winning the national championship once we get there," he said. "That's why I came to LSU. That's why all of us came to LSU . . . to win a national championship."

How tough had it been to bounce back after his struggles in Omaha? "Not tough at all," Bregman said. "That's baseball. Baseball is a game of failure. You have to deal with your failure. You have to learn how to get back up again."

That error he made in the first game of the College World Series—was it true that he still had a newspaper photo of it posted in his locker? "I see it every day," Bregman said. It had been mailed to him, apparently by a fan of a rival school, along with a note that basically said: "Nice job! Way to lose the game for your team!" Bregman threw away the note but not the photo. He taped it up as motivation. The image inspired him to practice taking ground balls with greater purpose. And the bold headline above it—"No margin for errors"—told him something he always wanted to keep in mind.

Toward the end of the interviews, a late-arriving reporter—late to Bregman—asked another question about the weight of expectations on him. Bregman smiled, his blue eyes lighting up, and he answered with the calm of a veteran: "I think pressure is a privilege."

The first big moment of his sophomore season looked a lot like his shining moments as a freshman. LSU was hosting the University of New Orleans in the February 14 season opener, and the game was scoreless when Bregman stepped to the plate with one out in the third inning. With men on second and third, he lined a single to right for LSU's first RBI of the year—scoring Conner Hale from third—and it would also end up being the game-winning hit in a 2–0 victory behind the pitching of Aaron Nola. With a paid attendance of 12,472—the second-largest attendance figure in LSU baseball history—there was joy in Alex Box Stadium.

One other large number caught my attention that evening. It was the number of people following Bregman on Twitter when he got his first hit of the year: 11,063. Nola (with 6,410 followers) was the only other member of the team who had half that many. Clearly, the combination of Bregman's playing style and his passion for tweeting was very popular with LSU fans.

Everything kept looking familiar—sometimes even redundant—through the first three weeks of the season. Bregman kept collecting hits. He was 20-for-48 (batting .417) through fourteen games. He had a team-leading 12 RBIs. And he had to be breaking some sort of record for use of the term "Rake City" on Twitter.

#RakeCity #WeTakinOver

#RakeCity the movement ain't stoppin

#RakeCityRevolution

In the parlance of baseball, raking is when a hitter consistently puts bat to ball and just keeps knocking the thing all over the yard. In the language of Bregman, Rake City originated back in New Mexico, at the Albuquerque Baseball Academy, an instructional practice facility that was basically his childhood home away from home. Some kids get into music or video games or just like to hang out with friends. Bregman mostly got into the batting cages at the ABA. He started going there when he was eight. As a high school freshman, he began working with hitting instructor Jason Columbus, a former LSU first baseman (2002) who became so close to Bregman he was like a big brother. Columbus also became known as the Rake City Boss.

"There was a rap song, 'Rack City,' and we just changed it to Rake City," Columbus says. "That's what we do here. We rake. We want our guys hitting line drives to every part of the park. No fear of the pitcher. You just go out there and you wear pitchers out. Every ball you hit, you just barrel it up and hit it hard. We strive for perfection, we work our tails off, and we have fun while we're doing it." After a while, whenever Columbus wanted to see Bregman for a hitting session—and *if* Bregman was not already at the ABA—all he had to do was send a text: "It's Rake City time! Let's go!" No further explanation was needed.

After taking his personal version of Rake City across state lines into Louisiana, Bregman initially made public references to it only on Twitter. That changed the night of March 8, after a 4–2 win against Purdue. Bregman had gone 2-for-4 and had played well in the field. But he was most excited by what the Tigers had done after trailing 2–0 deep into the game. LSU scored three runs in the seventh inning and one in the eighth (by Bregman) for its first late-inning, come-from-behind win of the year.

With reporters gathered around him in front of the LSU dugout, Bregman offered an opening statement: "All of our hitters, before the game, packed our bags, and we got on the train on the way to Rake City, OK? We unpacked when we got there, and I think we're going to stay for a while. OK?"

The next day, in the series finale against Purdue, Bregman went a step further. With Mark Laird on first base and no outs in the fifth inning, Bregman bounced a single up the middle and advanced to second when the center fielder tried—but failed—to throw out Laird at third. Standing on second base, Bregman pumped his right arm up and down in the pantomimed motion of a train conductor pulling a whistle. *Choo-choo!* The Rake City train was barreling through. And—just like that—the Tigers had a new way to celebrate a big hit. The leg chop of the 2013 team was out. The Rake City train whistle was in.

When it was time to start the SEC season—the Tigers had a non-conference record of 16–2 prior to leaving for Vanderbilt on March 13—Bregman (then batting .419 and leading the team in hits and RBIs) tweeted: *We gotta get a few thousand #RakeCity shirts made. . . . Who would wear one to the box!?!?* The Twitter response was swift and strong. Bregman loved it.

Then something unexpected happened in Nashville: Bregman went cold at the plate. After a fourth-inning single in the first of three games, he went ten straight at-bats without a hit, making him 1-for-12 in the series. Baseball just goes that way sometimes. But it almost never did for Bregman. After beating Vanderbilt 4–2 with Nola pitching Friday night, the Tigers lost both games of a Saturday doubleheader. As soon as Bregman got to his phone, he tweeted *#TTFU*—an abbreviation for Toughen The F--- Up. It was an instruction for himself. But he also knew that his dad would see it and know exactly what he was saying. For years, they'd been using that phrase as both a motivational jolt and a reminder of who they were.

This time a slogan was not enough.

In the next four games—Wednesday against South Alabama and a weekend series against Georgia (all at Alex Box)—Bregman went 3-for-15. He dazzled on defense. He never stopped hustling, always sprinting on and off the field as if his dugout exit and entry times were being recorded for a track meet. But he kept struggling with his bat. Pitchers were not giving Bregman much to hit. He wasn't getting nearly as many fastballs over the plate as he had the year before. He was seeing a lot more off-speed stuff. And he was probably pressing a bit—too eager to swing at whatever he could and to make good on all the lofty expectations (both his own and those of everyone else).

Three-for-his-last-25 definitely had people talking. After the last Georgia game—a 2–2 tie stopped after thirteen innings because the Bulldogs could not miss their flight home—Bregman was surrounded by reporters. He spoke calmly and nothing he said went beyond the expected. No, he had never struggled like this, but everything would be fine. He just needed to stay level-headed, keep competing, keep working. He couldn't wait to get back to practice the next day.

Once the reporters were done with their questions, though, Bregman and I walked toward the home-plate end of the LSU dugout, and he told me something I never could have imagined hearing: "It's actually good that this is happening." Huh? "Think about it," he said. "My whole life, I've never been in a slump. If I'm going to be the best ever, like I want to be, I'm going to struggle in pro ball at some point. That's how the game works. So it's better to experience it and learn from it now."

He had a plan. Instead of focusing on "the slump" or worrying too much about his overall production for the season, he would only look ahead in chunks of ten at-bats at a time. "Every ten, I need to square-up eight," he said, meaning he'd make solid contact. "Half of those eight will be hits. So that's .400 right there. On to the next group of ten. That's how I'm going to turn this thing around—ten at-bats at a time."

Can't enjoy the highs without the lows

Coach Mainieri kept getting asked about Bregman. "It's going to be hard for us to win a lot of SEC games if Alex Bregman doesn't hit," he said. "Hopefully he gets it going." The coach talked about the individual attention he was giving Bregman, working on a couple of minor things with his mechanics and on trying to keep the right mental approach at the plate. Mainieri repeatedly celebrated the way his shortstop continued to excel defensively even while his offense was down. He had high praise—as always—for Bregman's dedication and work ethic. He also offered this to reporters one afternoon before practice: "Hitting a baseball is the single most difficult thing to do in any sport, I promise you. And so even the best are going to have their struggles. I think Bregman is great, but he's not super-human . . . he's not perfect."

Things got worse.

The next night—Tuesday, March 25—Bregman went hitless as fourth-ranked LSU lost 3–2 in eleven innings to unranked Tulane. The Tigers then went to Florida for a weekend series. Bregman's birthday was that Sunday. He turned twenty. But there was not much to celebrate on the field. The Tigers lost all three games in Gainesville. That made it five in a row without a win—one of the worst stretches in Mainieri's eight years at LSU. And Bregman collected the same number of hits he would have had by staying home and eating cake: zero. His recent numbers were unthinkable: three hits in his last thirty-nine at-bats . . . a .077 batting average for someone who had spent his entire baseball life in exclusive neighborhoods north of .350.

Bregman did get a birthday gift that made him smile. His mom was sending Jason Columbus to spend a few days with him. The Rake City Boss would soon be in Baton Rouge.

Bregman had been hearing from all sorts of people. For the most part, he'd been flooded with the support of family, friends, and fans. He'd also had countless people offer what they considered to be valuable advice or assistance. (A Hungry Howie's Pizza delivery guy even texted him one day—after having brought him dinner the night before—with an offer to throw him extra batting-practice. "Seriously?" Bregman muttered.) Then there were the haters. He'd heard from some of them, too, usually on Twitter. They called him overrated, worthless, and a few other things that violated the boundaries of civility.

Bregman used softer language but was nonetheless strong in the few blanket responses he tweeted. For example: *A lion doesn't lose sleep over the opinion of a sheep. #StayTuned.*

At 11:23 the night of Monday, March 31—the night after returning from Florida—Bregman tweeted: *Trust few . . . Those that have been there since day 1 through the ups and downs . . . Those who never lost sight of the dream and still believe.*

Blake Dean, a former LSU All-American and member of the 2009 national championship team, saw that tweet. Dean was now coaching at the University of New Orleans, but having been an LSU undergraduate assistant last year, he knew Bregman well and wanted to share his support. Replying to @ABREG_1, he wrote: *keep believing!!! You're the heart beat of that team! You're one of the best I've ever seen and the best always figure it out!*

Bregman tweeted back: *never stopped, never will. . . .*

I know ya won't! Dean responded. *The game is truly humbling but when you come out of this no one will stop you!*

Baseball—more than any other major sport—has always been filled with superstitions. Don't dare mention that a pitcher has a no-hitter going—it'll be ruined! When a late-inning comeback is needed, players contort their hats into silly-looking rally caps. And so on. Bregman had never been a big believer in all that stuff. As his slump worsened, though, he was willing to try almost anything. He went with no eye black for a game. Then he returned to his usual look. He used batting gloves. Then he didn't. Then he did again. He tried wearing stirrup socks . . . tried a new pair of cleats . . . tried several different walk-up songs (the latest being Nelly's "Here Comes The Boom") to be played as he approached the plate at Alex Box.

None of it helped.

But Bregman was not worried about such minutiae as he prepared for a Wednesday-night home game—this was April 2—against McNeese State. All that mattered now was a late-morning arrival from New Mexico. His hometown hitting-guru, Jason Columbus, was in Baton Rouge to work with him. Columbus did not want to step on any toes—namely those of Mainieri or of LSU hitting coach Javi Sanchez, both of whom he greatly respected—so he initially worked with Bregman away from campus. They went to Traction Center for Sports Excellence, a local training facility co-owned by former LSU baseball star Ryan Theriot. Before Bregman began hitting, Columbus stressed two points he would touch on several times throughout the day. One: "You're playing baseball. Just be like a twelve-year-old. Have fun." Two: "You're the best. Nobody can get you out if you don't get yourself out."

Watching Bregman hit, Columbus confirmed a few mechanical issues he thought he'd seen while looking at video of some recent at-bats. Bregman was moving his hips too early. And the timing of his step—his front foot stepping into the pitch—was not right. Overall, Columbus thought Bregman was putting too much body into his swing. As a result, he had lost his normal hand path and was causing the barrel of his bat to hit around the baseball instead of straight through it. Columbus wanted Bregman to step "slow and early"—he kept saying that—and to trust the speed of his hands to get the bat where it needed to be.

Of course, a single hitting session—even with his favorite instructor—did not necessarily mean Bregman would immediately return to form. In the first inning against McNeese, he fouled out to the shortstop. In the fourth, he popped out to the first baseman. He had now gone seventeen straight at-bats without a hit and was 3-for-his-last-41. Watching from the concourse level above section 207 on the first-base side of Alex Box, Columbus texted with Sam and Jackie Bregman, who were at home in Albuquerque, but he did not have much to tell them.

LSU—as a whole—also continued to struggle. The Tigers trailed 3–2 when Bregman stepped to the plate with one out in the bottom of the sixth inning. Mark Laird was on first base. Christian Ibarra was on second. Wanting to eliminate any indecision Bregman might have about whether to wait for a certain pitch, Mainieri signaled for a hit-and-run, meaning there was nothing to think about. Bregman had to swing at the first pitch. It was a curveball that stayed up at eye level. Bregman unleashed. He made contact. And . . .

"He got it!" Columbus blurted out.

He was right. The ball sailed just over the left-field wall.

"A three-run homer!" Charles Hanagriff declared on the LSU radio broadcast. "And that's how you get out of a slump!"

Bregman rounded the bases as if someone were chasing him—and his home run ended up being the game-winning hit. Final score: 10–3 for the home team. The LSU winless streak was stopped at five games.

Bregman did interviews before going to the locker room. Then he sent out a tweet. *Freakin #RakeCity* was all it said—Rake City being a term he had not dared to use for quite a while. Bregman showered. He signed autographs outside the stadium. And then—walking with teammate Jarret DeHart—he met up with Columbus in the parking lot.

"You coming?" Bregman asked DeHart.

"Yeah," DeHart said.

It was almost 10:00. They still had work to do. But first they wanted to wait for everyone else to go home. They wanted privacy.

DeHart, a New Jersey native, had spent winter break with Bregman in New Mexico, and he too had worked with Columbus while there. The three of them now sat in a booth for a late dinner at Walk-On's Bistreaux & Bar, just down the street from Alex Box. If his condo and the stadium were the two places where Bregman spent the most time—and they definitely were—then Walk-On's was probably ranked third. Bregman ordered what he usually did: a Classic Burger with cheddar cheese and a Dr Pepper.

After dinner, the trio returned to Alex Box. At 11:15, the only other sign of life was in the equipment room, where student manager Shay Dubois was washing game uniforms. Perfect. Bregman could do his thing without anyone knowing, which would eliminate any chance of speculation and false conclusion about why he was working with his own instructor instead of the LSU coaches. To Bregman, working with Columbus was no slight toward Mainieri and his staff. It was simply something extra—an opportunity for help from the one person who knew his swing better than anyone else. But Bregman also knew that some sportswriter or broadcaster could easily twist things to create his or her own spin. As much as he cared about his coaches, it was the last thing he'd want to see happen.

Bregman and DeHart—with help from Dubois—spent more than twenty minutes getting everything set on the field. They turned on lights and music (Bregman selected country-rock singer Brantley Gilbert on Pandora). They rolled out two pitching machines, ran extension cords to power them up, and placed a protective screen in front of each machine. They rolled in the batting cage from its storage area beyond the centerfield wall and unfurled a giant mat to protect the grass in front of home plate. Dubois rolled out a big basket of baseballs for Columbus to feed into the machines. The stadium sprinklers were running on their regular automated schedule—spraying water in the outfield—but that would not bother anything. So what if some baseballs got wet?

Twenty-two minutes before midnight—after sending a few balls through the machines to check speed and location—Columbus turned to Bregman and DeHart: "All right, you guys got your helmets?" They did. Bregman stepped in first. He was wearing cleats, baggy workout-shorts, a T-shirt, batting gloves, and his purple helmet with "LSU" on the front. "Slow and early," Columbus said, going right back to his focus on Bregman's step into the pitch, and he started feeding balls into one of the machines. Bregman and DeHart took turns in the cage, each hitting for a few minutes and then taking a break while the other worked. With Bregman, Columbus concentrated on two things: the timing of his step and the movement of his hands. "Trust the hands," Columbus kept saying. "Get the hands to your spot."

Bregman pounded baseballs around the yard as if he were angry at them. Standing outside the cage during one of his breaks, he smiled while thinking how great it was to have Columbus in town: *Guy definitely knows his stuff.* After almost forty-five minutes of hitting, they were done. Bregman and company walked through the outfield, picked up balls, and loaded them into buckets. Then they put away everything they had set up and headed inside to the players' lounge.

Bregman had one more thing he needed to do before heading home for some sleep. While DeHart and Columbus sat on a couch and watched video of an old LSU game, Bregman got on a computer in the back of the room and worked on a school assignment. Later that morning, he would have to stand in front of his public-speaking class and make a presentation on how to decrease the use of tobacco in Louisiana. He'd already completed most of his preparation but wanted to find a few more facts to work in. Bregman was done in fifteen minutes. Still, by the time he and his friends finally walked out of Alex Box, it was

12:55 Thursday morning. Turning toward Columbus and smiling at the Rake City Boss, Bregman said: “Welcome to my world!”

Bregman and Columbus squeezed in four more hitting sessions the next few days—one night session at a high school in Plaquemine, the others in LSU’s indoor batting cages when nobody else was around. Columbus also got to see one more game before heading home to his wife and two sons. The night of Friday, April 4, he watched Bregman get singles in his first two at-bats—the second one knocked in a run—as the Tigers beat Mississippi State 3–0.

Of course, the end of a hitting slump is not often wrapped in a clean package. The next two days, Bregman went 1-for-8 to close out the Mississippi State series. In twenty-four days, his batting average had plummeted from .419 to .286. (At the same point a year earlier—thirty-three games into his freshman season—he was batting .439 and riding a twenty-one-game hitting streak.)

Bregman tweeted a well-traveled quote from author Christian D. Larson: *Believe in yourself and all that you are. Know there is something inside you that is greater than any obstacle.*

His recent struggles did nothing to stop a phone call he got the morning of Tuesday, April 8. It was Eric Campbell, general manager of national teams for USA Baseball, with an invitation. Campbell wanted to make Bregman the first position player—along with a few pitchers—named to the 2014 collegiate national team. Did he want to spend another summer playing for Team USA? “Absolutely,” Bregman said, as if there would have been any doubt. When they were done talking, Bregman tweeted: *Such an honor to be able to represent Team USA again this summer . . . #Pumped.*

That evening, Campbell told me that no matter how Bregman was hitting throughout any specific stretch of games—slump or no slump—it was clear to him and the USA coaches that they needed him on the team. "We're believers!" Campbell said. "Alex is just such a pure hitter. But it's also his history with USA Baseball. It's what he means to LSU—what he means to college baseball. He just has that 'it' factor . . . and it's contagious. He's a leader just by the way he does things."

Team USA was slated to play thirty games. It would host teams from Chinese Taipei and Japan. It would play a tournament in the Netherlands and travel to Cuba for a five-game series. With such formidable opponents on the schedule, Campbell was clear about Bregman's role: "He's the guy that we really want to build our team around."

The next half-dozen LSU games brought more of the same from Bregman: a combination of highlight-reel plays with his glove—he was part vacuum-cleaner, part acrobat in the field—and way too many delete-button results with his bat. No matter what happened, though, Bregman kept battling.

That made Sam Bregman proud of his son. Sam knew what it meant to have tough days. He thought of elections he had lost. He thought of what it felt like when a political matter or one of his high-profile court cases moved in a bad direction. And that made him think of a song he liked to play—Bob Seger's "Like a Rock"—whenever he wanted a reflective lift through the dark of disappointment and back to the usual light of his days.

Stood there boldly
Sweatin' in the sun
Felt like a million
Felt like number one

The height of summer
I'd never felt that strong
Like a rock

The lyrics always grabbed Sam.

Like a rock, I was strong as I could be
Like a rock, nothin' ever got to me
Like a rock, I was something to see
Like a rock

It had become a personal anthem of fortitude.

Like a rock, standin' arrow straight
Like a rock, chargin' from the gate
Like a rock, carryin' the weight
Like a rock

Sam was listening to that song the afternoon of Friday, April 18—he had it on in his car—and he called Alex. They only spoke for a few minutes. But this was not about dialogue. It was about hearing the music. "Bob Seger . . . 'Like a Rock' . . . says it all," Sam said. "No matter what's happening, no matter what people are saying, you gotta be like a rock, gotta stand strong. You need to really listen to the words. This is the motto now. Like a rock!"

After talking to his dad, Alex pulled up the song on his phone and listened to it a couple of times. Then he found a photo of the album cover and texted it to Sam. "Like a Rock" would indeed be the new motto.

Bregman started thinking of his battle against pitchers as a chess match. All season they'd been throwing him a lot of junk, and he'd been chasing too much of it. Then he got in bad habits—trying to hit with his body instead of his hands. He'd been working on correcting that. His work was already showing positive results. And now he tried another strategy in the ongoing chess game. He moved up in the batter's box. Maybe that would help him against all the off-speed pitches he was seeing. He could get to them before they moved—curved, dipped, whatever—as much as the pitchers wanted them to move. And he still had total faith that his hands could not be beaten by many fastballs.

In a stretch of six games—from April 22 against Tulane through a May 2 victory at Texas A&M—Bregman went 11-for-26 (a batting average of .423). He finally felt like himself again.

The ups-and-downs of sport were one thing—and they were unmistakably critical to Bregman's everyday existence. He also knew the difference between athletic challenges and true adversity. On Thursday, May 8, the tandem weights of loss and sadness found Bregman in the middle of the night. His beloved Zayde—forever his biggest fan—had succumbed after being hospitalized by a heart attack. Stan Bregman was dead at the age of eighty-three.

Alex was crushed.

Stan's encouragement—*Bang that ball! Bang that ball!*—had never left him. It never would. Alex had shared his whole childhood with his grandfather. They'd go to The Downs Racetrack together—one of their favorite things to do—and bet the horses. Stan taught Alex how to use the *Daily Racing Form*. Sometimes they'd eat at Mykonos Cafe & Taverna, Stan's favorite hangout in Albuquerque, a Greek joint where all the regulars called him Stan the Man. Alex started calling him that, too. It never really mattered what they did. It was just being together that made everything better for both of them. A day or two might pass without Alex seeing his grandfather, but almost never more than that—not unless Alex was out of town playing baseball.

This was the first time Alex had lost someone so close to him.

He cried.

He spent time on the phone with his mom and dad.

He tried to console himself by thinking that Stan would now have "the best seat in the house" whenever he played baseball.

Beyond that, he really didn't know what to do.

By late morning, Alex wanted to somehow express himself. He went to "Notes" on his phone and wrote directly to his grandfather. Then he took a screen shot of what he'd written and tweeted it: *You changed so many lives and were a role model to so many people. You had fun and made sure everyone around you did too. You loved unconditionally while being the most generous person I know. You will always be the man. RIP Stan Bregman*

After losing the previous Saturday and Sunday at Texas A&M—two tough, one-run games—the Tigers were in a precarious position. They were ranked anywhere from sixth to fifteenth in the nation, depending on the poll, but their conference record of 13–10–1 placed them third in the SEC West and left them vulnerable as far as post-season tournament seeding. Alabama—fourth in the same division (with a conference record of 13–11)—was due in town for LSU's final home SEC series of the season. The outcome would be huge for both teams.

Coach Mainieri told Bregman not to worry about any of that. He ought to do whatever was right for him—go home, be with his family, go to the funeral—even if it meant missing a few games. Of course, Mainieri also knew that Bregman voluntarily missing any baseball would be the equivalent of anyone else signing up to go without food or even air. Bregman told Mainieri that his grandfather never would have wanted him to miss a game. His family was trying to plan things so that he could attend the funeral without having to do that. Meanwhile, he would stay in Baton Rouge and play against Alabama.

Rain came Friday, making it impossible to play, so a doubleheader was set for Saturday. Bregman took the field with "STAN" written on the front of his cap, low and off to his right, but clearly visible. On the underside of the bill, only for him to see, were two additional reminders he'd written—"Stan The Man" and "Like A Rock"—in black marker. Bregman was now playing with an additional agenda. Whatever he could achieve on the field, he was dedicating it to the memory of his grandfather.

Perhaps he put too much pressure on himself to do something special in the first game that day. Instead, he went hitless: grounding out twice, striking out once, and flying out to center field. The game was still a good one for the Tigers. In his last regular-season start at Alex Box, Aaron Nola delivered a gem, yielding only four hits while pitching a complete-game shutout. LSU won 2–0. Although happy about that, and thrilled for Nola, Bregman had unfinished business to address in the second game of the doubleheader. He still needed to make some noise with his bat—needed to *bang that ball*—as a tribute to Stan the Man.

After more rain and lightning—three hours of delay—the second game did not start until ten at night. It did not begin well for the Tigers. Alabama scored three runs in the first inning. In the bottom of the first, Bregman stepped to the plate with two outs and nobody on base. On the fourth pitch from lefty Justin Kamplain—a 2-1 count—he swung and popped the ball up into foul territory to the right of first base. *Damn*, Bregman was frustrated. First baseman Austen Smith stayed under the ball as it drifted back toward the field, and he caught it at the edge of the coach's box to end the inning.

To anyone else watching the game, that was that. No big deal. But

Sam Bregman—watching at home on the LSU Geaux Zone—came unhinged. He was not upset about Alex making an out. That was just baseball. What set him off was the fact that his son had not bothered to run all the way through first base. What if that ball had drifted back into fair play and been dropped? What about the professional scouts seeing him take it easy like that? What about his own pride—the never-stop-hustling approach that had always defined him? Alex had just jogged down the line, and not even the whole way. About a dozen feet short of the base, he had broken off his jog and turned to the dugout, starting his turn before the ball had even been caught. Sam could not recall ever seeing Alex do something like that. All he'd ever seen was the embodiment of a powerful line that father and son had long carried with them and constantly shouted to the world: "Hustle never has a bad day!" Sam could hardly believe what he had just witnessed. He was so angry, he just turned off the game and went to bed. He did not see Alex go hitless in three more at-bats. He did not see LSU lose 5–1. But Sam fell asleep knowing he and Alex would be having a little talk.

When they spoke the next day, Alex had no good explanation for not running all the way to first base. "Obviously, I should have run," he said. "I guess I was just frustrated, feeling sorry for myself." Sam was stunned. Alex Bregman—the guy who would walk through hell in a gasoline suit to play baseball—did not hustle because he was frustrated and feeling sorry for himself? Was he really talking to his son? Sam was not about to sugarcoat anything. "You better start acting like you need a job, because right now you don't have one," he told Alex. "Is that how you'd act on a job interview?"

Alex would have loved to get right back on the field that day—would have wanted nothing more than to quickly make amends for his uncharacteristic slip—but the Sunday finale of the Alabama series was rained out. With no game until Tuesday night, Alex had a lot of time to think about what his dad had said. He kept returning to the thought that he was not only playing college baseball. He was also going to a job interview every time he stepped on the field.

Monday was a long day for Bregman. Stan the Man was very much on his mind. (The funeral would be Wednesday in California.) And now he was also going deep on himself. This was no longer about failing to run on a single play. It was about everything he'd been doing. It was about taking a good, long look in the mirror to see what that guy had to say.

By nightfall, Bregman was ready for his favorite refuge. He went to the Alex Box batting cages and hit baseballs for a while. After that, he retreated to the players' lounge and—still alone—went right back to introspection. Then he started writing. He wanted to share some thoughts with his teammates.

The result was one of the longest text messages—probably *the* longest—he'd ever written: 673 words covering everything from his childhood start in baseball to the situation he and his teammates now faced with only four games left in the regular season. Bregman was very tough on himself in what had somehow escalated into a passionate indictment of the way he had approached the entire season . . . and of how he had performed throughout.

He wrote in the text-speak of his generation—no need to worry about proper form—but his overall message was unmistakable: "from this point on the rest of the year i promise to be the old alex bregman. . . . not the guy that hit .370 and was whatever award. . . . not him. the alex bregman that ran out every groundball, hit for 752342398 hrs a day, took every groundball like somebody was coming for my job, and cared about winning more than what i did offensively that day. and i had fun doing that and that is what the game is about. I promise to be that guy for every pitch the rest of this season and the rest of my career."

Bregman said he might strike out his next 300 at-bats, but that he'd be the same guy every time he took the field. He wrote about how much he believed "in every single person" on the team "because i've seen everybody on this roster come through before." And that's why he still believed they could win a national championship—why he would do everything in his power to make it happen.

Bregman ended his next-to-last paragraph with this: "my life is you guys. my life is baseball and my best friends in that locker room. love you guys." Then he closed with a single line set alone—"i believe that we will win"—and sent the text to all his teammates.

It was 11:03 p.m.

Bregman's roommates, Aaron Nola and Henri Faucheux, were back at the condo, playing cards with another teammate, fellow pitcher Brady Domangue, when they got the text. "It kind of hit hard," Nola would later tell me. "Definitely gave us something to talk about. The biggest thing was, Alex was not telling others what they needed to do. He was saying what *he* was going to do. That's what makes other guys on the team respect him so much as a person and as a player."

But was Bregman being too hard on himself?

"That's why he's so good . . . because he's hard on himself," Nola said.

"After a while, you just kind of expect that out of Bregman," Faucheux said. "It can be almost irrational sometimes, the way he goes to extremes, but it's just the way he operates."

Extremes?

Bregman had two more issues he wanted to address.

While teammates were reading and responding to his text, he got on a computer in the players' lounge and went to Twitter. His profile showed that he had close to 14,000 followers, almost 3,000 more than at the start of the season, but all of them would now have to do without him. If Bregman were going to start approaching every day as a job interview—and that was his intention—then he wanted to eliminate the distraction of social media. At 11:10 p.m.—seven minutes after texting his teammates—Bregman sent out a farewell tweet: *Twitter it's been real. . . . Deactivating you.* He then clicked the account of @ABREG_1 into darkness. *nooo*, a high school girl in Ponchatoula quickly tweeted in response, the emoticons of a broken heart and three crying faces preceding the text of her protest. *who else am I gonna quote in chapel now*, a high school baseball player in California tweeted. But Bregman did not see the immediate flurry of responses intended for him. He was gone from the Twitterverse.

He also wanted to do something about what remained of his brown hair, which was faded on the sides and exaggerated on the top. He called it a mohawk. It was also a mess. *Idiotic*, he now conceded to himself. *Definitely not the way I'd want to look going into a job interview*. He would soon take care of that.

The next night—Tuesday, May 13—LSU had one more game to play before Bregman would depart for his grandfather's funeral. Prior to taking the field at Alex Box, Bregman asked one of the team's student managers, Andre Legrand, to shave his head for him. Legrand set up shop in the locker room, clippers in hand, and Bregman's dome soon shined like a cue ball. He did not tell anyone what had motivated him to get rid of his hair. People thought he simply wanted a new look. But Bregman now felt he was properly prepared for his about-to-be-played "job interview" against Northwestern State.

It ended up being a game for the record books. LSU hitters exploded for 27 runs while five Tiger pitchers combined for the first LSU no-hitter since 1979. The score of 27–0 was the largest margin of victory in school history. And it could have been even bigger: Due to lightning, the game was stopped in the bottom of the sixth inning.

Bregman's individual production was equally outrageous. After walking and grounding out in his first two trips to the plate, he batted twice in the third inning—hitting a sharp single to left field and drilling an RBI double to left-center—as LSU scored seven runs. But Bregman was only getting started. With two outs and bases loaded in the fourth inning, he blasted the first grand slam of his two-year college career. And—as if that were not enough for one game—he hit another homer in the sixth: a three-run shot that served both as encore and as a sign of things to come.

"It was a fun team win," Bregman told reporters. It also could have been the final home game of the year. That would depend on how many games the Tigers could win in their final road series of the regular season—at Auburn—and then in the SEC Tournament. Those outcomes would determine whether LSU was worthy of hosting a regional in the NCAA Tournament.

But Bregman had other issues with which to deal before any of that. By the time he was done with a late-night meal at Walk-On's—it was actually 12:35 in the *morning* when he exited—he had only a few hours left to sleep. His first of two morning flights en route to Los Angeles was set to depart Baton Rouge at 5:25. After connecting in Houston and making his way to the West Coast, Bregman would meet up with his family just in time for Stan the Man's funeral.

Sharing a room with his grandfather for the last time, Bregman would be hairless and Twitterless. But he would not be hitless—definitely not hitless.

Stan Bregman had moved to Santa Monica in 2012, and his service in the Coast Guard entitled him to a military funeral, so it was held in the Bob Hope Veterans Chapel at the Los Angeles National Cemetery. Alex cried. He also smiled and even laughed as certain memories were shared. He spent a low-key afternoon with his family. Then he went straight back to the airport. While his LSU teammates slept at the Hampton Inn & Suites in Opelika, Alabama—getting proper rest on the eve of starting their series at nearby Auburn—Bregman took an overnight flight from Los Angeles to Atlanta. Pitching coach Alan Dunn, already in Georgia to see a recruit, met Bregman at Hartsfield-Jackson International Airport, and together they drove ninety-five miles to join the team in Alabama.

After breakfast and a few hours of sleep, Bregman was ready to play baseball. That evening, he had two hits against Auburn, while the hit parade also continued for the team. The Tigers collected fifteen hits in a 10–0 victory. In back-to-back games, they had now outscored their opponents by an unthinkable total of 37–0. And the hits kept coming. LSU blasted Auburn two more times—11–3 and 8–1—for a series sweep to finish the regular season.

Next up was the SEC Tournament in Hoover, Alabama. The Tigers ran right through that, too, producing all sorts of big offensive numbers on the way to four straight wins and the tournament title. Bregman was a beast. In the field, he charged, spun, leapt, grabbed, and fired away with everything he had. At the plate, he was back at full force, pounding pitchers and wearing out the base paths.

In the tournament opener against Vanderbilt—an 11–1 win for LSU—Bregman went 3-for-4 (including a three-run homer) with five RBIs. In the seventh inning, when he ripped an RBI double down the left-field line, his batting average climbed above .300 for the first time since April 4. "His swing was just like lightning today," Mainieri said after the game. "I was scared for the health of their defensive players, to be honest with you."

The next day—in the third inning against Arkansas—Bregman crushed another double to left field and then scored to put LSU ahead. Luke Johnson, editor of *Tiger Rag*, offered immediate analysis in back-to-back tweets from the press box: *Y'all, college baseball is not happy with what's developing here in Hoover. Alex Bregman looks as though he's found his mojo. That's bad news for teams that might have to face LSU in the post-season.* A few minutes later, during a live interview on the television broadcast of the game, Mainieri said of Bregman: "He's the straw that stirs the drink for us."

The final accounting for four games in Hoover—LSU outscoring its opponents by a total of 31–4—was almost as preposterous as its domination in the last four games of the regular season. The Tigers had now won eight in a row since Bregman sent that heartfelt text to his teammates, shut down his Twitter account, and shaved his head. Coincidence? Was it simply his time to do what great players do—performing at his best when his best was most needed? Bregman would leave any such discussion to others. But his individual numbers did some talking of their own. In those eight games, Bregman went 15-for-36 (batting .417) with 13 RBIs.

Of course, the most important news had nothing to do with individual numbers. It was the announcement that came only because the whole team had played so well the previous two weeks. The Tigers would not only host an NCAA regional at Alex Box, they were also named one of eight national seeds—the last of the eight. It was a critical designation. If the Tigers could win their regional—hosting Houston, Bryant University, and Southeastern Louisiana—being a national seed meant that they would also play their super regional at home. The path was both clear and favorable. With two winning weekends at Alex Box, the Tigers would be headed back to the annual destination of their dreams: the College World Series. Two winning weekends, and the climactic stretch of that "Road to Omaha" Bregman tweeted about on June 18, 2013—a straight shot to the land of redemption—would finally belong to him and his teammates.

"Great time of year," Bregman said.

He was not talking about the heat and humidity of Louisiana. He was talking about everything that would make the NCAA tournament "so awesome" (his words). The atmosphere at Alex Box would be electric. His parents and both of his siblings—eighteen-year-old sister Jessica and fourteen-year-old brother A.J.—would be in from New Mexico for the regional. And school was done for the semester: The only thing that mattered now was coming up big in the biggest of games.

"I love it," Bregman said.

We had just settled into a booth at one of his other favorite places to eat, the California Pizza Kitchen in Perkins Rowe. We were having lunch on Wednesday, May 28, two days before the regional opener against Southeastern. Bregman was buoyant. Part of it was his excitement about how well the Tigers had been playing. Part of it was his anticipation of all that was about to unfold.

We touched on a wide variety of topics between bites of salads and pasta. Bregman spoke poignantly about what he'd learned and how he'd grown throughout the season. Most notably, he talked about having learned how to get through "struggles and tough times" as a player because he'd never really dealt with any of that before this year. He spoke quietly but strongly about "the people who really care" about him—his family and closest friends—and how they never stopped believing in him . . . never stopped flooding him with support.

The most remarkable exchange of the day had nothing to do with that. It came when I finally remembered to ask him something I'd been meaning to ask: "Without baseball—just pretend it didn't even exist—what would you be doing? What would be your goals, your aspirations?"

His eyes opened wide. His mouth opened, too, but only slightly, and he did not speak.

Bregman just stared into space. He was lost.

"No idea," he eventually said. "I've never even thought about it."

"Well, think about it," I said. "Without baseball, what do you think you'd be doing?"

This time he answered right away: "No clue!"

LSU kept rolling the first two days of the regional—defeating Southeastern 8–4 on Friday and Houston 5–1 on Saturday. The Tigers had now outscored their opponents 100–13 while winning ten straight games. Most important, they were in great shape to win their regional. Whichever team emerged from the losers' bracket—either Southeastern or Houston—would then have to beat the Tigers twice in a row to keep them from advancing to host a super regional.

The opponent turned out to be Houston. After defeating Southeastern in a Sunday afternoon game, the Cougars had to regroup and play the Tigers at 7:35 p.m. The short turnaround time plus the fact that LSU's pitching staff was not nearly as taxed as Houston's put the Tigers at a distinct advantage. Of course, playing in front of an energized crowd at the Box was yet another bonus for LSU.

In the first seven innings, Bregman went 4-for-4 (two singles and two doubles), Kade Scivicque and Tyler Moore homered, and the Tigers did not allow a run. Heading into the eighth, they led 4–0 and were only six outs away from the regional championship. Then the LSU bullpen suffered an uncharacteristic collapse. The Tigers gave up four runs in the eighth—all of them charged to senior Kurt McCune—and the game went into extra innings.

Leading off in the bottom of the tenth, Bregman hit a rocket—the ball was measured leaving his bat at 106 mph—and for a tantalizing moment he appeared to have a walk-off homer he'd someday tell his kids about. Alas, the well-traveled baseball met an untimely death in the glove of Houston center fielder Landon Appling, who made the catch while running into the wall. The Tigers went quietly in the tenth—three up, three down—and then Houston scratched out three hits in the eleventh for what proved to be the winning run. Final score: 5–4 for the Cougars.

The shocking turn of events meant that one more game had to be played last night: a winner-take-all contest for the regional championship and the right to keep moving toward Omaha.

Things did not go well for the Tigers.

The pitching staff—depleted—failed to do its job.

The offense—so hot the last couple of weeks—finally turned cold.

The game was not officially over when Houston broke a 2–2 tie with seven runs in the third inning. But the Tigers were in deep trouble. LSU never scored again and ended up on the wrong side of a 12–2 blowout. One night removed from what looked like the certainty of a regional championship—at least until late in *that* game—the 2014 Tigers were now relegated to the past tense. Season over . . . with a final record of 46–16–1.

Individually, Bregman stayed hot until the end. Two hits last night left him with a .451 batting average (23-for-51) in the final twelve games and a .316 average for the season (second best among LSU's regular starters). He led the team in hits (77), RBIs (47), and total bases (111). Clearly, he had struggled along the way, but what started as Rake City also ended as Rake City.

Of course, none of that mattered now. Bregman didn't even know about those numbers. Two was the only number he cared about. This made it two years in a row without a national championship. He was both stunned and pained, like a fighter who did not see the knockout blow coming, but Bregman had long since proven that he would never stay down on the mat for long.

He congratulated the Houston players. He went to the media room and answered questions. He shared some time in the locker room with teammates. He showered. Then he walked across the hall to the players' lounge . . . to the back of the room . . . to the tucked-away work area housing several computers. Bregman still appeared to be dazed, his steps slower than usual, his eyes glassy. Yet he knew exactly what he was doing as he settled down at one of the computers. It did not take long to have his Twitter account up and running again. At 11:39, he tweeted for the first time in three weeks: *Had a blast this year. Love my team. #ForeverLSU*

After a few minutes on the computer, Bregman gathered his belongings and went outside to the designated area—under the stands on the first-base side of the stadium—where fans always wait to collect autographs and take pictures. He was the last of the Tigers to make it outside—trailing just behind Aaron Nola. It was right at midnight when Bregman finally arrived. But close to a hundred people were still there to greet him. Bregman signed and posed and even managed to smile as he patiently worked the crowd.

Three eleven-year-old boys, friends on a baseball team in Gonzales, were last in line to meet him. They'd been talking about how cool they thought Bregman's bald head was—he had shaved it again before the final game—and now they had a request.

"Can we rub your head?" one of them asked.

"Absolutely!" Bregman said.

He leaned over for them. Each of the boys took a turn quickly rubbing his head—each laughing and celebrating the moment. But it was not only theirs. It also belonged to Bregman. At the end of a night defined by loss and finality, he was happy to let the innocence and joy of youth at least temporarily eclipse his heartbreak.

"Thank you," the boys said.

"No problem," Bregman said with a smile.

He walked with teammate Nate Fury to the parking lot on the other side of the stadium. Then he broke off, alone, toward his pickup truck, a red 2004 GMC Sierra with New Mexico plates and an interior he had long since transformed into both laundry bin and garbage dumpster.

Aaron Nola and his parents, A.J. and Stacie, were still lingering in the lot. Bregman told the Nolas he'd be looking for them when he watched the draft, meaning the Major League Baseball draft later this week, during which Aaron should be one of the top picks. "I expect to see you fully Hollywooded out on TV!" Bregman said. Then he said goodnight and got into his truck.

He did not leave right away, though. He first put his thumbs to work on his phone. At 12:32 this morning, Bregman tweeted: *Road to Omaha '15 starts now.* Then he pulled out of the Alex Box lot—one season in the rearview mirror, the next one already starting to form in the glow of his headlights.

With Alex Bregman leading the way, LSU won the 2015 SEC regular-season championship and advanced to the College World Series as the nation's top-ranked team. The Tigers were eliminated after three games, but Bregman performed well both at the plate and in the field. After three years as a Tiger, he then departed LSU the same way he stormed onto the college baseball scene as a freshman: with a collection of national honors. Bregman was a 2015 first-team All-American and recipient of the Rawlings NCAA Gold Glove Award for his defensive play at shortstop. He was one of four finalists for the Golden Spikes Award, which goes to the nation's top amateur baseball player of the year. On June 8, the Houston Astros selected Bregman with the second overall pick in the annual Major League Baseball draft. Bregman joined the Astros on June 25—with a signing bonus of $5.9 million—and began his professional career as a minor leaguer.

BUGA Nation

August 10, 2014

The youthful but already widely celebrated head of state—Leonard Fournette of BUGA Nation—settles on a folding chair at the twenty-two-yard line of LSU's indoor practice field. More than thirty writers and broadcasters scramble to form a crowded ring around him. They all want a piece of the top-ranked freshman football player in America—*need* a piece of him for their stories. They have an endless supply of questions for the rookie running back.

Was the first week of practice what you thought it would be?

How tough is it to learn the playbook?

What's the reception been like around campus?

This is how it works at LSU's annual preseason media day. Journalists come with questions. Seated football players offer answers. But the frenzy surrounding Fournette—literally surrounding him at the moment—is unlike anything else going on here. The young man has yet to play a down of college football. He is nonetheless the top interview target of the day. Fournette has been hyped to the heavens—the words "Heisman Trophy" even creeping into the conversation—and this is the first time since his arrival on campus that reporters have been allowed to speak with him.

Do you have personal goals for the season?

How do you handle all the attention?

Les Miles has mentioned Michael Jordan and Tiger Woods in the same sentence as you—what does that mean to you?

Fournette's bald head shines under the glare of television lights. His mouth opens into a big smile and his braces glisten. Making twin tracks across his top and bottom teeth, they are seemingly at odds with his dark beard—the braces a sign of youth, the thick facial hair a hint of manhood.

Your first taste of contact the other day . . . what was that like for you?

The adjustment you're making to the college game . . . is it a physical thing? Or is it more mental?

Are you the fastest player on the team?

The nineteen-year-old Fournette—six-foot-one, 224 pounds of chiseled hope and expectation—is wearing a white game jersey made perfect for him by the purple number sevens displayed on front and back. He chose his uniform number to represent the Seventh Ward of New Orleans. It was there that he grew up—known as "Button" before anything else because his parents adored his button nose. It was there—in a tough area plagued by poverty and crime—that family and faith combined with football to make him who he is.

How anxious are you to play in that first game against Wisconsin?

You think you'll be nervous?

Working with the older guys at your position—Terrence Magee and Kenny Hilliard—how has that been going for you?

Fournette answers with comfort and ease. He comes across as both confident and humble. Yes, he put up crazy numbers—rushing for 7,619 yards and eighty-eight touchdowns—during four years on the high school varsity at St. Augustine in New Orleans. Yes, *Sports Illustrated* recently declared him "the most highly touted LSU signee of all time" and he is often compared to NFL star Adrian Peterson of the Minnesota Vikings—so rare is his combination of size, speed, power, and moves. But there is so much more than that to Fournette. He already knows too much about death. He knows about struggling . . . about overcoming the odds of his environment. He knows about doing right things when others around him might not be doing the same. He has a mother who constantly texts him with Scripture. He has a powerful thought—"I express my pain through football"—that never really leaves him. He has his self-imposed standards of the nation he and his family created.

Long before the birth of BUGA Nation, there was Goretti Playground on Benson Street in New Orleans. At eight years old, little Leonard Fournette III started playing there in youth football leagues. Actually, calling him *little* Leonard is not exactly right. He was always one of the biggest, strongest, most athletic kids on the field. Coaches and parents from opposing teams sometimes suggested he should have to show a birth certificate to prove he was not older than everyone else playing. But so what? Leonard didn't mind. He was having fun. He was excelling at something people obviously cared about. And football kept his attention the way nothing else did. His parents—Leonard Jr. and Lory—had been told that he probably had ADHD and ought to be on medication. They said no to Ritalin and yes to a steady combination of sports and discipline.

There was also Hurricane Katrina. It hit New Orleans on August 29, 2005, when Fournette was ten. He and his family—he's the third of four children—had already moved several times within the Seventh Ward. Now they had to spend a few nights on a bridge before finding temporary refuge in a hotel. They ended up in Texas for a while, where things were better, but Fournette would always carry the grim images of his native city: Dead people floating in water. Seeing someone snatch a watch from the wrist of a dead man. Watching another man get shot in the head. Stealing food for himself and his family—just trying to survive. Attempting to describe how all of this affected him, Fournette would later say: "It kind of makes you stronger than what you really were."

There was personal loss—the worst possible kind of loss—in the years that followed. In 2010, Fournette's grandmother, Lorraine Tyler, died without him ever knowing she had been sick. What he did know was that he had learned more from her about the importance of family than he'd ever learned from anyone else. In 2012, one of his cousins—eighteen and full of life—was shot in the chest and gone before anyone could even say goodbye to him. Murdered. Fournette has known others—young people, his contemporaries—who have met equally senseless endings. His losses never leave him. They explain something he often thinks about and recently tweeted: "I wish heaven had visiting hours."

Long before BUGA Nation, there was just a made-up word spelled b-u-g-a and pronounced almost like the indelicate term for something stuck in your nose: *boog-uh*. In the personalized lexicon of the Fournette family, being buga meant "keeping it real," or staying honest and true to who you are. *Suga* was the opposite. That was being fake or putting on some kind of air to impress others. The Fournettes eventually employed the two words in a catchy motto that served as a family guidepost: *Buga no suga*.

As a St. Augustine freshman, Fournette immediately became a key player on the varsity football team. In his first game, he rushed for 238 yards and three touchdowns. "Incredibly gifted young kid," recalls offensive lineman Trai Turner, then a senior teammate who went on to play at LSU and is now an NFL rookie with the Carolina Panthers. "We definitely knew right away that he'd be great at whatever he wanted to do—offense, defense, special teams, whatever he wanted to play."

The fact that St. Aug lost a wild game in that 2010 season opener—59–56 to West Jefferson High School—would be inconsequential in the long run. But the presence of Frank Wilson that early September night at Tad Gormley Stadium would prove momentous in the life of Leonard Fournette. Wilson was both a St. Aug alum and the LSU running backs coach. He also served as recruiting coordinator for the Tigers—and he did something that Saturday night that he'd never before done. He offered a college scholarship to a high school freshman. Fournette was the youngest player to whom either Wilson or LSU head coach Les Miles had ever made such an offer. Of course, that was only the beginning of a four-year recruitment merry-go-round that drew countless coaches from across the nation and ultimately became a two-school battle between archrivals LSU and Alabama.

Humble. Hard-working. All about the team.

No matter how many yards and touchdowns Fournette piled up, no matter how much attention he got for his freakish athleticism and achievements, those were the labels his teammates and coaches consistently used to describe him.

There were also stories about him "clowning" a bit too much during classes in his early days of high school—just youthful silliness and inattention—but the structure and discipline of St. Aug did not take long to grab hold of him and set him straight. The all-boys parochial school had a long and celebrated history of helping students get locked in. Once Fournette settled down, he really enjoyed learning. He embraced the feeling that he was growing, maturing, gradually allowing himself to be more and more of who he truly was.

As Claranisha Goffner puts it: "Leonard has an old soul."

She would know. They started dating the summer before Fournette entered eighth grade at St. Aug and she entered tenth at Martin Luther King Jr. Charter School. They were boyfriend and girlfriend for more than four years until breaking up early this year.

"Leonard has a very kind heart," Goffner says. "No matter what happens, he's always going to be happy on the outside. He's not going to show any other emotions. He holds his family together. He held *us* together. That's just the way he is. He's a good friend."

There is one other word that quickly surfaces when describing her longtime boyfriend: leader.

"Everyone is so obsessed with Leonard not only because of his football talents, but because of his leadership skills," Goffner says. "He's like a father-figure before he's even a father. He's always making sure everyone else is OK. His cousins. His friends. His teammates. He's just like that with everyone. 'You good? You OK?' He's always checking on everyone else before worrying about himself."

The more Fournette accomplished as a game-changing running back—rushing for 1,735 yards and twenty-two touchdowns as a freshman, then for 1,957 yards and nineteen touchdowns as a sophomore—the more love he got from Louisiana football fans. Even his family motto—Buga no suga—started getting some play with followers of St. Aug football. Most people didn't even know what it meant. They just liked the ring of it and thought it was cool.

Then Fournette and two of his cousins, Reuben Evans and Renard Fournette, had an interesting talk during the summer of 2012. Leonard was by then living in Slidell with his immediate family—residing in a safer, more stable environment than anything he had ever known in the Seventh Ward—so he was commuting to school in New Orleans. During breaks in summer football practice, he would often stay in the city with his cousins—and on this day the three of them were at Reuben's house in New Orleans East.

The discussion started in the garage. With all the exposure Leonard was already getting, Reuben thought he should take the whole *buga no suga* thing and broaden it out to involve more people. Why not? It conveyed a positive message that could benefit anyone. And—thanks to Leonard's rising stardom—so many people were already interested in anything he did. Maybe they could even make some T-shirts with a logo. Reuben enjoyed designing Mardi Gras outfits and other specialty clothes. Why not try this?

They took the conversation inside, the three cousins sitting at the kitchen table and tossing around ideas. It was Renard who first came up with Buga Nation (not all capital letters on *Buga* at the outset because they had not yet made it into an acronym). Renard suggested the use of *Nation* because he thought that would allow the concept to go anywhere. It could be universal.

Leonard listened more than he spoke. He also laughed. He got a kick out of seeing Reuben and Renard so animated about their ideas.

"Me and my cousins, we're like brothers, so we were just having fun with it," Leonard says. "If they wanted to do Buga Nation . . . whatever they wanted to do with it, no problem. We could just have fun with it."

A polished team of corporate marketing executives probably couldn't have created what started that summer day with three young cousins brainstorming in the solitude of a residential garage. Then again, Leonard and his cousins never could have imagined the wild storm of popularity that was coming, either.

Nothing happened right away with Buga Nation. Fournette had more immediate priorities. First on his list was playing his junior season of high school football. He posted his biggest numbers yet—rushing for 2,135 yards and thirty-one touchdowns—and was honored with his biggest award to that point: Louisiana Gatorade Player of the Year.

St. Aug head coach Cyril Crutchfield knew he was working with a once-in-a-career kid. It was not only Fournette's physical attributes—

not only his ability to do so many things on a football field—that made him so special. It was also the way he handled himself. It was his mental approach and his everyday demeanor. "Leonard is a very conscientious young man . . . a student of the game," Crutchfield says. "He has a tremendous work ethic. He has this relentless pursuit to be successful."

College recruiters kept calling. They kept filling his mailbox with letters.

Fournette just kept doing his thing—staying steady in his relentless pursuit.

He also gave more thought to what he and his cousins had talked about. He prepared for the birth of a nation.

When Fournette started making a "B" sign with his fingers and flashing it for all to see—he calls it throwing up B's—most people had no idea what he was doing. The sign was simple: Using either hand, he would make a circle out of the thumb and forefinger while pointing the other three fingers up to form the shaft of a lowercase B. But what did it mean? Why was he doing it?

He would sometimes tell people the B was for Buga Nation—maybe even offering a brief explanation of what that was. Other times he would just allow his personal signature to hang in the air as a mystery. Either way, Fournette kept smiling and laughing about it, clearly enjoying the process of introducing his old family concept to others. Fellow students were soon imitating him. So were St. Aug football fans and others who knew the star of the team. They were all throwing up B's of their own.

Then—as Fournette began his final season of high school football—two ever-growing forces combined to take Buga Nation to a level he had never envisioned. One was the power of the sports platform in America—our national obsession with games and the most talented people who play them. Thanks to the coast-to-coast reach of college recruiting services and the constant escalation of TV and Internet sports coverage, Fournette was already widely known. The other force was social media. People all over the country saw what Fournette was doing and started tweeting photos of themselves throwing up B's. When Fournette retweeted their photos, that encouraged even more people to participate.

With the "population" of Buga Nation rapidly growing, Fournette decided to take another step. He assigned additional meaning to Buga by elevating it to acronym status—all capital letters now (BUGA)—and declaring that the word stood for a positive message of togetherness for all: *Being United Generates Attitude*.

"It's still about being real, which is something everybody can do, something everybody *should* do," Fournette says. "And then it's also about the togetherness of people. It's about the effort you can make when people are all together in something. It's about always sticking together as a family. It's about all those things."

Les Miles had no idea what BUGA Nation was. He had heard Fournette use the term but thought that being BUGA just meant that someone was a "cool dude" from New Orleans. Lack of clarity aside, the coach fully understood that one of the most important players he'd ever recruited had a strong connection to the concept. So he wanted to show his support. At 10:18 the night of December 18, 2013, Miles sent a tweet saying "#Geaux Buga Nation" with three exclamation points to emphasize his enthusiasm.

Fournette was surprised when he saw that. He could hardly believe that someone like Miles—such a high-profile college coach—would put out something like that for a high school kid. Fournette remembers laughing with his mom about that tweet and thinking that the rise of BUGA Nation was getting pretty crazy. He liked that.

For the number-one high school football player in America—so named by ESPN and multiple recruiting services—BUGA was not only a label or a slogan. It was his way of life. Fournette constantly reached out to others and united with them. He consistently lifted attitudes.

There was the time a teammate's mom died and the boy had to miss a game to be with his family. Fournette played the game wearing the boy's number 86 jersey instead of his own number 5.

There was the award he gave away to a player from a rival school. Soon after Fournette and St. Aug were defeated by Archbishop Rummel High School in a Division I semifinal of the 2013 state playoffs—crushing Fournette's state championship dreams and ending his high school career—the Greater New Orleans Quarterback Club named him the city's prep player of the year. When given his award at the club's banquet, however, Fournette immediately presented it to Eugene Wells, the East Jefferson High School quarterback who had led his team to the Class 4A state championship. Wells was understandably stunned—as was everyone else in the crowd. Lory Fournette told her son: "You deserved that award." Leonard's low-key response was short and simple: "So did he."

There was the celebratory assembly he attended at the school that had broken his heart. Fournette had been devastated when the clock hit 0:00 in that state semifinal game and the scoreboard showed Rummel forever ahead 31–28. He took a knee on the field and dropped his head, his eyes leaking, everybody's All-American temporarily transformed into a solitary figure of anguish. Fournette crumbled to the turf and came to a rest on his back—staring silently into the night sky. His emotional fog then carried him somewhere he never would have intentionally gone: off the field of Metairie's Joe Yenni Stadium without first shaking hands to congratulate his opponents. He later felt bad about that. Then he got a chance to show his true self. After Rummel went on to win the Division I state title, the school made plans to honor the team at a big assembly. Rummel president Brother Gale Condit had an unusual idea: Why not invite Fournette and allow him an opportunity to apologize for skipping the customary handshakes? Fournette accepted the invitation and spoke from the heart in a packed gymnasium—both saying he was sorry and sincerely congratulating everyone at the school for its championship. Rummel students and faculty responded with strong applause and a newfound appreciation of Fournette. "What guy would stand up and admit he was wrong in front of a whole student body of another school?" Condit says. "Our students admired him greatly for what he said. I certainly admired him for it. What an example he set for everybody who was there."

There was the night Fournette walked in a Mardi Gras parade—Orpheus—with the renowned St. Aug band known as the Marching 100. The band members had always been so supportive of him and the football team. Now it was his turn to reciprocate. "It was fun!" Fournette says. It was also a bit nutty: people along the parade route constantly shouting his name and cheering for him, countless screams of "BUGA Nation," a steady flow of people running up for handshakes and photos. "Leonard was smiling a lot," says his uncle, Corey Scott, who walked the entire route with him. "I mean, everyone was treating him like a rock star, and he embraced every single person who approached him."

There was the way he encouraged younger students at St. Aug—most notably a group of sixth-graders who first caught his attention one day when they were in trouble for being rambunctious on the way out of an assembly. Two teachers had about sixty boys doing push-ups—outside on the blacktop of the school courtyard—when Fournette happened to walk by. He was curious why the boys were being punished. The teachers, Chad Smith and Sharon Hudson-Neveu, explained what had happened. Then Fournette asked if he could talk to the youngsters about their behavior. He spent a few minutes doing that—stressing to the students that no matter what was going on around them, they always needed to know when to turn off the fun and act right. "They were totally locked in, totally engaged, because these young men idolize Leonard like he's already made it to the NFL," Smith says. "Once he finished speaking, Leonard went around and gave each one of them a firm handshake, and he kept telling them, 'Hope you remember everything I said.'" This was only the beginning. For months after that, Fournette just showed up at Smith's classroom every now and then—unannounced—and knocked on the door to see if he could speak to his students for a few minutes. Fournette talked about the importance of staying organized and showed everyone the binder he used to keep his class assignments in order. He discussed what things would be like for them once they reached high school. He talked about life in general—pretty much anything that was on his mind and might be of use to a room full of sixth-graders.

There was the blood drive for St. Aug students—the one Fournette initially planned to skip because his fear of needles trumped any desire to donate. When he realized that his involvement might encourage other students to participate, Fournette rolled up a sleeve and took a needle for the cause. Most of his peers—more than ninety percent of the students eligible to give blood—ended up doing the same.

There were the hours he spent learning to dance the waltz—then helping a few fellow novices who were still having trouble with it. This started when a cousin, Jacqueline York, then a senior at Warren Easton Charter High School, asked him to be her escort for the school's 2014 cotillion at the Sheraton New Orleans Hotel. Rehearsals were held on Saturday mornings leading up to the event. Edith Carbo, a Warren Easton guidance counselor and coordinator of the ball, knew of Fournette as a highly publicized football star and was initially concerned about whatever ego and attitude he might bring. She feared that working with him would be difficult. "But I was so wrong," she says. "You just don't find too many young guys these days with the manners Leonard has—and especially when it's someone who's gotten so much hype. Leonard is just different. He's such a sweetheart."

As the popularity of BUGA Nation increased—the concept becoming pretty much synonymous with Fournette and his rising fame—his family wanted to protect the term from anyone else who might try to use it for personal gain. With that in mind, Lory Fournette applied for a federal trademark.

Soon thereafter, BUGA Nation enjoyed its biggest breakout moment. It came on January 2 during the Under Armour All-America Game in St. Petersburg, Florida. ESPN televised the game, and it repeatedly promoted the fact that Fournette would announce his college commitment—live on air—during the fourth quarter. With 7:48 left in the game, Fournette caught a pass coming out of the backfield and ran untouched into the end zone for a thirty-six-yard touchdown. He could not have scripted a better lead-in to his widely anticipated announcement.

Fournette walked with his St. Aug coach, Cyril Crutchfield, to a large TV platform overlooking the field. ESPN announcer Dari Nowkhah was waiting there for them. So were Fournette's parents, his brother, Lanard, and a few other family members—all of them wearing BUGA Nation T-shirts and sweatshirts in an assortment of colors. The family attire alone basically made for a free commercial on national television.

Then came the big moment: Who would win the Fournette Sweepstakes? Nowkhah listed LSU, Alabama, and Texas as the finalists (although Fournette would later reveal he had actually narrowed it down to the first two).

Fournette sat in what looked like a director's chair. Everyone else stood around him. After thanking God and his parents, Fournette calmly said he would "take my talent . . . for the next three or four years" to . . .

Leonard Jr.—his dad—held out a plastic bag for him.

Fournette reached into it for the hat representing his choice—announcing "LSU" as he pulled out a purple cap with gold letters on it.

Then all the Fournettes started throwing up B's.

"BUGA Nation, baby!" Leonard Jr. said.

"BUGA Nation, baby!" repeated his brother, Corey Scott.

With B's flying and smiles frozen, the Fournette family was in full glory.

Countless viewers who'd never heard of BUGA Nation could not help but wonder what all the commotion was about. Fournette was soon trending on Twitter. BUGA Nation was blowing up.

Recruiters from other schools still pursued Fournette after he made his oral commitment to LSU. They kept calling and texting him until February 5, which was National Signing Day for high school football players moving on to college ball. St. Aug held a signing ceremony in its gym. Sitting behind a table, wearing a purple-and-gold sweatshirt and hat, Fournette threw up a B with his right hand. Then he used the same hand to sign a letter of intent that officially bound him to LSU. When a television reporter asked him what BUGA Nation meant, he explained what the letters stood for and finished with this: "It's a movement."

People were definitely moved enough to keep throwing up B's and tweet photos of themselves in action—often tagging Fournette so he would see that they were on board. On signing day, LSU President F. King Alexander and Student Government President John Woodard were together in Washington, D.C. Respectably dressed in dark suits, white shirts, and ties for meetings with members of Congress, the visiting presidents took a moment to throw up B's and tweet a photo in celebration of Fournette. "I didn't know what the B was for until John explained it," Alexander says. "But I certainly knew who Leonard was . . . and I was thrilled he signed with us."

Fournette continued retweeting some of his favorite photos.

Five girls from Archbishop Rummel, the school at which Fournette spoke after its football team ended his senior season, throwing up B's while posing with a confused Mickey Mouse during a visit to Disney World. "Mickey ain't got nuthin on Buga," Emily Hickman tweeted along with their photo.

Three members of a state championship football team in Ohio—the Loveland High School Tigers—throwing up B's at their team banquet. "State Champs keepin it Buga up in Ohio," tweeted Jeff Prifti, a junior cornerback who had heard about BUGA Nation and introduced his teammates to it.

Two-year-old Chloe McKenzie, hair wrapped in a green bandanna, her green dress punctuated by a string of SpongeBob beads, throwing up a B—holding it over her right eye—before heading out to a big parade. "Chloe repping #BugaNation on St Pattys day," tweeted her dad, Casey McKenzie, a Baton Rouge insurance agent and dedicated fan of LSU sports.

Five boys throwing up B's while standing in an aisle of a New Orleans church.

Three LSU football fans throwing up B's while scuba diving—about sixty feet down in the water—during their vacation to the Caribbean island of St. Kitts.

An out-of-town group of LSU students—fifteen young men and women in Florida for a fraternity formal—throwing up B's on a beach.

A Baton Rouge youth baseball team—eleven-year-olds—throwing up B's after winning a tournament in Gonzales.

A bunch of tuxedo-wearing boys throwing up B's at a high school prom in Colorado.

Nine hikers proudly displaying their B's while standing high up on a mountain.

There was so much BUGA Nation celebration—so many people throwing up those B's and joining in—that a popular LSU instructor even talked about it in his introductory class on the principles of marketing. Dr. Tommy Karam was that impressed by what he called the "personal branding" of a high school kid. One of the students in the large class, Kelsey Gremillion, tweeted of Fournette: "(H)e ain't even here yet and he already the talk of this school #LSU #BugaNation." Classmate Jacob Hebert tweeted his own assessment of BUGA Nation: "The Movement is real!"

Fournette remains amazed at how quickly BUGA Nation has spread—in awe of the way so many people have so readily embraced the concept. He smiles about that. "We never knew it was going to be like this . . . so big," he says. "I mean, it's kind of worldwide."

Worldwide might be an exaggeration. Neither the open plains of Africa nor the crowded streets of Tokyo have been besieged with the B's of BUGA Nation. But the hype related to Fournette has certainly been real within our own borders—and it has continued to climb off the charts in the football-loving state of Louisiana.

When Fournette graduated from high school on May 21—throwing up B's as he crossed a stage to receive his St. Aug diploma—he had 20,520 followers on Twitter.

When he arrived at LSU for summer school—checking in at the West Campus Apartments on June 6—that alone was defined as news. Local reporters and photographers were there to document the occasion. The next morning's *Baton Rouge Advocate* ran a color photo of Fournette—casually dressed in a black T-shirt, grey shorts, white socks, and Nike sandals—doing nothing more than showing up at his new home.

When *Tiger Rag* featured him on the front of its football preview magazine, the cover design was inspired by an old concert poster promoting Elvis Presley: *The Leonard Fournette Show . . . Starring in Person . . . Leonard Fournette*. "Great Expectations" was the headline of the big story on him, which must have made for an all-time first in sports journalism: Elvis Presley and Charles Dickens being paired up in the coverage of a college football player.

When Fournette finally took to an LSU practice field for his first official session as a Tiger, reporters tweeted away madly, moving in a pack as they breathlessly shared photos and videos of him. Hunter Paniagua, a recruiting analyst for Tiger Sports Digest, included this summary with a photo he took: "The man. The myth. The Buga . . . Leonard Fournette debuts at LSU."

Scott Rabalais of the *Advocate* had a little fun that afternoon with the opening of his column: "Would you believe that Leonard Fournette parted the Mississippi on Monday and walked across its dry river bottom on the way to his first LSU football practice? Or that he leaped over linebackers at said practice in a single bound? Or even that he killed him a bear when he was only three?" Rabalais also assigned a new moniker to the freshman sensation: His Leonardness.

All of this was in advance of a new documentary soon to premiere on New Orleans Public Television—*Road to Stardom: The Leonard Fournette Story*. When was the last time a film had been made about a college football player before he'd even played any college football?

It is no wonder that some of his new teammates enjoy teasing him about all the attention. "Oh, my God, it's Leonard!" they'll practically squeal with feigned excitement. Fournette just laughs when they do that. Cornerback Rashard Robinson playfully calls him "Superstar" and wanted to take a selfie with him. Fournette will make a big play or a flashy move in practice, showing a glimpse of greatness, and the two players he already calls his "big brothers"—senior running backs

Terrence Magee and Kenny Hilliard—start right in on him: *BUGA Nation! I see you, BUGA Nation!* "Just to mess with him," Magee says. "It's all in fun."

Sports information director Michael Bonnette has seen a lot of highly publicized athletes come and go in his twenty-one years with the LSU athletic department. He has seen nothing like the exposure Fournette and BUGA Nation have already gotten.

"Leonard Fournette steps on campus as the most well-known athlete we've ever had," Bonnette says. "I'm not saying he's the best athlete we've ever had. I'm not saying that he's going to *be* the best athlete. I'm talking about the situation that comes with the day we live in. With the Internet and social media—just because of that reach that now exists—Leonard is already better known than any other athlete we've ever had."

With that in mind, the crowd still surrounding Fournette at media day actually seems to make sense. Exposure leads to more exposure. Hype leads to more hype. So the questions—no matter how redundant or inane—just keep coming.

Leonard, your first touchdown in Tiger Stadium, how much have you thought about that?

Is it tough for you to insulate yourself from all the hype and expectations?

How would you describe yourself, as a running back, to somebody who has never seen you and has just heard all this stuff about Leonard Fournette?

The singular moment of the day comes late in the media session when most of the real reporters have finished with Fournette and a faux journalist steps up with questions. It is actually LSU kicker Colby Delahoussaye. Accompanied by punter Jamie Keehn, long snapper Logan Boudreaux, and defensive tackle Maquedius Bain, Delahoussaye playfully introduces himself as a radio reporter and pretends to record the proceedings with his phone. After some initial talk about special teams,

Delahoussaye abruptly shifts gears and hits Fournette with a critical question: "Pancakes or waffles?"

"Pancakes," Fournette says.

"OK, syrup or no syrup?" Delahoussaye says.

"Syrup!"

"OK, what kind of syrup?"

"Uh, the original."

"Is that maple or cane?"

"Maple."

"Now, is that sugar or no sugar?"

"Sugar!"

"Corn starch or no corn starch?"

"Corn starch!" Now Fournette can no longer contain himself. He is laughing out loud—at the absurdity of this individual scene, yes, but also because he understands the bigger picture of what Delahoussaye is doing. He is poking fun at the entirety of the media frenzy surrounding Fournette.

"OK, all right, thank you," Delahoussaye says. "Thank you, Mr. Leonard."

There are laughs all around. Then running back Melvin Jones—standing nearby and taking it all in—does the only thing that makes sense at a time like this. Facing Fournette, he throws up a B.

Leonard Fournette set the LSU record for rushing yards by a freshman (1,034) and led the 2014 team with eleven touchdowns (ten rushing and one on a kick return). He led the entire Southeastern Conference in all-purpose yards per game (137.4). Fournette was named a freshman All-American by the Football Writers Association of America.

BACK STORIES

When I finished walking, I decided to include two additional stories in this collection: one from another book I wrote (*The Long Snapper*) and one by former LSU football player John Ed Bradley.

The Long Snapper

He never really liked the idea of keeping his cell phone on while teaching. He certainly would not tolerate such behavior from the seventh-graders in his Bible class at Parkview Baptist Middle School in Baton Rouge, especially not now, while reviewing for the end-of-semester final exam that was only two days away. But Brian Kinchen had a wife and four young sons. He could not imagine being unreachable in an emergency. The phone was tucked away, on silent, in the front left pocket of his slacks, when he felt it vibrate at 9:20 the morning of Monday, December 15, 2003. The little screen showed an unfamiliar out-of-state number.

"Hello?"

"Hey, Brian, it's Scott Pioli."

An old friend from a previous existence.

Kinchen was an ex-jock. At the age of thirty-eight, after thirteen years of professional football and almost three years of searching for whatever might be next, he was new to teaching. He and Pioli were friends from their long-ago days together with the Cleveland Browns—Kinchen when he was a young player doing everything he could to keep his spot on the roster, Pioli when he was a young personnel assistant trying to move his way up in the front office. Pioli still worked in the NFL but now operated on a whole different level. As vice president of player personnel for the New England Patriots, he was one of the most respected executives in the league, working closely with head coach Bill Belichick, who was on his way to becoming the NFL's winningest coach of the decade. Together they had orchestrated the franchise's first Super Bowl victory after the 2001 season. And now—with only two weeks left in the 2003 regular season—the Patriots were well positioned for another championship run.

Kinchen and Pioli had not spoken for nearly a year. *Why this out-of-nowhere call at a time when his schedule has to be crazy?* Kinchen wondered. *Must be about that hat I asked him to have Belichick sign for that lady I met.* After the obligatory small talk, Kinchen cut to the chase: "Hey, man, where's my hat? I never got the hat."

Pioli had an entirely different agenda.

"Listen," he said. "You're not gonna believe this, Brian, but we need to get a look at you. Bill wants to get a look at you."

Kinchen was familiar enough with football-speak to know exactly what that meant. His old coach—Belichick had been head coach in Cleveland when Kinchen and Pioli were there—wanted to fly him into Boston for a tryout. Kinchen was absolutely stunned. He paced in front of his class.

"You're serious?"

"Our long snapper got hurt," Pioli said.

Most of the two dozen students were distracted from working on their review material, trying to figure out what in the world their teacher was dealing with on the phone.

"I'm thirty-eight years old," Kinchen said.

Pioli already knew that, of course, but Kinchen was only thinking out loud. "You realize how long it's been since I've played football? I mean, I still work out, just went to the gym before school this morning, but I'm probably down about twenty pounds from the end of my career."

Kinchen stood almost six-foot-three and now weighed less than 220, big for everyday life, but not for someone banging heads with defensive linemen in the NFL.

"Not a problem," Pioli said. "We just need you to snap. We don't need you to block. Don't need you to cover. Just snap. Just get the ball back there."

"Really?"

"Wouldn't be calling if I didn't mean it."

Kinchen was excited but also wary. Those painful memories he'd been trying to push away—the indignity of rejection and the empty feeling of worthlessness—came rushing back, once again washing all over him. What to do? What to tell his friend?

"I really don't know if I want to do this," Kinchen said. "I'll have to think about it. Can you give me a couple hours?"

"I'll call you back," Pioli said.

The teacher turned to his curious students and took in a deep breath. Gathering himself as best he could, Kinchen said, "You guys are not gonna believe who that was. This guy from the New England Patriots, Scott Pioli, he wants me to fly up there and try to make the team. He wants me to play football again."

It is not often that a Bible class turns into a free-for-all. Students shouted and cheered, so many voices competing for attention that Kinchen could not immediately make out the particulars of what anyone was saying. All that registered was the overall excitement emanating even from those who did not have a clue about football. But then came a voice of clarity through the cacophony. It belonged to a boy in the back of the classroom: "The Patriots have the best record in the league. Everyone's picking them to win it all this year." That was an overstatement; not everyone was picking the Patriots. But New England was indeed projected to be one of the strong favorites heading into the playoffs. The Patriots had won twelve of fourteen games—including their last ten in a row—and were tied with the Kansas City Chiefs for the best record in the NFL. Kinchen had no idea about any of that. He had not been paying much attention to professional football. Turning his back on the game he loved was the only way he could deal with its having unceremoniously dumped him after all those years.

"What do y'all think?" Kinchen asked.

"Awesome," one of the girls shouted.

"You gotta go," one of the boys said.

Then came a chorus of concurrence.

"Yeah, go, Mr. Kinchen."

"You have to. You have to."

Kinchen settled everyone down and shared an idea. He would take a vote: "Raise your hand if you think I should go." There was no need to count. Every student—boys and girls—had at least one hand up. Some were enthusiastically stabbing the air with both hands. The vote was unanimous. And the students erupted again.

"We'll watch you on TV," one of the boys blurted out. "How cool is that?"

If only it were that simple for Kinchen. Of course, none of the kids knew about the ugly ending and the string of rejections he had already endured. Kinchen had not only been a long snapper in the NFL. He had been a decent tight end as well, gaining recognition primarily for his blocking and tenacity, but also catching as many as fifty-five passes in a single season, 1996, while playing for the Baltimore Ravens. The apparent end to his playing career came four years later with the Carolina Panthers, after a knee injury and months of clinging to the false hope that his job would still be there for him the next year. Instead, after surgery and rehabilitation, Kinchen was cut loose. For a while, he remained optimistic about catching on with another team. But nobody called. Kinchen was crushed.

Professional athletes almost uniformly voice the desire to retire "on their own terms," a vague and shifting goal that is rarely realized. And they are often filled with regret and separation anxiety when closure does not come so neatly wrapped. Kinchen was by no means the first to struggle upon departure from the high-profile world of professional sports. Back in his hometown of Baton Rouge, where he had attended LSU, he certainly enjoyed the extra time with his family and the practically endless freedom to play golf. But Kinchen missed the intensity of the NFL and the camaraderie of teammates. He missed having a schedule and a specific purpose every day. He became depressed. And that was before the onslaught of disappointments.

His second year out of football, 2002, Kinchen decided that he would no longer sit around waiting for someone to invite him back into the NFL. He would start calling people himself. So what if his thirty-seventh birthday would arrive before the start of the season? Surely someone could use a long snapper who had been steady and dependable for thirteen years as a professional. So he started reaching out to people he knew.

The first thread of hope was extended by a former college teammate who was now working in player personnel for the Dallas Cowboys. Toward the end of summer training camp, right after their long snapper had struggled in a preseason game, the Cowboys invited Kinchen in for a tryout. He thought he snapped as well as he ever had. The *Dallas Morning News* even reported that the Cowboys were expected to sign him. But they decided to go with a younger player, and Kinchen was sent home without so much as a hello or goodbye from head coach Dave Campo.

A few weeks later, Kinchen got another shot, this time with the Pittsburgh Steelers. Their long snapper, Mike Schneck, was expected to miss six weeks with a dislocated elbow, and their special-teams coach, Kevin Spencer, had started his NFL coaching career in Cleveland while

Kinchen was playing with the Browns. Kinchen's confidence was further bolstered by the fact that he'd played for three other Pittsburgh assistants either in college or in the NFL. That only made the outcome all the more frustrating. After throwing what he considered perfect strikes in his tryout and thinking the job was his, Kinchen was offered nothing but a ride back to the airport. Once again, he had not even been allowed an audience with the head coach. Having been told that Bill Cowher was "in meetings" and too busy to see him, Kinchen seethed the whole way home. After all those years in the NFL, he thought that he should be treated with at least some degree of respect. He was devastated by the Pittsburgh trip.

One more blow was yet to come. Midway through the 2002 season, the Denver Broncos were looking strong after winning six of eight games. Less than thrilled with the play of his kicking teams, however, head coach Mike Shanahan wanted to make a few changes. He was in the market for a new long snapper. Kinchen knew Shanahan and again thought he had a reasonable chance of being signed. He was invited to Denver for a tryout. He felt that his snaps were flawless. Then—without explanation and without ever seeing Shanahan—he was again passed over for a younger guy. Was it simply a matter of opting for youth? Was Kinchen considered too risky because of his less-than-perfect knee? Did league salary rules—his thirteen years of NFL service dictating that he'd have to be paid considerably more than a newcomer—have anything to do with it?

"I don't know what the deal is," Kinchen told his wife, Lori, on the phone. "But I'm not putting myself through this anymore. Too much of an emotional roller coaster. I'm done."

It was not until the flight home that both the reality and the finality of that really hit him. His dejection stemmed not only from the worthlessness he felt after going zero-for-three in tryouts or from the absolute belief that he was unmistakably done this time. No, Kinchen struggled with something much bigger and broader and more debilitating than that—a blindness. It was simply impossible to see himself the way almost anyone else would view him: as a highly successful athlete who had parlayed his Hercules-like build and considerable abilities into a remarkably long (for football) and prosperous career. It was impossible because—after all the dreaming and the training and the stretching of limits and the sacrifices—Kinchen could see only one word hanging over the entirety of his efforts: *failure*. All he'd ever wanted was to establish himself as an impact player, someone who would long be remembered and who might even accomplish something worthy of mention in the football history books. The mere thought of that desire now brought such discomfort and sorrow. Kinchen had a beautiful wife and four healthy children waiting for him at home. He had a profound spiritual grounding that had guided him and served him well for as long as he could remember. Yet there was nothing he could do on that plane to shake that one word—*failure*, *failure*, *failure*—and the depth of hurt that it triggered.

The thoughts kept taunting him: *I was just another guy who wore a jersey. Nothing really spectacular ever happened in my career. All I ever did was try to legitimize myself. But now I'll never get what I've always wanted, what I've always* needed. *I'll never have that stamp of approval that I really made it. No validation. No finality on my own terms.*

Speaking for the broad universe of professional athletes, Hall of Fame quarterback Steve Young describes retirement from the NFL as the emotional equivalent of falling off a cliff. "You're at the top of your field, and then suddenly you're done," he says. "I was great at football, but I haven't been that great at anything since. And once that sinks in, that realization is really hard."

Kinchen had done the best he could to pack away the emotional residue left from his fall off the cliff. And teaching seemed to be the right "next thing" for him. He truly felt he was employing his talents exactly as God intended. And he had even found several avocations—coaching middle school football at Parkview, helping the LSU football staff as a volunteer assistant, playing celebrity golf tournaments all over the country—that again allowed him to enjoy all that was good in sports. Now, though, he was flooded with confusion and doubt. Sure, he felt a lift from the blind affirmation enthusiastically offered by his students when he explained the phone call from the Patriots. He also felt a jolt of hope that perhaps there was still something left of his football career, maybe even the defining moment that had always somehow eluded him. But then there was the dread: *What if I'm just being set up for yet another letdown? If I really found what I'm supposed to be doing, teaching, then how can I justify just picking up and taking off from school simply because some football team needs a long snapper, just because* I *might deep inside be starving for one final shot at the NFL?*

His students would have been stunned had they known the turmoil that churned inside him. After all, he was always big, strong, confident Mr. Kinchen to them, Coach Kinchen to some, a former professional athlete whose exterior walls were built with layer upon layer of absolute certainty. The boys who were into sports thought he was just about the coolest guy they'd ever known. The girls focused on his rugged good looks—the overall build, the chiseled face with pronounced chin and well-defined jaw lines, the hazel eyes and thick brown hair, the radiant smile. But physical shell and emotional façade meant nothing now. Kinchen felt extremely vulnerable.

He called his wife, who was only a building away. Lori often worked as a substitute teacher at Parkview and had also been coaching fifth- and sixth-grade cheerleading. She happened to be teaching that morning in the elementary school.

"You'll never guess who called me," Brian said.

"Who?"

"Scott Pioli. They want me to go to New England."

"To coach?" Lori said.

"No, to *play*."

"Shut up, Brian. There's no way."

He offered details and convinced her that he was telling the truth. Then the conversation turned to making a decision. Brian explained that Pioli would be calling back shortly and wanted him at the airport as soon as possible.

"I really don't think I want to go," Brian told his wife. "I just don't want to deal with the rejection again."

"Well, what about living the rest of your life wondering what might have happened?" Lori replied. "I mean, let's say you go and then they don't sign you. At least you tried. It's a lot easier to live with something you at least tried than to live with the regret that you didn't even give it a chance. If you don't go, you'll have to live with that regret your whole life."

"True. I guess I need to think about that."

"The worst thing that happens is you're gone for a couple days. Maybe they'll let me take your classes for you. I already know most of the kids. It wouldn't be that big a deal."

"No."

"And then if the Patriots end up signing you and you're up there for a while, with Christmas break coming, you wouldn't even be missing that much school."

Brian paused. Then he said, "Let's talk again in a little while. I want to go get a football and see what it feels like."

By this point, the students had a pretty good feel for their first-year teacher. They knew that Kinchen was unmistakably serious when it came to the understanding of Bible stories and concepts, but they also appreciated that he consistently tried to foster a fairly light atmosphere in the classroom. The first day of school he had been asked by one of the students what they were supposed to call him. This was a somewhat confusing matter because many of the kids had already known him before he started teaching. He had coached some of the boys in football. His wife had coached some of the girls in cheerleading. And some of the kids had long been friends with his two oldest sons: Austin was now in eighth grade, and Hunter was in sixth. "Okay, we have a few choices," Kinchen told his first class. "You can call me Mr. Kinchen, Mr. Brian, Coach Kinchen . . . or Professor." Everyone laughed. "Yeah, I like the sound of that," Kinchen said, with mock seriousness. "*Professor*. Really stuffy, formal guy. That's me." It was so *not* him that some of the students got a kick out of calling him that and still did sometimes.

Even knowing Kinchen the way they did, they were still surprised when he announced that they were taking a break from reviewing for the final exam. He was going to get a football from the athletic department, and they were all going outside so he could show them what a long snapper does. Actually, Kinchen also had another reason—the one he'd shared with Lori—that he wanted to get his hands on a football. Before hearing back from Pioli, he wanted to be certain that he could still throw it between his legs with the same power and precision that had always come so easily to him. Kinchen had no reason to think it would be a problem, but he wanted to make sure. Fortunately, he was in a climate that would comfortably allow for a spontaneous class outing in the middle of December. The sky was clear, and the temperature was fifty-three degrees.

Kinchen led his students outside to an open stretch of grass, dirt, and gravel between their two-story brick school building and the collection of swings, slides, and climbing apparatus that filled the playground. He marked off fifteen yards and explained the measurement to those who didn't know what it represented: the distance a long snapper typically throws the football from the line of scrimmage—where a play begins—to a punter who will kick the ball away to the other team.

"Come catch some for me," Kinchen said to one of his students, Wesley Perkins, who was one of the better football players in the seventh grade.

Kinchen stretched his arms and shoulders. Standing upright, he threw a few passes—just as a quarterback would—to make sure he was loose. Then he tugged at his dress slacks for better mobility and bent forward toward the ground. He gripped the football with both hands and stared back through his legs at Wesley's outstretched hands.

"Ready?" Kinchen asked in an upside-down shout.

"Ready," Wesley said.

Kinchen fired away and . . . *thwack* . . . Wesley felt the hard leather and unforgiving laces of the football violate the soft skin of his palms.

"Wow," Wesley said.

The other students oohed and aahed. None of them had any idea that the ball would be zipping so fast through the air. The average NFL snapper requires between seven- and eight-tenths of a second to cover the fifteen yards from his grip to the hands of a punter.

"How was the spiral?" Kinchen wanted to know.

"Perfect," Wesley said.

"Let's do it again."

Wesley caught close to a dozen snaps.

"Where was it?" Kinchen asked after each.

"Right down the middle," Wesley kept reporting. Only once did a snap move slightly off center. But then the next one was right on target again.

"Spiral was good?" Kinchen said.

"Better than my passes!" Wesley answered.

Other students stepped in to try catching a snap or two. A couple of the boys were able to hold on. None of the girls had much success, usually just knocking the ball down or even jumping out of the way before it reached them, but they had no problem screaming and laughing and playfully wrapping themselves in the excitement of it all. After a while, four girls decided that they would stand together—one big target—and that one of them would somehow come up with a catch. "We're getting it this time," Ashley Thornton said. But when Kinchen let loose of the football, one of the other girls simply swatted it to the ground and they all went right back to giggling.

Kinchen still had work to do. He cut the distance almost in half, marking a spot about seven and three-quarters yards away, right where he would want a holder positioned to catch and place the ball for a kicker to attempt a field goal or an extra point after a touchdown. Wesley got down on a knee and held out a hand for Kinchen to target.

Thwack. Thwack. Thwack.

With a shorter distance to travel, the ball was coming in even harder now. Lower and harder. Right on target.

Pretty amazing, Wesley thought. *Does he ever miss?*

When the bell rang to signal the end of class, Kinchen's students returned to the normal flow of their school day, gathering up books and knapsacks, scurrying off to their next classes. Kinchen stayed behind for a few moments, staring at the ground, pondering his predicament: *I want to submit to God's plan, but what is it? I thought I was supposed to be here at the school, and I made a commitment to teaching. But now am I supposed to go?* Kinchen silently asked for help: *Please, Lord, give me some kind of clarity.*

Kinchen soon found that clarity in the form of encouragement from others. He spoke to his dad on the telephone. He called an old LSU teammate—Tommy Hodson, one of his best friends from college—who had gone on to play quarterback for the Patriots in the early 1990s. He visited with the school principal, Cooper Pope. Their responses were all similar: "What a great opportunity. What are you even thinking about?" When Kinchen explained to Pope that he was struggling with the thought of breaking his commitment to the school, the principal encouraged him not to look at it that way. "It's a no-brainer," Pope said. "This is something you need to do. You gotta go play if you can. And, no matter what happens, the experience will serve the school and the kids well. This might be a God-created opportunity for you to go do something and then bring it back to share with the kids." That made Kinchen feel better. By the time he was done processing, he was certain he had to go for the tryout. He was also sorry he had ever asked Pioli for time to think about it: *What if he's already found someone else while he's waiting to call me back?*

Kinchen had two more classes before lunch. He opened each with an explanation of what was happening with the Patriots. Then he did the best he could to concentrate on reviewing. Really, though, all he was doing was waiting for his cell phone to ring. When it finally did, he was relieved to see Pioli's number on the screen.

Kinchen had a question for him: "Is there any way you can guarantee that I'm actually gonna get the job?"

"Can't promise you anything," Pioli said. "You know how it works."

"Yeah, I understand," Kinchen said. "But you can at least promise me I'm gonna see Belichick, right? I mean, if I'm going all the way up there, I am *not* leaving without at least a 'hello' from the guy."

After those three painful tryouts the year before, three straight rejections without even seeing the head coaches, Kinchen was doing emotional damage control.

"Not a problem," Pioli said. "You'll definitely see Bill. You have my word on that."

"Good," Kinchen said. "So what do I need to do?"

Pioli put an assistant on the line to discuss travel plans. Only a few days after sitting at a computer and putting together the final exam for his seventh-grade Bible students, formulating questions about miracles and morality and free will, Kinchen now had all of about three hours before he had to be at the airport.

After making final arrangements with school administrators—Lori would indeed handle his classes while he was gone—Kinchen went home for toiletries and a change of clothes. That was it: just one day's worth of essentials. If he ended up signing with the Patriots, Lori would ship more clothes to him. But there was no reason to get ahead of himself. He and his family had been around football plenty long enough—three generations' worth of blocking and tackling and life-changing drama—to know that virtually anything could happen.

Brian Kinchen signed with the Patriots the next day. Seven weeks later, he was the oldest player in Super Bowl XXXVIII. With nine seconds left on the clock, he snapped the ball on Adam Vinatieri's game-winning field goal as the Patriots defeated the Carolina Panthers 32–29. After the victory parade in Boston, Kinchen returned to his job as a seventh-grade teacher—proud owner of both a championship ring and one of the most improbable stories in Super Bowl history. He and his family still live in Baton Rouge.

The Best Years of His Life

By John Ed Bradley

It ends for everybody. It ends for the pro who makes $5 million a year and has his face on magazine covers and his name in the record books. It ends for the kid on the high school team who never comes off the bench except to congratulate his teammates as they file past him on their way to the Gatorade bucket.

In my case it ended on Dec. 22, 1979, at the Tangerine Bowl in Orlando. We beat Wake Forest that night 34–10, in a game I barely remember but for the fact that it was my last one. When it was over, a teammate and I grabbed our heroic old coach, hoisted him on our shoulders and carried him out to the midfield crest. It was ending that day for Charles McClendon, too, after 18 years as head coach at LSU and a superb 69% career winning percentage. The next day newspapers would run photos of Coach Mac's last victory ride, with Big Eddie Stanton and me, smeared with mud, serving as his chariot. Coach had a hand raised above his head as he waved goodbye, but it would strike me that his expression showed little joy at all. He looked tired and sad. More than anything, though, he looked like he didn't want it to end.

We were quiet on the flight back to Baton Rouge, and when the plane touched down at Ryan Field, no cheers went up and nobody said anything. A week or so later, done with the Christmas holidays, I went to Tiger Stadium to clean out my locker. I brought a big travel bag with me, and I stuffed it with pads, shoes, gym trunks, jockstraps, T-shirts and practice jerseys. I removed my nametag from the locker. Then I studied the purple stenciling against the gold matte. In one corner someone had scribbled the words TRAMPLE THE DEAD, HURDLE THE WEAK. The source of the legend eludes me now, but it had been a rallying cry for the team that year, especially for my mates on the offensive line.

The last thing I packed was my helmet. I'd been an offensive center, and the helmet's back and sides were covered with the little Tigers decals the coaches had given out as merit badges for big plays. I ran my fingertips over the surface, feeling the scars in the hard plastic crown. There were paint smudges and streaks from helmets I'd butted over the years. Was the gold Vanderbilt or Florida State? The red Alabama or Georgia, Indiana or USC?

When I finished packing, I walked down the chute that led to the playing field, pushed open the big metal door and squinted against the sudden blast of sunlight. I meant to have one last look at the old stadium where I'd played the last four years. Death Valley was quiet now under a blue winter sky. I could point to virtually any spot on the field and tell you about some incident that had happened there. I knew where teammates had blown out knees, dropped passes, made key blocks and tackles, thrown interceptions and recovered game-saving fumbles. I knew where we'd vomited in spring scrimmages under a brutal Louisiana sun and where we'd celebrated on autumn Saturday nights to the roar of maniacal Tigers fans and the roar of a real tiger, Mike IV, prowling in a cage on the sideline. We'd performed to a full house at most every home game, the crowds routinely in excess of 75,000, but today there was no one in sight, the bleachers running in silver ribbons around the gray cement bowl. It seemed the loneliest place on earth.

I was only 21 years old, yet I believed that nothing I did for the rest of my life would rise up to those days when I wore the Purple and Gold. I might go on to a satisfying career and make a lot of money, I might marry a beautiful woman and fill a house with perfect kids, I might make a mark that would be of some significance in other people's eyes. But I would never have it better than when I was playing football for LSU.

Despite this belief, I was determined to walk away from that place and that life and never look back. You wouldn't catch me 20 years later crowing about how it had been back in the day, when as a college kid I'd heard the cheers. I knew the type who couldn't give it up, and I didn't want to be him. He keeps going to the games and reminding anyone who'll listen of how things used to be. His wife and kids roll their eyes as he describes big plays, quotes from halftime speeches and embellishes a "career" that no one else seems to remember with any specificity. He stalks the memory until the memory reduces him to pathetic self-parody. To listen to him, he never screwed up a snap count or busted an assignment or had a coach berate him for dogging it or getting beat. In his mind he is forever young, forever strong, forever golden.

Standing there in Tiger Stadium, I squeezed my eyes closed and lowered my head. Then I wept.

Hell no, I said to myself. That wasn't going to be me.

I still remember their names and hometowns. And I can tell you, almost to a man, the high schools they went to. I remember how tall they were and how much they weighed. I remember their strengths and weaknesses, both as men and as football players. I remember the kinds of cars they drove, what religions they practiced, the music they favored, the hair color of their girlfriends, how many letters they earned, their injuries, their dreams, their times in the 40-yard dash. In many instances I remember their jersey numbers. On the day last August that I turned 43, I wondered what happened to Robert DeLee. DeLee, a tight end from the small town of Clinton, La., wore number 43 on his jersey when I was a senior. During my freshman year a running back named

Jack Clark had worn the number. Jack Clark, too, I thought to myself—where on earth has he slipped off to? I had seen neither of them in more than two decades.

That was the case with almost all of my teammates. Last summer I attended a wedding reception for Barry Rubin, a former fullback at LSU who is a strength coach with the Green Bay Packers. It had been about eight years since I'd last had a face-to-face conversation with a teammate, and even that meeting had come purely by chance. One day I was waiting in the checkout line at a store in suburban New Orleans when someone standing behind me called out my name. I wheeled around, and there stood Charlie McDuff, an ex-offensive tackle who'd arrived at LSU at the same time I did, as a member of the celebrated 1976 freshman class. A couple of shoppers separated Charlie and me, and I couldn't reach past them to shake his hand. "How are things going?" he said.

"Things are good," I said. "How 'bout with you?"

I felt uncomfortable seeing him again, even though we'd always gotten along well back in school. The media guide had listed him at 6' 6" and 263 pounds, but in actual fact he was a shade taller and closer to 275. Even after all these years away from the game he had a bull neck and arms thick with muscle. His hair was as sun-bleached as ever, his skin as darkly tanned.

I paid what I owed and started to leave. Then I turned back around and looked at him again. "You ever see anybody anymore, Charlie?" I said.

"Yeah. Sure, I see them. Some of them. You?"

"Not really."

He nodded as if he understood, and we parted without saying anything more, and two years later Charlie McDuff was dead. My sister called, crying with the news. Charlie had suffered a pulmonary embolism while vacationing with his family at a Gulf Coast resort. He left behind a wife and three young sons. I wanted to call someone and talk about him, and I knew it had to be a player, one of our teammates, and preferably an offensive lineman. But I couldn't do it, I couldn't make the call. Nobody wanted to remember anymore, I tried to convince myself. It was too long ago. So instead I pulled some cardboard boxes out of a closet and went through them. There were trophies and plaques wrapped in paper, letters tied with kite string, a short stack of souvenir programs and a couple of plastic-bound photo albums crowded with news clippings and yellowing images of boys who actually were capable of dying. If Charlie McDuff could die, it occurred to me, we all could.

At the bottom of the box I found a worn, gray T-shirt with purple lettering that said NOBODY WORKS HARDER THAN THE OFFENSIVE LINE. Charlie had had that shirt made, along with about a dozen others, and handed them out to the linemen on the '79 squad. The year before, we'd lost some outstanding players to graduation, and Charlie had hoped the shirts would inspire us to pull together as a unit. We wore the shirts at every opportunity, generally under our shoulder pads at practice and games. It seems crazy now, but there was a time when I considered stipulating in my will that I be buried in that ratty thing. I was never more proud than when I had it on.

I learned about Charlie's funeral arrangements, and I got dressed intending to go. I started down the road for Baton Rouge, rehearsing the lines I'd speak to his widow and children, and those I'd tell my old teammates to explain why I didn't come around anymore. I drove as far as the outskirts of Baton Rouge before turning around and heading back home.

Are there others out there like me? I've often wondered. Does the loss of a game they played in their youth haunt them as it's haunted me? Do others wake up from afternoon naps and bolt for the door, certain that they're late for practice even though their last practice was half a lifetime ago? My nightmares don't contain images of monsters or plane crashes or Boo Radley hiding behind the bedroom door. Mine have me jumping offside or muffing the center-quarterback exchange. They have me forgetting where I placed my helmet when the defense is coming off the field and it's time for me to go back in the game.

If it really ends, I wonder, then why doesn't it just end?

I suppose I was doomed from the start, having been sired by a Louisiana high school football coach. The year of my birth, 1958, was the same year LSU won its one and only national championship in football, and the month of my birth, August, was when two-a-day practices began for that season. Although my parents couldn't afford to take their five kids to the LSU games, we always listened to the radio broadcasts, usually while my father was outside barbecuing on the patio. He'd sit there in a lawn chair, lost in concentration, a purple-and-gold cap tipped back on his head. Not far away on the lawn I acted out big plays with friends from the neighborhood, some of us dressed in little Tigers uniforms. We played in the dark until someone ran into a tree or a clothesline and got hurt, then my dad would have me sit next to him and listen to the rest of the game, the real one. "Settle down now," I remember him saying. "LSU's on."

When I was a kid I always gave the same answer to adults who asked me what I wanted to be when I grew up. "I want to play football for LSU," I answered. Beyond that I had no clear picture of myself.

Nor could I fathom a future without the game when it ended for me 23 years ago. One day I was on the team, the next I was a guy with a pile of memories and a feeling in his gut that his best days were behind him. I shuffled around in my purple letter jacket wondering what to do with myself, and wondering who I was. Suddenly there were no afternoon workouts or meetings to attend. I didn't have to visit the training room for whirlpool or hot-wax baths or ultrasound treatments or massages or complicated ankle tapings or shots to kill the never-ending pain. If I wanted to, I could sit in a Tigerland bar and get drunk without fear of being booted from the team; I didn't have a team anymore. Every day for four years I'd stepped on a scale and recorded my weight on a chart for the coaches. But no one cared any longer how thin I got, or how fat.

That last year I served as captain of the offense, and either by some miracle or by a rigged ballot I was named to the second team All-Southeastern Conference squad. The first-team player, Alabama's Dwight Stephenson, went on to become a star with the Miami Dolphins and a member of the Pro Football Hall of Fame, and I'd seen enough film of the guy to know I was nowhere in his league. At the end of April, in the hours after the 1980 NFL draft, a scout for the Dallas Cowboys called and asked me to consider signing with the club as a free agent, but by then I'd already shed 30 pounds along with any notion of myself as an athlete. I gave some excuse and hung up. "You don't even want to try?" my father said.

I could've yelled at him for asking, but there was genuine compassion in his eyes. He and my mother were losing something, too. One of their sons had played football for LSU, and where I come from nothing topped that. "It's over," I said.

My father nodded and walked away.

Number 50 was Jay Whitley, the pride of Baton Rouge's Lee High. Fifty-one was Lou DeLaunay, then Albert Richardson; 52, Kevin Lair, then Leigh Shepard; 53, Steve Estes and Jim Holsombake; 54, Rocky Guillot. Fifty-five was linebacker S.J. Saia; then after my freshman year the number went to Marty Dufrene, probably the toughest offensive lineman ever to come out of Lafourche Parish. My number was 56. When we left the stadium after games, fans were waiting outside under the streetlamps, some of them with programs and slips of paper to sign.

Even a lowly offensive lineman was asked for an autograph. "Number 56 in your program, Number 1 in your heart," I'd write, disgracing myself for all eternity but way too ignorant at the time to know it.

I don't recall how I first learned about what happened to Marty. Maybe it was from a news story about efforts to raise money to help pay his medical bills. Or maybe it was another tearful call from a relative. But one day I found myself punching numbers on a telephone keypad, desperate to talk to him again. Marty was living in LaRose, his hometown in the heart of Cajun country, or "down the bayou," as the natives like to say. His wife, Lynne, answered. "Lynne, do you remember me?" I said, after introducing myself.

"Yes, I remember you," she answered. "You want to talk to Marty? Hold on, John Ed. It's going to take a few minutes, because I have to put him on the speakerphone."

A speakerphone? When he finally came on he sounded as though he was trapped at the bottom of a well.

"Marty, is it true you got hurt?" I said.

"Yeah," he said.

"You're paralyzed, man?"

"Yeah," he said, raising his voice to make sure I could hear. "I broke my neck. Can you believe it?"

It had happened in July 1986, some five years before my call. While in his second year of studies at a chiropractic college then based in Irving, Texas, Marty was injured in a freak accident at a pool party to welcome the incoming freshman class. He and friends were horsing around when a pair of them decided to bring big, strong Marty down. One held him in a headlock, the other took a running start and plowed into him. Marty smashed through the water's surface of a shallow children's pool and struck his head on the bottom, shattering a vertebra. He floated in the water, unable to move or feel anything from his neck down, until his friends pulled him out.

As he told me about the accident I kept flashing back to the kid I'd known in school. Marty had been a lean, powerfully built 6' 2" and 235 pounds, small by today's standards but about average for a center in our era. On the field he'd played with a kind of swagger, as if certain that he could dominate his opponent. The swagger extended to his life off the field. Marty liked to have a good time. He spoke with a heavy Cajun accent, the kind of accent that made girls crazy and immediately identified him as a pure Louisiana thoroughbred. Football schools from the Midwest featured humongous linemen brought up on corn and prime beef. At LSU we had guys like Marty, raised on crawfish from the mud flats and seafood from the Gulf of Mexico.

The son of an offshore oil field worker, Marty was an all-state high school center in 1976. He was a highly recruited blue-chipper coming out of South Lafourche High, just as I had been at Opelousas High the year before. Marty had vacillated between committing to West Point and to LSU before he realized there really was only one choice for him. Air Force was the military academy that had tried to lure me before I snapped out of it and understood what my destiny was.

The only problem I'd ever had with Marty Dufrene was that we played the same position, and he wanted my job. Going into my senior year I was listed on the first team, Marty on the second. One day after practice he told me he was going to beat me out. I couldn't believe his gall. "I want to play pro ball," he said.

I shook my head and walked off, thinking, Pro ball? To hell with that, Dufrene. I'm going to see to it you don't even play in college.

Now, on the telephone, I was telling him, "I'd like to come see you, Marty."

"Yeah," he said. "It would be great to see you again."

"I'll do it. I promise. Just give me some time."

"Sure, whatever you need. I'd like to catch up."

But then 11 years passed, and I didn't visit Marty or follow up with another call. Nor did I write to him to explain my silence. How could I tell the man that I was afraid to see him again? Afraid to see him as a quadriplegic, afraid to have to acknowledge that, but for the grace of God, I could be the one confined to a chair, afraid to face the reality that what we once were was now ancient history.

I might've played football, in another life. But in my present one I had no doubt as to the depths of my cowardice.

At some point I decided to turn my back on it all, rather than endure the feeling of loss any longer. Marty Dufrene wasn't the only one I avoided. There were years when I tried to stay clear of the entire town of Baton Rouge. Travelers can see Tiger Stadium as they cross the Mississippi River Bridge and enter the city from the west, and whenever I journeyed across that elevated span I made sure to look at the downtown office buildings and the State Capitol to the north, rather than to the south where the old bowl sits nestled in the trees. I struggled to watch LSU games on TV and generally abandoned the set after less than a quarter. Same for radio broadcasts: I tuned most of them out by halftime. On two occasions the school's athletic department invited me to attend home games as an honorary captain, and while I showed both times, I was such a nervous wreck at being in the stadium again that I could barely walk out on the field before kickoff to receive my award and raise an arm in salute to the crowd.

Love ends, too, and when the girl invites you over to meet her new beau, you don't have to like it, do you?

I received invitations to participate in charity golf tournaments featuring former Tigers players; I never went to them. Teammates invited me to tailgate parties, suppers and other events; I never made it to them. The lettermen's club invited me to maintain a membership; except for one year, I always failed to pay my dues. Even Coach Mac tried to get in touch with me a few times. I was somehow too busy to call him back.

It wasn't until December of last year that I finally saw him again, and by then he was dying. In fact, in only three days he would be dead. Cancer had left him bedridden at his home in Baton Rouge, but even at the worst of it he was receiving guests, most of them former players who came by to tell him goodbye. One day I received a call from an old college friend, urging me to see Coach Mac again. She said it didn't look good; if I wanted to talk to him and make my peace, I'd better come right away.

So that was how I ended up at his doorstep one breezy weekday morning last winter, my hand shaking as I lifted a finger to punch the bell. I wondered if anyone in the house had seen me park on the drive in front, and I seriously considered walking back to my truck and leaving. But then the door swung open and there standing a few feet away was Coach Mac's wife, Dorothy Faye. I could feel my heart squeeze tight in my chest and my breath go shallow. My friend had called ahead and told her I might be coming; otherwise she surely would've been alarmed by the sight of a weeping middle-aged man at her front door. "Why, John Ed Bradley," she said. "Come in. Come in, John Ed."

She put her arms around me and kissed the side of my face. Dorothy Faye was as beautiful as ever, and as kind and gracious, not once asking why it had taken her husband's impending death to get me to come see him again. She led me down a hall to a bedroom, and I could see him before I walked in the door. He was lying supine on a hospital bed. His head was bald, the hair lost to past regimens of chemotherapy, and, at age 78, wrapped up in bedsheets, he seemed so much smaller than I remembered him. His eyes were large and haunted from the battle, but it was Coach Mac, all right. I snapped to attention when he spoke my name. "Come over here and talk to me, buddy," he said.

I sat next to the bed and we held hands and told stories, every one about football. He was still the aw-shucks country boy who'd played for Bear Bryant at Kentucky before going on to build his own legend in Louisiana, and the sound of his rich drawl made the past suddenly come alive for me. I named former teammates and asked him what had become of them, and in every case he had an answer. "Your old position coach was here yesterday," he said.

"Coach McCarty?"

"He sat right there." And we both looked at the place, an empty chair.

"And you're a writer now," he said.

"Yes sir, I'm a writer."

"I'm proud of you, John Ed."

I didn't stay long, maybe 20 minutes, and shortly before I got up to leave he asked me if I ever remembered back to 1979 and the night that the top-ranked USC Trojans came to Baton Rouge and the fans stood on their feet for four quarters and watched one of the most exciting games ever played in Tiger Stadium. "I remember it all the time," I said. "I don't always want to remember it, because we lost, Coach, but I remember it."

"I remember it too," he said in a wistful sort of way.

The Trojans that year had one of the most talented teams in college football history, with standouts Ronnie Lott, Charles White, Marcus Allen, Brad Budde and Anthony Munoz. They would go on to an 11–0–1 season and finish ranked second nationally behind Alabama, and White would win the Heisman Trophy.

In his bed Coach Mac lifted a hand and ran it over the front of his face in a raking gesture. "They called face-masking against Benjy," he whispered.

"Sir?"

"That penalty. The one at the end."

"Yes, sir. They sure did call it. And it cost us the game."

He swallowed, and it seemed I could see that night being replayed in his eyes: the yellow flag going up, the 15 yards being marched off, the subsequent touchdown with less than a minute to play that gave USC the 17–12 win. "Benjy Thibodeaux didn't face-mask anybody," I said, the heat rising in my face as I started to argue against a referee's call that nothing would ever change.

Coach Mac was quiet now, and he eased his grip on my hand. I stood and started for the door, determined not to look back. His voice stopped me. "Hey, buddy?" he said. I managed to face him again. "Always remember I'm with you. I'm with all you boys." He lifted a hand off the bed and held it up high, just as he had so many years ago after his last game.

"I know you are, Coach."

"And buddy?" A smile came to his face. He pointed at me. "Next time don't wait so long before you come see your old coach again."

Now it is summer, the season before the season, and Major Marty Dufrene, Civil Department Head of the Lafourche Parish Sheriff's Department, motors his wheelchair to the end of a cement drive and nods in the direction of a horse barn at the rear of his 38-acre estate. Five horses stand along a fence and wait for him, just as they do every day when he rolls out to see them after work. "I'm going to be riding before the end of the year," he tells me. "I've got a saddle I'm making with the back beefed up for support, so I can strap myself in. Of course I'm going to have to use a lift to put me in the saddle. But I'm going to do it."

By now I have been with him for a couple of hours, and already the force of his personality has made the chair invisible. After the injury his muscles began to atrophy, and over time his midsection grew large and outsized, his face swollen. But the fire in his eyes hasn't changed. Marty is exactly as I remembered him. "One thing about him," says his wife, "Marty might've broken his neck, he might be paralyzed and in that chair, but he is still a football player."

Their large Acadian-style house stands only a stone's throw from Bayou Lafourche, the place where they met and fell in love as teenagers. Lynne and their 17-year-old daughter, Amy, are inside preparing dinner, and outside Marty is giving me a tour of the spread when we come to rest in the shade of a carport. I reach to touch the top of his shoulder, because he still has some feeling there, but then I stop myself. "Marty, you must've resented the hell out of me," I say.

He looks up, surprise registering on his face. He bucks forward and then back in his chair, and it isn't necessary for me to explain which of my failures might've led me to make such a statement. "No, never," he says. "I saw you as my competition, but I always have a lot of respect for my competition, and I did for you, too. You were standing in my way, standing in the way of where I wanted to be. But even then I knew my role and accepted it. I was going to push you as hard as I could. That was my duty to you and to the team. I looked up to you as a teacher, just as you looked up to Jay Whitley as a teacher when he was playing ahead of you. We were teammates, John Ed. That was the most important thing."

Lynne and Amy serve lasagna, green salad and blueberry cheesecake in the dining room, and afterward Marty and I move to the living room and sit together as dusk darkens the windows. He revisits the nightmare of his accident and the rough years that followed, but it isn't until he talks about his days as an LSU football player that he becomes emotional. "Nothing I've ever experienced compares to it," he says. "That first time I ran out with the team as a freshman—out into Tiger Stadium? God, I was 15 feet off the ground and covered with frissons. You know what frissons are? They're goose bumps. It's the French word for goose bumps." He lowers his head, and tears fill his eyes and run down his face. He weeps as I have wept, at the memory of how beautiful it all was. "It was the biggest high you could have," he says. "No drugs could match it. The way it felt to run out there with the crowd yelling for you. I wish every kid could experience that."

"If every kid could," I say, "then it wouldn't be what it is. It's because so few ever get there that it has such power."

We are quiet, and then he says, "Whenever I have a down time, or whenever I'm feeling sorry for myself, or whenever life is more than I can bear at the moment, I always do the same thing. I put the Tiger fight song on the stereo, and all the memories come back and somehow it makes everything O.K. All right, I say to myself. I can do it. I can do it. Let's go."

Marty and I talk deep into the night, oblivious to the time, and finally I get up to leave. He wheels his chair as far as the door, and as I'm driving away I look back and see him sitting there, a bolt of yellow light around him, arm raised in goodbye.

I could seek out each one of them and apologize for the vanishing act, but, like me, most of them eventually elected to vanish, too, moving into whatever roles the world had reserved for them. Last I heard, Jay Blass had become a commercial pilot. Greg Raymond returned to New Orleans and was running his family's jewelry store. Tom Tully became a veterinarian specializing in exotic birds, of all things. And Jay Whitley, somebody told me, is an orthodontist now, the father of four kids. If they're anything like their old man, they're stouthearted and fearless, and they eat linebackers for lunch.

When the pregame prayer and pep talks were done, we'd come out of the chute to the screams of people who were counting on us. The band would begin to play; up ahead the cheerleaders were waiting. Under the crossbar of the goalpost we huddled, seniors in front. I was always afraid to trip and fall and embarrass myself, and for the first few steps I ran with a hand on the teammate next to me. Arms pumping, knees lifted high. The heat felt like a dense, blistering weight in your lungs. If you looked up above the rim of the bowl you couldn't see the stars; the light from the standards had washed out the sky. Always in the back of your mind was the knowledge of your supreme good fortune. Everyone else would travel a similar course of human experience, but you were different.

And so, chin straps buckled tight, we filed out onto the field as one, the gold and the white a single elongated blur, neatly trimmed in purple.

This story originally appeared in Sports Illustrated *on August 12, 2002. Five years later, encouraged by the positive response of readers and the enthusiastic pleas of New York book editors, John Ed Bradley published his LSU football memoir,* It Never Rains in Tiger Stadium. *It, too, drew rave reviews, and is one of my favorite books.*

ACKNOWLEDGMENTS

This is challenging. Six times I've had the good fortune of completing a book and sitting down to thank the people who helped me with it. Never before, though, have so many people been involved in so many meaningful ways. If I tried to name everyone here, I would run out of space long before completing the process. With that in mind, I begin with a blanket "thank you" to the numerous people—hundreds of folks—who helped me with this book. I am enormously grateful for the input and support of all who participated.

None of these pages could have been filled—none of these stories told—without the cooperation and kindness of the people I wrote about. They gave me their time and their trust—the greatest gifts any writer could ever want. I am indebted to all who gave me these gifts. I am also grateful for the friendships developed along the way. To the Rhymes family of Monroe, Louisiana . . . the Bregman family of Albuquerque, New Mexico . . . Stanley Roberts . . . Frank and Liz Brian . . . Mikie Mahtook and his mom Mary Ann . . . and many others: I will always cherish the time we spent together. You are now stuck with me!

People in the LSU athletics department were—as I have always found them to be—extremely kind and accommodating. Big thanks go to athletic director Joe Alleva and his assistant (my friend) Wanda Carrier. Thank you, also, to the coaches and other LSU staffers who helped, most notably the following members of the sports information office: Michael Bonnette, Kent Lowe, Bill Franques, Jake Terry, Clyde Verdin, and student-assistant Brandon Berrio (a rising star).

My team of editors is the best in the business. Carl Cannon has somehow managed to edit all six of my books—beginning in 1989. Thank you for sticking with me, Carl. John Carroll has been the single biggest influence in my writing career—part editor, part mentor, always a friend. Thank you, John, now and forever. Ray Walker is a wonderful copyeditor—kind, committed, and always dependable. Thank you, Ray, for your many contributions through the years.

I have enjoyed working with Michelle Neustrom, who designed both the cover of this book and its pages. Thank you, Michelle, for taking my pile of paper and making it look so good.

Matt Moscona of ESPN radio in Baton Rouge has been remarkably supportive throughout this project. Thank you, Matt, for sharing your audience with me as we did our "Walking with Tigers" segments on your show—and also for your friendship.

Brandon Landry and Kelly Parker of Walk-On's Bistreaux & Bar are tremendous partners on the "Walking with Tigers" team. Thanks to their leadership and support, thousands of young people throughout Louisiana will benefit from our books-to-schools program. Thank you, Brandon, Kelly, and everyone else at Walk-On's.

Finally, I want to thank friends and family for being patient with me as I worked on this project. I thank the following for being so supportive and understanding: John Ed Bradley, Dale Brown, Tom Connolly, Bill Corwin, Joe Ehrmann, Chris Elkins, Lee Feinswog, Rusty Gorman, Bert Jones, Greg Katz, Sam and Sally Lavergne, Carl Lewis, Mitch Loveman, Peggy Marx, Richard and Leslie Marx, Keith Meister, Eric Mogentale, Mike and Beth O'Shea, Peter Ripka, Bret and Lori Talbot, Jim Walsh, and Mike Woodrow.

Of course, my biggest bundle of gratitude is reserved for the two people with whom I most closely share my days: Leslie (my awesome wife) and Alex (my remarkable stepdaughter). To them I say: Thank you for always being here whenever I need you most. Thank you also for allowing me the time and space to do my thing.